I Love You Still

Myron Krahn

I Love You Still

Myron Krahn

Myron Krahn
Sexsmith, Alberta

This book is dedicated to Stacy, Halle and Layla

Table of Contents

Chapter 1

Growing up in the house I did meant you had to learn to work and you had to go without a lot of things that most would find essential. If you couldn't work all day in the hot summer sun doing physical labor you were not likely to succeed in life. That's what I was taught. If you had a task in front of you, you had to get it done one way or another. Wasting time to cool off or warm up was unproductive and if you wanted any free time you better not waste a moment being lazy; get it done and move on.

I spent a lot of hot days packing square bales by hand and loading them onto trucks, pounding posts into dry ground with a 20lb post maul, stringing out tangled up rolls of barbed wire. I was small for my age so the work seemed endless and impossible, but, if I kept my head down and focused on what was in front of me, eventually the work would get done. My dad never accepted laziness as an excuse to not complete a task and he always had a list of things that needed to be done. He was not always the best planner or the most organized so sometimes my brother and I would have to wait to have enough staples to get the barbed wire tacked into place on the freshly pounded posts. Many of those staples were old, rusty and bent and would have to get straightened out by hand before we could use them again. But we never dared to complain. Sometimes those moments waiting for dad to get organized were the only chance to rest before the work really began.

My brother and I had a slightly different view as to how to get the work done in an efficient manner. I wanted to get it done as fast as possible, just barely good enough to pass inspection, so I could go hang out with friends. Travis was better at taking water breaks, assessing what we were doing and making damn sure it was going to be acceptable so we wouldn't have to do it over again. It drove me crazy.

Our chores didn't end when we got home either. My mom, forever neat and tidy, would not let us stand idly by when there were dishes to wash, rooms to clean or grass to cut. It was just me and Travis, we didn't have any sisters to pawn that 'girly work' off on. She would stand for no less than perfection in whatever was asked of us.

My parents loved us. That was never a question. Sometimes that love came in different forms. It could be a hug, a word of encouragement or an ass whipping you weren't soon to forget. I learned right from wrong at a very young age, but that didn't stop me from testing those boundaries on a regular basis. Being raised by parents with soft hearts and hard hands made me who I am today. There was never a loss of trust or respect because of their way of disciplining us. They made sure to explain what we had done wrong. I was not always fond of them after getting a whooping that I surely deserved, but I came to understand their point as I grew older.

Some kids got the belt, some got a wooden spoon, and some lucky kids only got an open hand on the rear end. My folks had the bottom two inches of a Kenworth mud flap. Let me tell you, that got our attention real quick. One time as young mischievous boys, my brother and I messed up. I can't recall exactly what we had done, but we knew we were in for some discipline. Having a few moments before my dad figured out what had happened, we decided the best thing to do was to hide that evil piece of rubber mud flap in a place where Dad wouldn't find it. That way we would get the open handed swat, which was much less severe.

Dad came into the house absolutely fuming and properly pissed off, and started digging for that strap. Travis and I stood by, nervously waiting for our punishment, hoping to get the hand instead of that terrible strap. Dad rummaged through drawers and searched all around the kitchen. I knew it would only be another minute or so before he would give up and go to plan B. Out of the corner of my eye, I watched as my brother slowly made his way over to where we had hidden the strap. I wasn't sure what his plan was. I thought maybe he was going to stand in front of what was possibly visible of the evil chunk of pain. Then, to my horror, he reached over and pulled it out.

"Is this what you're looking for?" he said.

I nearly soiled my pants and thought oh my god we're gonna die. My dad gave us a look that said you're gonna feel this for a week. I thanked God that my brother was first up to bat, which was only fitting. After all he did throw us both under the bus by pulling that thing out of its hiding spot. After I had my turn, though, I was sure I had gotten it just as bad. I definitely did feel that one for a week. I can laugh about it now - with my dad and Travis giggling right along. It's the way us hard headed boys learned. After all that we still loved our parents and knew that they loved us.

We never had a lot of anything growing up, although we never really knew it. Both my folks worked hard for every dime they earned, but times were tough. We had Christmas without gifts, and dinner was a far cry from what anyone would consider to be a hearty meal on Christmas Day, but my mom did the best she could to scrape something together. She was never happy with it, but we never noticed that it wasn't up to her standards. Coming from a family where love meant everything and material things meant nothing will teach you about what cannot be bought at any big box store.

For as long as I can remember we always had horses around. Many days were spent working with them, trimming their hooves and feeding and riding them. Some days were awesome, riding through new terrain, across unexplored creeks and enjoying Mother Nature. Other days I wanted to make glue out of those retarded jugheads. They'd throw you off, step on you, kick you in the thigh and send you to the hospital. But you had to suck it up, get back on and show that long faced piece of dog food that you were not about to give in to its shitty attitude. If nothing else, those critters taught me some patience and a fair bit of pain tolerance which would come in real handy later in life.

We took in the local rodeos whenever they came to town. I took an instant liking to the bull riding event. There was nothing quite like a pissed off, 1500 lb. bag of horns, hooves and hate. I had to get on it and stay there for eight seconds and try not to get myself killed. This sounded like the most awesome thing in the world to me. I was too young to ride bulls but I was old enough to start riding steers. I'd get on scared half to death. I'd hit the dirt and bounce back up, ready to do it again. I was around 13 when I used my wrist to break a fall. I waited three days before complaining to my mom enough that she finally took me in to get it checked out. Yup, broken. My mother was thoroughly impressed since I had just had a second surgery to repair my other elbow that I had broken in a tobogganing mishap during the previous Christmas holidays. My poor mother. To this day I don't know how she survived me and my brother's great ideas. Once I turned 14 I was old enough to sign up for the high school rodeo club. I couldn't wait to get my chance at an actual bull. I was ready to leave those little steers behind for the kids. I was ready to take on the baddest bulls in the pen. That's what I told myself anyhow. I usually ended up gimping my ass into school on Monday with another story of how I got beat up by a monster bull. One with horns eight feet long, or maybe I just got off at a bad time and got stepped on…Nah, eight foot long horns sounded way better. Some of my friends went camping or played video games. They liked hanging out with the in crowd. Not me. I was doing something I absolutely loved, even though it was dangerous and caused me a lot of pain sometimes. I couldn't get enough of it. Nothing compared to the rush I'd get from crawling on the back of a bull. I craved those near death experiences.

I'd stand behind the bucking chutes, waiting for my turn and watch as they'd load the bull I had drawn. I'd eyeball that big bastard while I worked another chunk of rosin into my bull rope, doing my best to not look nervous. I'd take my time getting my rope around the bulls belly, making sure it was set just right. Doing it slowly, I could concentrate and it helped me not look as terrified as I felt. I'd gently slide my legs down behind the bull's front shoulders, get my hand into my rope and set my pinky finger on his spine. Some big fella in a cowboy hat would start pulling the tail end of my rope tight against my hand and around the bull. I could feel every muscle in that beasts back flex and twitch as it began to get angry. Then the adrenaline would start hammering through my veins at full force. I'd wrap the tail end of the rope around my right hand, slamming it in with my left to ensure my grip was solid. Then I'd make sure the bull was looking in the right direction and the flank man was all set. I'd slide up on my rope and nod my head. The gate would rattle open as it swung wide to turn us loose. I'd dig my spurs into the side of that monster as we exploded from the gate. Then the world around me would go silent. My focus was so intense that the only things visible to me were my hand tied in that rope and the bull's neck. Everything else was blacked out and nothing else mattered in that moment. Keeping my chin down, chest out and grabbing a new hold with my spurs at every jump, I did my best to stay over top of the bull and ride him jump for jump. The bull would twist and turn, buck and kick doing everything it could to get rid of this lightweight teenager on his back. Many times the bull would succeed, but when I had my mind set on winning, there was nothing that animal could do to toss me off before the whistle blew. I wouldn't let it happen. It was a mental game; it was mental toughness. I didn't need to be physically strong, I had to be mentally tough to stay on. If I wasn't 110% focused, I wasn't going to stay on, and I usually knew it before I ever crawled on in the first place. I was either switched on completely, or I may as well have packed my bag and gone home.

I suffered several injuries, as most bull riders do. I've broken my ankles, ribs, and arms. Concussions were pretty normal. Getting my face smashed in was just another day in the sport of bull riding. In spite of all the pain, I still had the time of my life. My folks would drive my brother and me to a rodeo and watch us attempt our rides. Then they would haul us to the nearest hospital to mend our broken bodies.

My brother rode in the saddle bronc event back then. Bucking horses tend to be short and stocky, but I remember Travis once drawing an unusually tall horse. He saddled up ready to give it his best. He was expecting the horse to start bucking, but the lousy nag took off at a dead run. Just when Travis thought he'd start bucking, the horse stopped in its tracks and shot straight into the air. Travis came unglued from his saddle and landed under the animal with one foot stuck in the stirrup. I saw the horse stomp on his back and stretch him out before his boot finally popped out of the stirrup's grasp. When the dust settled, my brother was laying there motionless. I jumped the fence and ran to him with my heart was pounding in my ears as I raced across the arena. He slowly rolled over onto his back. He couldn't say anything. His lips were blue and he couldn't get air into his lungs. I frantically waved to the medical staff and they rushed over to haul him away in the meat wagon. The ambulance sirens echoed around me as I realized it was almost my turn to ride. I did my best to clear my head, but jumping off and heading to the hospital was what I really wanted to do. Let's go with that, I decided. Better luck next time.

Travis suffered 4 broken ribs, a collapsed lung and a broken arm just below his shoulder. It was his last ride. He hung up his spurs after that one. I didn't blame him. My Dad tried his best to convince me to pick a different event, calf roping maybe. Yeah right, Dad, haven't you heard? I'm the toughest SOB around, I can take any kinda pain. I got this! In hind sight, I should have listened to his advice.

I continued to ride, learning a lot of lessons the painful way, but I got better. By the time I was seventeen I had improved tremendously. I had learned a thing or two about the sport and how to not die. Occasionally I'd come home with 1st place cash in my pocket I may have even become a little bit cocky, but that's debatable. I was well on my way to qualifying for the finals that year and I was completely focused on my goal. I ate, drank, slept and dreamed bull riding. I was driven to do well and become one of the best.

Even as a seventeen-year-old full of hormones, my energy and drive was spent on practicing and getting better. Now, I'm not saying I didn't celebrate a good ride by chatting with some random girl who caught my eye. Who wouldn't want to hang out with the best bull rider around, right?

By this time, I had a couple buddies I traveled with to rodeos. My folks had turned me loose and I got to chase my dreams and ride bulls wherever the rodeos would take me. Together, Chris, Ryan and I would tear down the highway in my rusty old F-150, blasting a scratched up CD of Chris Ledoux all the way to the next event.

Ryan was a bareback bronc rider. He was as focused and determined as I was. He was a second generation rodeo cowboy and wore the label with pride. Chris rode bareback broncs as well and was very focused…on the barrel racers. One, in particular, caught his eye, and he turned on the charm and swagger for her. To us it looked more like he had one leg shorter than the other and spoke with a lisp, but eventually the charm worked (or she took pity on him) and they started dating.

Rodeo season ended for the winter. The cold November snow had arrived leaving us with a lot of energy and not much to do. Ryan drove three hours south to Grande Prairie, Alberta to hang out for the weekend, we all crashed at Chris' mom's house. We had a few drinks, or maybe a few too many, and watched old rodeo videos. We laughed at all the wrecks and good times we had. The next morning, Chris woke us all up way too early. I mean, eleven a.m. is a ridiculous time for a teenager. He wanted to go to some damn horse auction to meet up with his barrel racer girlfriend, Angie. Much to my disgust I gave in to his pleading. I fired up my old piece of junk a 1980 F150. It barely had a working heater but I couldn't let Chris miss seeing his girl.

We wandered around for a while. Chris and I looked over the horses being sold while Ryan checked out the saddles and tack. Then we headed to the concession stand for our favorite meal: greasy burgers and fries. After filling up on the perfect breakfast, our heads were less painful. Feeling human once again, we made our way to the holding barn to find Angie. We found her near a pen of animals of some sort. It may have been horses, I couldn't say for sure. Someone else had caught my short, adolescent attention span.

Sitting up on the fence, talking to Angie was a young lady. I was instantly drawn to her natural beauty. Her long brown hair was a bit messy. She wore no make-up and dressed in basic blue jeans and a sweater. But the softness in her eyes and infectious smile made my heart race. She saw me coming and hopped down and said, "Hi, I'm Angie's friend, Stacy." She held out her hand to me in greeting. I took it and was barely aware of gently shaking it up and down. I said, nothing. My brain couldn't form a coherent word.

Angie laughed, "Stacy, this is Myron"

Dammit, I thought. I should've said that. Stacy laughed, "Okay, nice to meet you Myron"

"Yes, you as well," was all I could muster up. Crap, what was her name again?

Man, I'm terrible at this. I guess it's back to focusing on bull riding, right? I don't have to talk sweet to those bulls.

Angie turned toward me and gave me a funny look. I must have been staring at the beauty in front of me a little longer than I realized.

"Myron, did you drive your truck here?" Angie asked, breaking the awkward moment.

"Oh yeah, I did." Suddenly, I was unsure where this was going.

"Let's go hang out there, I'm getting bored in here." Angie turned and headed to the exit.

I didn't think there was any way we'd all fit in my regular cab truck. I was proven wrong. We all crammed inside, with Angie on Chris's lap. Stacy was uncomfortably squashed beside me, but I, on the other hand, was right as rain. Up to this point I hadn't thought too much about any girl, but Stacy was terribly easy on the eyes. But I had rodeos to go to, bulls to slaughter, and dreams to catch. There was no time for a girlfriend in my mind, but then again, minds can be changed.

Chris and Angie finally bailed out of the truck, laughing and throwing snow at each other. Ryan slid out and spat his wad of chewing tobacco onto the ground to make room for a fresh one. It was the moment I put a pinch of the nasty stuff in my lip that I realized I was alone for the first time with Stacy. The fact that she hadn't moved an inch surprised me. My hip bone dug into the door of my truck, it was the best pain in my ass I'd ever felt. Shit, I now I had to make idle chatter.

"Are you here with your folks?" I asked, trying to sound much more mature than I was.

"Yeah my brother is buying a horse. He's with them."

"I see. Do they know where you are?" The last thing I wanted was to find out that her father had a 12 gauge in his truck while she was sitting in mine!

"They know I'm with Angie"

Close enough for me. What's the worst that could happen?

We hung out in my truck all day long. The parking lot had started to clear out and it was now dark. Angie had already left and Chris was ready to go too. But Stacy was still in my truck and there was no way in hell I was going to rush her out the door. She had captured both of my attention spans by this point. Since I had a lot of respect for my own father, I was starting to wonder where hers were and how angry he would be when he found her in my truck.

"Are you sure your folks know where you are?" I asked again, hoping I didn't sound like I wanted her to leave, because that sure wasn't the case.

"Oh yeah, they're just…" She trailed off for a second, looking across the lot towards the front doors of the auction house. One bright yard light shone down on a lady using crutches and a man who appeared to be in a serious state of anger. "Gotta go." Stacy clambered out of the truck and slow jogged towards the pair standing in the light. Once she was within arm's reach of that angry looking man, he grabbed her by the ear and dragged her off to their truck.

Ryan looked at me. "Well, that looks like it went well for you." He laughed, knowing that if that man ever caught me, I'd likely have a nice funeral.

I had no idea where this day would end up taking me, but I was hoping for something that didn't end up with death by pissed off farmer.

I was 17, Stacy was 15. It was November 21, 1999. A day that would forever change my heart and soul.

Chapter 2

The next week was terrible. No matter what I did I couldn't get this girl off my mind. I needed to get my mind back on track. Bull riding was the priority in my life. I needed to practice during the off season if I wanted to make the finals that year. Did it have to be all or nothing? Why couldn't I spend time with a girl I liked and practice? What could it hurt? Maybe I should could call her up and just talk. Friends do that kind of thing all the time. I'm a friendly kind of guy. But I didn't have her number, I never asked Stacy for it before she had to go. Would it be weird if I got her number from Angie and just randomly called her? Only one way to find out. I got a hold of Angie and asked her for Stacy's number. Angie of course thought this was funny and had to tease me about it a little bit before giving it to me.

Now that I had her number, I couldn't decide if I should call her right away or not. If her dad answered what would I say? Holy crap! What if he started asking me questions? I had no idea how this all worked. I wanted a guarantee that she'd answer, even though I had no idea what I'd say to her. Dammit, this was stupid. Bull riding was less complicated. Taking on one thousand pounds of pure muscle was easy compared to talking to a pretty girl.

I waited another day and finally dialed the number.

"Hello?" a lady answered

"Hi. Is Stacy home?" I asked

"Yes, just a minute." She replied

In the background I heard, "Stacy, the phone's for you. It's a boy and it's not Trevor."

Well, who the hell was Trevor? I wondered. Maybe this was a bad idea after all.

Stacy picked up the phone. "Hello?"

"Hey, I uh, do you know who this is?" I asked, suddenly unsure of this crazy idea.

Stacy giggled. "Yeah, this is Myron." She paused suddenly, as if she had just realized the words that came out of her mouth. Had she expected me to call? How would she have known it was me? "Angie said she gave you my number and mentioned you might call me sometime."

The conversation didn't last a long time, but by the end of it she had invited me to a dance at her high school the following weekend. Of course, I played it cool. I told her I would have to get back to her, even though I knew there was no way I'd miss seeing her. But who was Trevor? I called Angie right after I hung up. I had to know what I was getting into. Angie informed me that she had a boyfriend, but they hadn't been seeing each other long and didn't seem serious. Okay, but she asked me to come to the dance? Isn't that odd? Maybe this was just a friend thing to her, maybe she is not looking for anything more than just friends.

The following week passed and before I knew it, it was the night of the dance. I had no idea what the invitation meant, but I guess I was about to find out. Chris and I strolled in, wearing our finest plaid shirts, boots and cowboy hats. It was a typical high school gymnasium, basketball nets on one end, a stage at the front and bleachers along one side. The speakers blasted some kind of new pop music that we were not well acquainted with, not our flavour of music.

We found Angie right away. She grabbed my hand and pulled me toward the back of the gym where Stacy stood. She looked gorgeous. She was naturally beautiful and didn't wear a lot of makeup. I liked that about her.

"Hey, you made it!" Stacy said with a smile.

Unfortunately, I had very little to say. I had no experience charming anyone. Flirting with a beautiful girl was out of my comfort zone. Stacy on the other hand had the gift of gab. She easily carried the majority of the conversation. She was easy to talk to, though, and I was comfortable around her. There was something about her that just made her easy to be with. She was relaxed, and she didn't act all crazy like most of the other girls did. We danced to a few songs. She didn't seem to mind my limited dancing skills. It helped that most of the music was country. I kept wondering when this Trevor fella would show up and be pissed that I was dancing with her.

The evening was coming to a close and it was getting time for us to head home. I ran outside to fire up my old truck and let it warm up. Usually I would have just said bye and been on my way, but as I lingered by the door waiting for Chris, Angie ran up to let me know that Stacy wanted to say goodbye and I had to go to her.

Well alright then, I suppose I could do that. I didn't want to leave anyway. I was thoroughly enjoying spending time with Stacy at this point. I wandered back through the crowds of kids, feeling a little out of place since I didn't know any of them, though they all seemed to know who I was for some reason. There she stood, off in the corner by herself.

"Hey, I guess we gotta head out now. I had a really fun time with you though," I said, impressed that it sounded all right.

"Me too," she said. "I'm glad you were able to come. Maybe we could hang out sometime?"

She smiled up at me and I couldn't help but stare. Her smile was so genuine and beautiful.

"Sure, we could go hang out with Angie and Chris sometime again I'm sure."

Now what? How do I leave? Do I give her a hug or just wave goodbye and walk away?

Stacy grabbed my arm and pulled me in. She put one hand around the back of my neck and pressed her lips against mine.

My mind was now racing! I wasn't sure how people said goodbye where she came from, but this was so awesome! That first kiss lasted longer than I had expected, but I didn't want it to end either. That was it, this girl was amazing and I was now a puddle of mush.

She let go of me and smiled that beautiful smile again, "Call me again sometime."

There was no question there. I'd definitely be calling her again.

We said our goodbyes and left, Chris smacked me on the shoulder as we headed to the truck. "Nice going man, I saw that, but you know she has a boyfriend right?"

Shit! I had forgotten about that.

A few days later Stacy called and told me she had broken up with her boyfriend. It was nothing serious and was only a short term thing anyway. I was relieved. I wasn't sure what that made us, but it didn't really matter I guess. She was free to spend time with me and that's what I cared about.

I asked her out to a movie, which, of course, she needed to get permission from her parents to do. She asked her mom who had no issue with it. She would get a ride into town with her older sister and meet me there. Stacy hadn't told her father about our plan and she was hoping to avoid even mentioning it. Her sister Twila insisted. "You have to tell him or he's gonna be pissed when we get home."

"I will. Just let me do it when the time is right." Stacy was trying to figure out how to not say anything about it. He still wasn't happy about the auction and she never told him about the dance.

As Stacy and her sister were heading out the door, she hurried to say, "We're going to the movies. I'm meeting a boy there. Mom said it was okay."

Twila instantly followed that with, "The one from the auction mart."

"Freeze! You're not going anywhere." He demanded.

"Mom said I could go as long as Twila went with me." Stacy protested.

Her father glared at his wife, Debbie with disapproval. He looked over at Stacy's brother Trenton. "Here's twenty bucks, go with them, and don't let her out of your sight."

We met up at the theatre and found some seats. I expected to sit next to her brother and sister, but thankfully, they took seats in front of us. *How nice of them*, I thought. The movie started, but I didn't pay much attention to it. I was more concerned with deciding whether to hold her hand or not. I finally got up enough courage and slipped my hand into hers. She didn't pull away so I took that as a win. When the movie ended I leaned over and whispered something in her ear. Everyone was leaving making all kinds of noise and she didn't hear me.

"What?" Stacy asked leaning toward me. The look on her face made me think she heard me but wanted to make me say it again.

"Will you go out with me?" I asked loud enough for the other theater to hear. I grimaced as I waited for her answer, she took a moment before replying.

"Yes, of course I will."

I wasn't sure if I was shocked or just dumbfounded but I didn't know what to say. I smiled the biggest goofball smile I could and said nothing. I held her hand as we walked out of the theater. I felt like I had grown a foot taller. I was doing the best I could to not break out into a happy dance. We kissed and said goodbye, she went off to her sister's car and I made my way to my junky old truck. I fired it up, hoping the heater would work this time as it was insanely cold out. I couldn't stop myself, I had to do it. I put that piece of crap in 3rd gear, slammed the gas pedal to the floor and side stepped the clutch. The poor 300 ci inline 6 cylinder motor had never seen so much rpm. I whipped that truck into some figure eight donuts in that empty parking lot covered in snow. Happy dance complete and engine making some heat to take the bite out of the cold inside the cab, I headed for home. I was a happy kid.

New Year's Eve was just around the corner, Stacy and I hadn't talked much through the busy Christmas weekend. We were both preoccupied with our own families but we still managed a few calls in the evenings. Stacy asked me to come to the New Year's Eve dance at a hall near their farm.

This was going to be my first time actually meeting her parents face to face. I needed a game plan. Chris was coming with me so he could meet up with Angie. He was a rowdy, loud mouthed buddy who could be a bit quirky. I figured if I brought him along, my quiet, shy demeanor would likely look pretty good in their eyes. I dressed up in a new pair of wrangler jeans and a decent shirt, I threw on my high school rodeo jacket with my name and event embroidered on the sleeve. I wanted Stacy and everyone else to know I was a Bull Rider.

After all, it was still my favorite sport and I still had plans to become the best.

I swung into Chris' driveway and ran into the house. I didn't want to be late for the first meet and greet with Stacy's parents. When I turned the corner into his kitchen, I found Chris chugging down a bottle of booze. *Just great*, I thought, this evening was already going downhill.

"Hey buddy! Let's do this!" Chris was already half in the bag. I wasn't sure what to do but I wasn't going to waste time trying to figure it out.

"Dammit man" I groaned. "You couldn't wait until we got to the hall?"

We loaded up and headed for Stacy's. It was about a 30 minute drive from Chris' house. I had hoped that he would sober up somewhat before we got there, but I was so wrong. We pulled into the yard. Stacy ran out to meet me. Chris fell out of the truck and stumbled around trying to catch his balance.

"What's up with Chris?" Stacy asked nervously.

"He's plastered already. He was slamming them back before I got to his house." I said, hoping it wouldn't cause a problem.

"Oh boy," she said with raised eyebrows. "Why don't we put him in the back room and try to keep him there. We'll have to sneak him through the house."

"Chris" I snapped, "keep your mouth shut and be polite," I warned, trying to keep him on his feet.

"I'll be a perfect angel, you won't even know I'm here." he slurred.

I didn't believe him but there was no turning back now. We walked into a house of chaos. It was full of family all taking turns using the washroom, doing hair and whatever girls did to get ready for a dance. *Must be a pretty big deal around here*, I thought to myself. Stacy grabbed my hand and rushed into the kitchen.

"This is Myron, and that's Chris. We will be in the back room." Stacy quickly blurted it out and attempted to drag me away before anyone would notice. She was successful, almost. Chris half fell as he made it up the first two steps, but missed the third.

"Whoa, are you alright there fella?" One of Stacy's cousins reached out to catch him.

"He's fine. Come on Chris." Stacy grabbed him by the collar and shoved him in the direction she wanted him to disappear.

We sat down in the spare room, away from the crowd. I kept my mouth shut. I knew better than to say anything just yet to avoid any sort of unwanted attention.

"Stacy, come on out here! Bring your boiyfrieenndd!" hollered someone from the kitchen.

Oh shit, here we go. Stacy looked terrified but put a smile on her face and started leading me back to the lion's den.

"Chris, you stay here and be quiet," she ordered.

Chris looked up and saluted her, "Yes, Ma'am," he smirked.

Stacy had a large family and it seemed they were all there getting ready. We walked into the kitchen full of her aunts, uncles, cousins. Even her granny was there. She was the youngest and it seemed they were all curious to know who I was.

"So, you're the new boyfriend, huh?" asked one of her older cousins who seemed like a giant to me at the time.

"Hey, Jamie?" someone asked, looking over at Stacy's father. "Did you tell this kid about your nut collection jar?"

Jamie raised his eyes at them, then scowled at me.

"Nope."

I was officially nervous now. My family was very quiet and conservative and the hustle and bustle in this house was foreign to me. Lots of loud talking, dirty jokes and tons of laughter. It was a warm feeling home, but I was feeling chills up and down my spine.

Another cousin piped up. "You see, Jamie has this jar that he keeps out back in the parts shed. It's nearly full of nuts taken from boys that come around here causing trouble, but I believe there would be enough room for a couple more. What do you think Jamie?"

"Yup, I'd say so."

Phew, tough crowd. Stacy flipped them all off, laughing a little to try and lighten the uncomfortable moment, and excused us from the situation.

We retreated to the safety of the back room where Chris was quietly singing to himself. We sat down and waited for the time to leave for the hall. Stacy's mom, Debbie, came back and said hello. She was a short statured woman with thick dark hair and wisps of grey that I assumed were caused from raising three kids on a farm. She introduced herself and shook my hand. I was pretty sure they had caught on to the fact that I had brought a drunk friend with me. In my parents' house, that would not have gone over very well, but Stacy's family were surprisingly unfazed by his state. They had to have taken notice. I wasn't sure yet if it was going well or not, but I was hoping for at least a half decent first impression.

We finally got the green light to head to the hall. Stacy walked outside with me and Chris. She headed straight for my truck and her dad hollered at her. "Where do you think you're going?"

"I'm just gonna ride there with Myron. See you there." She smiled and jumped into the truck. I wasn't sure what to do. I wanted her to ride with me, but the last thing I wanted to do was annoy her father any more than he already was.

"Come on, let's go," she insisted. "He'll get over it." She rubbed her hands together trying to generate some heat. I hurried and climbed inside and followed her family. I knew they were critiquing my every move. I don't remember ever driving so carefully in my life.

We all walked into the hall, and quickly found a few more of our friends to hang out with. It was a pretty big event, being 1999. The theme was Be With the One You Want Forever, which, of course, we all took far too seriously as immature teenagers. One of Stacy's friends, Jenny, constantly bugged me. She kept tapping me on the shoulder, asking me weird questions, being a general pain in my ass. But the night was going well. Chris had sobered up some and wasn't being a complete buffoon, so things were looking up. Suddenly a song came on and all the young women lost their damn minds. Redneck Girl was the tune and I was instantly jerked off my chair nearly dislocating my shoulder. Apparently, this was a thing and my beautiful girlfriend wanted to dance. I wasn't going to let her down. We tore around the dance floor, knowing that there were many eyes on us but by this time, we didn't care. We were having the time of our lives.

17

Midnight was getting close. I knew my mom wanted me home by 12:30 but I also knew that probably wouldn't happen. We were off to the side of the dance floor when the countdown began. Five! Four! Three! Two! One! Happy New Year! The entire hall erupted with noise from the half-drunk crowd. Stacy looked me in the eyes and put her arms out. This time I wasn't going to let her do this on her own. I met her in the middle and pressed my lips to hers. We made out for a few seconds before I felt this tap on my shoulder…again. Why would her friend not leave me alone? Did she not notice that we were having a moment here? I brushed her away, hoping she would take the hint. She tapped me again, for fu….I turned to see Debbie, Stacy's mother smiling at me. Oh shit.

"Happy New Year, you two!" She smiled and wrapped her arms around me in a big warm hug. I was stunned. Stacy started laughing her ass off at what I can only assume was the look of total fear and shock on my face. When Debbie walked off, I turned to Stacy who was still giggling.

"I just brushed your mother off while making out with you, and then she hugged me!" I was in total shock. Stacy said nothing while covering her mouth trying to control her laughter. Oh I totally got this now! I was completely confident that I had won her momma over.

"Ha! She totally loves me, I can tell" I said with absolute confidence.

Stacy's annoying friend popped up out of nowhere and said "Nah, that's Debbie. She loves everyone. You're not anything special."

We danced a few more times, though I knew I needed to leave. I was already late for my curfew that my parents had set for this particular event. If I didn't head home soon, I'd get grounded. The thought of not being able to see Stacy helped me push Chris's drunk ass back into my truck. As I drove away after saying a mushy goodbye I realized, I was falling in love... And it felt amazing.

Chapter 3

The next few months were filled with lengthy phone calls, frequent visits to her high school and planning every weekend as best we could. We wanted to spend every moment together. Our conversations had grown deeper and more personal than I'd ever thought possible. We talked about everything; nothing was kept a secret between us. We talked about the smallest of details regarding our relationship. By this time my parents had met her and had become comfortable with her hanging around and taking up a lot of my time. Although my folks would get a little frustrated when I would volunteer to go out and help clean the barn, check cows that were due to calve or find any other excuse to be with her and not at home, they let me go. The chores that I needed to look after and just about everything else, including school work, took a backseat as I was completely infatuated with her.

Our comfort with each other had grown so much, she was someone that I could talk to about the oddest details or subject matter. We had a way of talking about anything that may come up in our relationship with each other, including what it meant to introduce the 'I love you' into any relationship. We had witnessed many friends throwing it around with someone they had just met and we found it to be shallow with no actual meaning. We talked about it at length and at some point I realized what she was actually trying to tell me. I was sometimes a bit slow to catch on when she didn't always want to come outright and say it. She was trying to tell me that she wanted to know that I loved her, because she was in love with me. I had loved her from the first moment I saw her, but saying it made it real for both of us and I hadn't said those three words to her yet. Although we were still very young and I'm sure many would say the same thing at that age, I was head over heels for this girl and I truly did love her.

Our conversation was coming to a close after what seemed like minutes but was likely closer to hours. We had discussed this particular subject at length and had pretty much come to the conclusion that we were both okay with saying those three words to each other, but hadn't actually been very specific about it. As we were saying goodbye, she said it for the first time.

"I love you."

I panicked.

"Ok, talk to you later. 'Bye." And I hung up. What the... What in the hell is wrong with me, I wondered. She just said those beautiful words and I said bye? I'm such an idiot!

What should I do now? Do I call back just to say it back to her? I suck at this!

I felt terrible. We had spent so much time talking about this and I completely dropped the ball when she had said it to me. I slept very little that night. Although it seems like such a minor thing now when I think about it, for her I was certain that it was a big deal that I hadn't said it back. She was probably thinking that I didn't love her, which was so far from the truth. I had been in love with her much longer than she would ever know.

I could hardly wait to call her the next day and try and explain how I panicked. When I got home from work the next afternoon, I barely got my boots off my feet before the phone was in my hand.

"Hi, is Stacy home?" I asked as soon as the phone was picked up.

"Yes, but she's out at the barn right now," Debbie answered. She had become accustomed to my phone calls. "I'll let her know you called when she gets back in."

Great now I had to wait. I was never the most patient person, especially when I really had something to say. I waited in agony all evening and had nearly given up when she finally called back at eleven o'clock.

"Hey, Listen," I said before she could start talking. "I know we talked about this for a long time and we were both on the same page, but I kinda panicked when you said it. I didn't mean to just hang up. I got scared, but you need to know I love you too." I blurted it all out before she could say a word.

"Oh, okay I'm glad you said that because when you hung up I was thinking I should just forget the whole thing."

I felt that guilty gut punch.

"No, no, I just wasn't used to us saying it and just didn't think before hanging up." I was hoping she wasn't upset with me.

"Okay, so we are good? We are in the same place?" She sounded like she was about to cry.

"Yes! I am so sorry. I didn't mean to do that. I am completely in love with you."

Stacy started to giggle. She was happy and somewhat amused at my groveling.

I had finally said it. I told her what I had been feeling for so long but was afraid to say. She completely consumed my mind and I thought about her constantly. She was perfect. She worked hard, she loved the outdoors, she had a great sense of humour, and she had picked me to be her boyfriend. She was the most incredible girl I had ever met. And now she knew that I loved her.

Spring was just around the corner, which, for me, meant rodeo season. I needed to make few more good rides to make the finals, I was in 7th place in the standings but I needed to be in 5th to qualify. It was time to get my head back in the game. I needed to get focused and be ready to kick some ass. I signed up for bull riding school like I had for the last couple years. It was a great way for me to knock the rust off and fine tune my motor skills before I entered the first rodeo. There was only two weeks before the first one, and it was in my hometown. I wanted to be at the top of my game since it'd be the first time Stacy would see me ride.

My parents and I drove eight hours south to Uncle Howard's ranch near Calgary where the school was held. The guys teaching the school knew me by name. I was considered a veteran there even at my young age since I had been riding for a few years already. Several of the other riders there hadn't been on a bull yet. We did our basic training and warm up before they loaded the first round of bulls into the bucking chutes. I was itching to get back on and couldn't wait. One of the instructors pointed at a bull already loaded up and said, "Myron, jump on that one there. He's a real good one for you, but he's a bit rank in the chutes." (Meaning the bull fought inside the chutes. He would smash your legs to pieces if you didn't know what you were doing.) I didn't hesitate, it was time to ride! I was excited. I had done this so many times before that I was no longer scared to climb on. I was always nervous, but that's what heightens your senses and makes you react faster to every move that bull makes.

I slung my rope around that bulls belly and waited my turn. Kids were getting tossed left and right. Everyone was rusty or new to the sport. I would soon find out how much I had forgotten over the winter. Finally my turn came and I climbed over the chute and stayed above the bull to avoid pissing him off and getting my legs smashed. I knew I'd have to jump on his back as I nodded my head. Everyone called this move 'taking a jump at him.' I slammed my riding hand tight with my free hand, just as I had done so many times before. I took a quick glance around, nodded and jumped down. The gate swung wide and we were right back to my favourite place, sound muted, surroundings invisible, just me and this beast. Did I mention I was rusty? The bull started spinning hard to the left, away from my riding hand and I was too slow to react. I slid down to the outside of the bulls spin landing underneath. I knew better than to just lay there, but before I could move the hooves of that beast came slamming down on the inside of my right knee. I rolled out of this death tunnel, got to my feet and started running, the adrenaline still pulsing through my veins. I made it about three strides before I knew something was wrong. I stumbled and fell, still looking for the bull to make sure it wasn't coming after me. He was gone. I hit the dirt in excruciating pain. One of the trainers grabbed me and pulled me through the fence before the next rider came out on his bull. The medics looked at me briefly, but the next rider had been knocked out cold and stomped on badly. That kid was in bad shape, much worse than me, so they ran to his aid.

I pulled my jeans back over my swollen knee and hopped to where my folks were waiting on the other side of the pen. They loaded me up and headed to the hospital. The doctor that looked at my injury had plenty of experience with bull riders and all the injuries that we brought him. After all the x-rays and examinations he looked at me and said "You tore some ligaments. You need to stay off of it for four weeks. When is your next event?"

"I have two weeks Doc, and I can't miss the next one." I was worried my parents would cancel it on me if he gave me more bad news.

"Okay. Ice it, stay off of it and wrap it up really well. I know telling you guys to stay off the bulls is useless because none of you ever listen to me. Take it easy and be careful. It's not in good shape and you could damage it severely, which would require surgery."

I didn't want that. I didn't want to miss the finals either. I was going to do everything I could to get it healthy enough to ride again. It wouldn't be my first time riding injured; that was just something that came with the sport. You either put the pain out of your mind and got the job done, or you became a calf roper. That wasn't going to happen. It would've been a better idea to brush up on my roping skills, but at this moment I wasn't thinking very far ahead.

We headed back to the ranch and I pressed a bag of frozen peas against my knee. Dad and I settled on the sofa to review my ride on video. About half way through it my dad got a phone call. I thought it was odd, but didn't pay much attention. When he hung up the phone, I knew something was wrong. His mother had just passed away. I didn't know my grandmother all that well, but I could see my dad was hurting. We left first thing in the morning and headed home.

I could tell Dad didn't feel well. He hadn't slept much and my mom was upset. I could barely walk, but I could still drive, so I got behind the wheel and started the journey home. We stopped for fuel only. The further we went, the more pain my dad appeared to be in. I didn't know what he was going through, but seeing my dad in so much pain wasn't normal. This went beyond the emotional pain from him losing his mother. He was one of the toughest men I knew and I was getting worried. I passed our turn off to head home. I wasn't stopping there.

Much to my dad's objection, he needed a doctor. I got to the hospital and went to get out of the vehicle, but my knee couldn't support my weight. Using the car door to hold myself up, I did what I could to help mom get Dad into the hospital. Dad ended up there for a few days with some kind of intestinal issue that caused all the pain. After he was released we had to travel up north for my grandmother's funeral. I wished I had time to call Stacy and let her know what was going on, but we didn't have time to stop. All I wanted to do was sit next to her and let her fuss over my injuries. Knowing that my parents would be staying up north for a while and I would need to get home sooner, I jumped into the truck with my brother and followed them to High Level.

The next week was spent with some family I knew and a lot I didn't. I was never big on family reunions, and even less of a fan of funerals. But this was my dad's mother. I felt like I needed to be there. The few days in the hospital had cleared my dad up and he was doing better. I, however, was still in a lot of pain. I was doing my best to stay off of my leg, ice it, stretch it out and baby it. I only had a week before it was time to ride again.

Chapter 4

Another week passed and my knee was better, but still sore. I could walk without a limp and it felt strong enough to ride, which I had full intentions of doing. Not all rodeos had trophy buckles up for first prize; a lot gave out cash prizes. That was great for getting down the road to the next one on a full tank of gas, but I had my mind set on that bull riding champion buckle. This one was gorgeous, and I wanted it. It was going to be mine. My mind was set. Nothing was going to stop me from getting it (aside from drawing a crappy bull, but that was out of my control).

My dad had volunteered to be the director of this rodeo, which was also another reason I wanted to win. He'd be the one to hand me the buckle if I won it, and I was going to get that damn thing. Sometimes you rode two or three days and the person with the most points wins the buckle. This time you won it on the first night. I had to ride my best because I had no chance to improve my score the next day.

I had hoped that Stacy was going to make it for the Friday show but with school and their cows still calving, she was unable to make it. I wasn't going to let that bother me and, although I wanted her to be there, I had to focus. This was my time. I needed a couple more good rides to qualify for the finals and I was going to make this one count.

I drew a short horned, Black Angus bull, a bit on the small side for my recent growth spurt. My legs had grown longer over the past year making smaller bulls a bit tougher for me to grip with my spurs, but that didn't matter. I had done it before, and I was going to do it again. They ran my bull into the chutes, I performed my regular pre ride stretch and rope prep. My mind was set right and I was as ready as I had ever been. I sat down on his back, taking extra care to keep my right knee safe from getting reinjured in the chutes and I worked rosin into my rope to get it sticky. I wanted no chance of my rope slipping and coming loose. I had a quick glance around and it was go time. I slid up and nodded my head.

"Let's go boys" I hollered.

They swung that gate open hard. I heard it crash into the fence as my bull smashed it with his head on the way out. I stayed top and center, grabbing a new hold with my spurs at every jump. I was one step ahead of every move that monster made, left spin and back to the right. I felt the bull weaken towards the end of the ride. Not what I wanted. I needed every point I could muster to get the win. The whistle blew and just as it did, the bull gave one last hard kick. It caught me off guard as I was preparing to eject from this roller coaster ride. I lost all grip with my spurs and flipped forward over the bulls head. Twisting my riding hand upside down and was not able to get my tight grip loosened enough to get out of the rope, I was hung up. I knew I had to get on my feet and get my hand out before I got into a serious wreck. I managed to get to my feet as the bull jerked away from me, pulling me along and dragging my off my feet again. I had to get out of this situation. I got to my feet one more time and that bastard turned hard right, straight towards the fence. There wasn't much more I could do but try to hug close to the bull and wait until we got away from the steel fence panels. I used whatever strength I had left to try and get close to the bull and not get dragged under his hooves.

Last time that happened I ended up with a dislocated ankle broken in 5 places. I didn't need a repeat. The bull got right up beside those steel panels. It jumped and belly rolled into the fence, smashing me against it. My hand ripped from its death grip in my rope and sent me to the dirt. I saw the bull take off across the arena so I was in no rush to get up. I waited a few moments for my heart to stop racing. I didn't want to move until I knew nothing hurt. I had the wind knocked out of me, but I felt okay. Surprisingly, my knee didn't seem to hurt yet. I stood up and the crowd cheered. I picked up my rope and dragged it behind me, satisfied that I had done my best. It was up to the judges now to decide if it was good enough to win that buckle.

It was between me and another buddy of mine. Matt and I stood in the arena waiting for the verdict. The judges came up to us after adding up the tally.

"Myron, you got it, by one point"

Matt turned to me, shook my hand and slapped my shoulder. We had travelled together numerous times, he was one of the most hilarious guys to be around and a helluva bull rider.

"Good ride buddy, you're a tough sonuvabitch." Matt walked off, a true sportsman.

My dad walked out, holding that prize that I had wanted so badly to win. I had dodged a bullet with that wreck and was happy to be able to stand in front of him and shake his hand as he handed me that trophy buckle. I had done what I set out to do. I set my mind on a goal, I believed in myself and I accomplished my goal. I was pretty damn happy with myself. The only thing that could've made this moment better was if Stacy had been there to see it. She still had not seen me ride.

I packed up my gear and headed home. My focus had been so centered on getting that buckle. I couldn't wait to tell Stacy it was mine. But I had another bull to ride the next day and I needed to switch gears and work on points for the finals. Making this ride had put me in the top 6 contingent and I needed to be in the top 5. I found ice for my knee which was now starting to swell again and went to bed.

The next morning I got up early and headed out to Stacy's family farm, I was picking her up and taking her to watch me ride. I was excited. I hadn't had time to call her the night before, so she had no idea how I had made out. I slowly hopped out of the truck, hoping the sun would gleam off my shiny new trophy buckle.

"Ha-ha, why are you so smiley?" She asked, as if seeing her wasn't enough reason for me to smile.

"What?" I asked "You didn't notice it?" I was almost offended that she hadn't.

"Well, you're walking. That's a good sign," Stacy said jokingly. She was the best ball buster- she kept my ego in check, which I probably needed more often than not.

"I won dammit! See the buckle?" come on woman, you gotta give me some credit!

"Oh that's awesome! Good job babe. I'm happy for you, wish I could've been there." She seemed a bit bummed out that she had missed it. I was as well, but I was happy to be with her then. I hadn't been able to see her much in the last couple weeks.

She jumped into the truck, taking her normal spot in the middle by my side. We chatted all the way into town. I was so happy to have her with me again. I parked close to the arena and dragged my heavy gear bag out of the box of the truck. My knee was not feeling great and I was a bit worried that it wasn't going to stay healthy for the weekend, but I had another couple weeks to rest after this event. I just had to get through the next couple days. We walked back to where the bull riders got ready. I got my rope out and tied it to the fence panel and started preparing my gear right away. Once I was all set, I hopped up over the fence. Stacy had been standing on the other side patiently waiting for me. As my feet hit the ground, my knee gave out and I ended up in a crumpled mess in the dirt.

Uh oh.

"Are you okay?" Stacy reached down to help me back up.

"I'm not sure. My knee just popped." The pain had rushed back into my knee and instantly started to swell. I couldn't put any weight on it. This was bad. I wasn't concerned about being able to walk. After all you have to ride the bull, not lead him around. But if I drew on a head hunter who wanted nothing more than to smash me into the dirt with his head, I would need to be able to run. I needed to sit down and get some ice.

She helped me limp to a nearby bench. Thankfully, I carried instant ice packs in my gear bag, an essential piece of kit for this sport. She ran and grabbed one for me, cracking it and got it onto my knee. I had to make a decision pretty quick. I knew what I wanted to do-- I wanted to ride-- but injuring my knee bad enough to need surgery would end my chances of riding at the finals.

I sat there, not saying a word, hoping the pain would go away. It didn't. It got worse. Soon my knee was so swollen people were asking what was up with it. What was I going to do? The bull I had drawn was one that I wanted to ride. He made nice tight turns, spinning hard to the right, which was perfect for me as I rode with my right hand. But with my right knee in the state it was in, Spinning to the right would put even more strain on it and I needed my right knee to be strong so I could spur. My outside leg would kick encourage the bull to spin harder. I knew what the right decision was. I just didn't want to say it out loud. But what did I want more? Did I want to try to win the rest of this weekend and give Stacy the chance to see me ride? Or bow out of the competition, heal up for the next one and continue my road to the finals?

"I gotta turn my bull out." I felt so defeated, like such a failure. I went from feeling like an absolute champion to a quitter and I was anything but that.

I let the judges know. They hadn't known about my injury and questioned my decision, which made me feel even worse. I wasn't scared and they should've known that by now. These judges had watched me ride many times before; they knew I wasn't a quitter. They also knew that injuries had never stopped me before. But I had to look at the bigger picture. I would get to ride again and I still had a chance at the finals. I just had to make it count once I could heal up.

I packed up my gear, Stacy carried it to the truck for me and sat by my side as I pouted for the rest of the weekend.

I may have been upset, but having her with me and share my grief made me feel a bit better.

"Don't worry about it babe," she encouraged. "Just get healed up and ready for the next one. You got some points now. You're going to make it no matter what." For someone that hadn't seen me ride yet, she was becoming my biggest fan.

Chapter 5

I spent a couple weeks babying my knee. I was being extra cautious and made sure to follow the book to heal it up as quickly as possible. Spring was in full bloom, which meant it was my busy season. I was getting close to my graduation, I had rodeos to get to, finals to prepare for and I needed to figure out what I was going to do with myself after school. I had a list of things I needed to take care of: packing, future planning, and fixing up my old truck. My folks found an acreage they wanted to move to as well.

Stacy's life wasn't much easier. She was in 4H and had cows to show and speeches to write. Plus, she had to stay on top of her own school work. She was more focused on her education than I ever was. I spent the majority of my last semester skipping school so I could work, saving up all I could so I would have funds to travel around to rodeos. I had all the credits I needed to graduate, so I wasn't too worried about it. Although I probably could have slacked off a bit less for my English and math classes, I didn't see how that was really going to affect my future. Who really needs that stuff to ride bulls anyway?

The next couple rides went well. I placed in each event. I was now qualified for the finals and I had enough points that I wasn't going to get beat out by anyone that could take my spot. I skipped a couple events to take some extra time to heal up now that the pressure was off a little bit. I spent time at the farm with Stacy. I got a kick out of her with her messy ponytail and torn up clothes she'd wear for chores. She didn't give a damn how she looked. It was function over form at that point. I still thought she looked beautiful. There was just something about a girl who wasn't afraid to get cow shit on her jeans, which was rare. So many girls were more focused on how they looked and less on their own personality which made them much less desirable in my eyes.

I wasn't into 4H. I wasn't into showing animals-- I wanted to ride them. But Stacy loved it and since she had been there to see me ride (even though I was unable to) I said I would go to her achievement day. I had to ask what it was. Basically it's like a finals rodeo, except you're showing off your prized steers, cows, calves or whatever else you had raised. They led the animals around an arena while a judge critiqued it and their showmanship. Once that part was done, they auctioned off the steers for meat. Stacy had done quite well. She took top prize in showmanship and runner-up for confirmation with her steer and I was proud of her. But then it was time to auction off her animal that she had raised from a baby. She spent hours training it to lead and be calm. I didn't realize that this was going to be rough. She led her steer in, and led him back and forth in front of the buyers while the auctioneer rattled of the rising price as the bids poured in. Once the bidding was done she led him out and tied him to a fence with the rest, they would go to the meat market from there. I walked up to her, smiling because she had done so well. Stacy turned to me and burst into tears. I was so confused.

"What's wrong?" I asked. "You did really well!"

Stacy hugged me and sobbed into my shoulder. I didn't know what to do besides wrap my arms around her until I figured out what was wrong.

"They're going to eat my steer," she cried.

I had to bite my lip to keep from laughing. I knew that would just piss her off and make the situation worse.

"It's okay, honey. You got a good price for him." Not the best choice of words, I would've been better off not saying anything.

"That's not helpful. Just shut up and hug me."

Okay, fair enough. I can do that, I thought. I kept my mouth shut and just hugged her. Thankfully, she didn't cry for long. We went back to the stall she'd setup for her animals and started the cleanup process.

This 4H thing was like work. I'd rather ride bulls. I only had to spend a few seconds getting the job done and it was way more exciting.

I had been watching the rodeo schedule to see where I was going to go after the high school rodeo finals were done. That would be my last time riding at that level. I had already registered to be a member of the next league up. The prizes were bigger, the bulls for the most part were tougher and a lot of the riders were better. But I was ready for it. Stacy's folks had been a huge part of their local rodeo, which was one of the better known shows to go to. I wanted to make sure I went to that one. Her dad had always been skeptical of this kid who was dating his youngest daughter; some cocky boy that came around all the time, claiming to be a bull rider. Unless he witnessed it, he wasn't about to believe it. I wrote down the dates for all the events I wanted to enter. I found the date for their rodeo and cringed. Dammit, it was the same weekend as the finals. This was terrible. Their hometown rodeo was a huge deal in her family. They planned on being there a full week, camping out, running the event and drinking beer. What should I do? I wondered. I didn't want to miss out on the opportunity to ride there and prove my claim of being a good bull rider.

This really bothered me. I would end up being in another town nowhere near this event. Stacy would spend an entire week basically alone while I was at the finals. If I hadn't been so in love with her, it would have been no big deal, but man, this sucked. I asked Debbie if the date had been confirmed or if it is still tentative. I already knew the answer but I was hoping for good news. No such luck. This bothered me so much I could tell it was messing with my focus. That is never good for a bull rider. I had to get back on track. That local show will be there next year and I could ride then. For now, the finals were all that mattered. I tried to convince myself of that over and over, not that it worked very well. There was nothing I could do to change things. I wasn't about to skip the finals after I'd worked so hard to qualify.

The day before the finals I checked through all of my gear. I made sure everything was ready to go. Then, I packed everything up and threw it into my mom's van. As we headed south the weather turned bad. Rain came down in sheets and never let up. We got to our hotel and it continued to pour. Even though we had traveled several hours south, it seemed that the entire region was getting soaked. Thank goodness the finals were held in an indoor arena.

We had finally made it. The show was much bigger than I had anticipated. It seemed like an endless line of horse trailers, pickup trucks and cattle. Kids from all over Alberta were here to compete. Winning here meant getting into the nationals. I hadn't thought that far ahead yet. I had learned that planning too far ahead would take my focus off of what was in front of me at that moment. This moment was for this weekend, but I was still not feeling like I was as charged up as I should've been for this. I'd been pushing myself so hard to get here and now that I had arrived I felt only half ass ready. I was still bummed out that I wasn't going to be with Stacy this weekend at their rodeo. I had to try and get that out of my head. Now was not the time to be feeling sorry for myself. Tomorrow would be my first of three attempts to prove that I belonged here.

I called Stacy to let her know we made it and to see how things were going with their show.

"We got rained out, my parents are postponing this rodeo for a couple weeks."

Seriously? This was great news for me! Probably not what her family wanted after months of planning and organizing, but now I had the chance to ride there!

Now the problem was getting my focus razor sharp. Some people were able to switch on within minutes. Not me. It took days, sometimes weeks to get myself mentally ready. Now I was trying to do it over night. I should've been ready for this weeks ago but I let one stupid thing get into head and ruin it. Rather than focusing on the finals I had used my mental energy to stress over missing the rodeo at home.

The first bull I drew was barely worth speaking about. They swung the gate open and I hit the dirt. What the hell was I even doing here? I wondered. I had to get my shit together. I made it here, I worked my ass off to qualify. I would prove to everyone that I earned my right to be here.

I woke up the next morning in a better state of mind. I wouldn't make it easy for any bull to throw me today. The stock they brought in for the finals was top notch. There was no reason I couldn't score some good points today. I knew that, I also knew that I had to stay on to get those points. I had full intentions of making that happen that day. I overheard one of the bullfighters mention the name of the bull I'd drawn and my ears perked up.

"You rolling that bull in here?" I asked them.

"Yeah, this side here," the bullfighter said pointing toward a chute, "This bull has been on fire this year. No one has been able to stay on him."

Perfect, I thought. That's the one I needed. Scoring on a bull like him was a sure way of earning some great points. This bull was no rookie. He walked into the chute and stood there as if he had been there a hundred times. This meant that he would not thrash me in the chutes before they got the gate open, which was good news for my knee. I would have the best chance at making a good ride right now.

I did my usual pre ride warm ups the exact same way as I always did. I took my time to make sure my rope was set just right, like I had a hundred times before. This one needed to count for something. This ride had to be perfect. I set my knees down on top of the bulls back, testing him to see if he would start to thrash or not. He didn't budge. He stood perfectly centered in the chute. This made my job much easier. It also raised my awareness that much more. I could feel the tension in the animal's muscles. He knew what was coming. It felt as if he could explode at any moment. But he stood completely still. I had my rope pulled tight and my grip was perfect. This was it. I slid up slowly onto my rope, I didn't want to startle this monster and have him start smashing around. I was set. I nodded my head.

The gate latch clicked open and that beast exploded out of the chute. He kicked his rear legs high up in the air and I set my spurs again. With such an aggressive move, my feet had moved back to where I couldn't get a good bite with my spurs. I quickly shuffled them forward and grabbed another hold. He leaped hard into the air. I had never felt an animal with this much athleticism before. It was incredible to feel the power that this bull had. We were in the air long enough for me to start wondering how long it would take before he touched ground again. When we finally came back down, I felt slightly out of the sweet spot where I needed to be to stay on top of this thing.

I quickly smashed my spurs into his side again to try and grab a better hold with my feet. I reached far forward trying to work my upper body into a good position for the next jump. The bull leaped with all four feet high up in the air and twisted his body completely sideways. I knew I was in trouble. My feet had slid too far back again. My upper body had not recovered enough to sustain this obscure maneuver. My brain couldn't comprehend what this animal was doing. I'd never been on one quite like it before. As we started descending back to earth, I started to think this bull was going to slam his whole body down on his side, right on top of my leg, but at the last possible moment he flipped back straight leaving me behind. I slammed into the dirt.

The bullfighter ran up to me, helping me up off the ground.

"Holy shit, kid, there ain't no shame in getting tossed from that bull. That was incredible!" he said slapping me on the back.

I sure didn't share his point of view. Yes that bull was something else, something I had never encountered before. That was the kind of bull I needed to stay on. Drawing a bull like that is great, but I didn't stay on long enough to make it count. I felt like I wasted my time. I was pissed off with myself. I had come so far, I had tried so hard and the only person I could blame for my failure was myself. I had one more bull to ride, but now the chances of getting to the nationals was pretty much gone. I could feel the disappointment in my parents on our way to the hotel that night. I felt bad. They were taking time out of their busy lives to bring me down here, they paid for the hotel, they'd spent many days at the hospital with me after getting beat up, and they'd listened to my constant chatter about riding. They had put up with it all, now I was at the finals and failing.

The next day, I decided the nationals didn't matter, all I needed was one decent ride and I would go home happy. Put all the other stuff aside, just ride because you love to do it, don't ride for any other reason. I wanted to do this one for myself. I got on again one more time. One last chance. It just wasn't meant to be. I got hung up in the rope. The bull was big enough I could barely get my feet to touch the ground. I eventually got loose and landed in front of the chute gates. There was nothing left to do but pack up and go home. I felt completely defeated. This was not how this was supposed to turn out. I just wanted to go home, review the videos and see where I went wrong and try to focus on where I was going next. I already knew the destination. I was going to be riding in front of a packed crowd. And Stacy's dad. No pressure though, right?

After being home for a couple weeks and feeling sorry for myself, I decided it was time to retire my embarrassment of a truck and get an upgrade. I had been saving up what I could and had found the truck I wanted. A friend of mine had shown up to school one day with a bright yellow 1979 ford F-250, it had a lift and big mud tires on it. This was more my style. Now that we were out of school, he was selling it and I wasn't going to waste time thinking on it too much. My brother drove me out and I handed over the funds. It had some rust and it was a little rough, but nowhere near as bad as my other truck. I drove this beauty home, cleaned it up and called Stacy to tell her about my exciting purchase. She was about as excited as I was at the 4H event, not her thing. Oh well, this truck had a stereo in it and a working heater and it was a 4x4 so we wouldn't get stuck so easy.

"Uh huh, that's great Hun. Are you coming out tomorrow?" Stacy asked.

"Well, hell yeah I am. I gotta show you the new wheels right?" I was starting to think she was really not all that interested in the truck. I was sure she would love it once I drove it out there.

Next morning I was itching to get out the door and head to the farm with my new pride and joy. I rolled into the yard proud as ever. Stacy met me in the driveway, the look on her face was a little less than impressed.

"It's yellow."

"Yeah, isn't it cool?" I asked in excitement.

"I don't like it," she replied

How could she not like it? It was a million times better than my last truck in every way. What's not to like about it? I wondered.

Jamie walked out to see who was in the yard with this strange vehicle. After realizing it was mine, he took a little closer look at it, knowing full well that his daughter would be riding in it. It would need to pass his safety inspection. He didn't say much about it; just grunted a few words and walked off. I took that as a solid approval.

I smiled at Stacy "Come on, let's go for a drive."

She rolled her eyes "Alright fine. Let's go take big bird for a drive."

She walked over to the driver's door and assessed the height of the jacked up truck. She stretched one leg up into it and was struggling to get in. I took this opportunity to help out and grabbed a handful of her ass to hoist her in.

"Nice, babe, real nice," she said, laughing at my attempt at helping her in. I knew there would be benefits to having a lifted truck. This was the best one yet.

We cruised in that truck all day. By the time we had wasted all the gas in the tank, she had started to warm up to my new ride. It was much nicer to ride in than the old truck and it did have a decent stereo. That's pretty much all that is really required as a kid for any type of vehicle. Little did I know that stupid truck would become a huge part of our lives.

Chapter 6

With my graduation from high school wrapped up, my family packed up everything and we moved out to our new place. The house was old and ugly, the yard was a mess and we had a ton of work to do to get it suitable for our horses. The best part about this new place? I was now only a few short miles away from Stacy's family farm! I had quit my job in town. We were now a fair ways out of town and I didn't want to drive that distance every day with my new gas guzzling pig of a truck. I found a job working at a ranch. Working with cattle was fun for me, but the field work was not my favourite. I found it terribly boring and monotonous. The ranch was a few miles past Stacy's house which was perfectly convenient for me. I'd head out first thing in the morning, work all day, then head back to her place to have dinner and hang out. What a perfect situation for a teenager in love!

The rodeo that I had so desperately wanted to ride at was coming up quick. I had licked my ego wounds from my complete failure at the finals and started to focus on the next ride again. I was very excited for this one, an entire weekend spending time with my pretty lady and her family and getting the opportunity to show that I could actually do this. By this time Stacy had seen me ride a couple times at different events, I had come to realize that she would get very nervous and quiet before I rode. She'd go from her usual chatty self to completely shut down and wouldn't say a word. I was all jacked up and hyper and she would just stand off to the side, arms folded and not looking particularly happy. I would ask her if she was okay, she'd just nod and give me one word answers. Once my ride was over she would go back to normal.

She had seen me get tossed around a bit. Nothing serious as far as I was concerned; just bumps and bruises.

"How do I know if you're actually hurt?" Stacy asked me.

"If I don't get up, or try to get out of the way of the bull, I'm hurt. But you shouldn't worry about that, I'll be fine" I replied.

I was pretty confident by this time. I had been riding for years and knew when it was time to get out of a bad situation. I had been hung up enough to not panic and was able to ride smart enough to avoid injuries for the most part. Stacy was not convinced, but what would you expect her to believe? She was helpless when it came to what happened inside that arena. The only thing she could do was sit and watch to see what happened and wait to see if I got up after I got off the bull.

With her folks busy setting up for the event and spending the majority of their time getting setup, I made sure to keep Stacy company every chance I got. I'd help her with whatever she needed to do around the farm. She'd listen to my constant chatter about the bull I'd drawn. She would begin to get a knot in her stomach and get quiet again. She was happy that I loved this sport and she admitted she thought it was pretty damn hot when I would make a good ride and strut back across the arena, dragging my bull rope behind me, cocky as ever. But it scared her. She didn't want to see me get hurt. I assured her over and over that I would be fine. Still, she was not convinced.

I packed up my gear again. I had hardly slept the night before the event; I was too excited about the ride. I drove to the farm, picked up my sweet heart and headed a few miles down the road to the rodeo grounds in Teepee Creek. Since she was with me and her folks were a part of the committee for this event, she had full access to the grounds. I held her hand and carried my gear bag over my shoulder as we headed to the back of the bucking chutes. Most of us rough stock riders were not a shy bunch. When you go behind the chutes you were in our 'locker room.' We would be half naked, changing into our riding gear, talking tough, cussing, spitting chewing tobacco on the ground. Not the most comfortable place for Stacy to hang out, but she was with me and she found it amusing to see me and my riding buddies talking smack, acting tough and getting worked up for our rides. I talked to the stock contractor a bit about the bull I would be riding. He said to make sure the bull is looking out as he was notorious for coming out backwards and slamming your knee into the gate, which would ruin your ride not to mention your knee. But if you got out on the bull okay, he was a good one to get on. Not the biggest points bull, but if you stay on you were very likely to place in the top three. That was good enough for me. I just had to make sure I didn't fall off, but my mind was set, that wasn't going to happen today.

They started rolling the bulls into the bucking chutes. One of the judges walked up and pointed at my bull. "Hey Myron, this one is you, you're up first."

I hated being the first one out. I preferred to be in the middle somewhere. It seemed to help my focus even more. But that didn't matter too much. I was going to do this and I was going to do it well. By this time I had realized that Stacy's dad was the gate man, he was standing beside me as I got down on the bull. He was watching for my nod to turn us loose. *Great*, I thought, *I better not mess this up…no pressure at all.* This would be my chance to show him that I wasn't a bull shitter; I was, in fact, a bull rider.

I slung my legs up over the chute gate, glanced over to the side of the arena and saw Stacy sitting up on the fence, nervously chewing her nails. Time to get the job done in front of a huge crowd and all her family. I pulled my chaps back away from my knees as I sat down on the bulls back. The bull fussed and kicked as I got settled in. My hand felt at home in the rope. I pulled the rope tight and felt completely confident. I ensured everything was just as it should be. I had done this so many times that it was all muscle memory now. I slid up on my rope and glanced at the bulls head, he was looking straight ahead. I remembered what the stock contractor had said about making sure the bull was looking out at the gate before I turned loose. Now I had a 50/50 chance of whether this bull would head out the gate or turn around backwards and ruin my ride.

Jamie stood with his hand on the latch. "You ready?" He yelled.

"Rattle the gate, get this son of a bitch looking out towards you" I didn't want to chance it.

Jamie shook the gate to get the bulls attention, the bull stood solid and wouldn't turn his head to look. I was sitting right, I was ready to go, but I wanted the best chance to get out on him.

"You ready?" Jamie hollered, sounding a bit impatient now.

"Get his damn attention first! I need him looking out!" I insisted.

With this bull not cooperating like I wanted and Jamie itching to see if this kid could stand up to his claims, I heard one last thing...

"Fuck it, he's ready."

The gate flew open.

Here we go! Luckily that bull turned out towards the gate and we were on our way. He jumped hard and kicked. I dug my spurs in and reached up over the bulls head. Now I was a little pissed that I hadn't given my nod, I started riding angry. I jabbed that bastard in the ribs every jump, encouraging him to jump harder. He snorted, spewing snot from his nose as he leaped and twisted left and back to the right. Bulls are smart and can feel when you are not centered on their back. A bull that has been ridden enough will turn away from you and get you off quickly. I was sitting perfect this time, every turn he made I would make my moves to stay in that sweet spot. I had an answer for every trick this beast tried. I continued to slam my spurs into his side at every jump. This ride felt incredible, some rides feel like they take minutes. This one felt like it was over too soon. The buzzer sounded and it was time to make my exit. Riding right handed meant that you should try to get off on the right side of the bull. The chances of getting hung up are next to nil that way. But we were now close to the fence on my right side, not a good place to get off. Getting off on the left side is ok as long as you get your death grip released first. I dove off to the left, my feet hit the dirt. My right armed jerked away, death grip still holding strong. I reached up and yanked the tail end of the rope as the bull jumped again and I managed to release myself with no further drama.

I walked over and picked up my rope from the ground. I slung it over my shoulder dragging the bells behind me in the dirt. I felt 10 foot tall, chest puffed out and completely bullet proof. I had accomplished what I had set out to do. It wasn't the best bull I had ever been on, not by a long shot, but it was an okay ride and I was satisfied with it for now. I walked past Jamie, he had a half grin when he saw me walking up. He gave me a slight nod and moved over to the next chute gate as the next rider was set to go. No words were exchanged. I was not about to call him out on his decision to turn me loose without my nod. I had still stayed on and that's all that mattered.

I walked back behind the bucking chutes, tossing my rope on top of my gear bag. Stacy walked back to meet me there, smiling, but still coming down from her nervousness.

She slapped my shoulder. "You did that on purpose!"

I looked at her puzzled.

"Huh? I did what on purpose? Stayed on and kicked the shit out of that bull? Hell yeah, I did!"

"No, you jackass, you got hung up when you jumped off, you did that on purpose just to scare me."

I laughed, what should I tell her? That I kind of messed up there by not releasing my grip before exiting on the off side? Nah.

"Ha-ha yeah, well I just wanted to see your face when I got back here. Everything else went way too well, I had to add at least a little bit of excitement to it."

Stacy glared at me. "You're such an asshole." She wrapped her arms around me. I could tell she was proud of me.

I left the rest of my gear on, waiting to come down from my adrenaline rush before I stripped down. We stood up at the end of the chutes, watching the other guys take a crack at the bulls they had drawn. I helped a few buddies in the chutes, pulling their ropes tight or holding on to them while their bulls thrashed and bucked inside the chutes as they prepared to make their rides. We watched as one after the other attempted their rides, they were all falling off. No one else had stayed on their bulls by the end of the day. Things were looking good for me, but there was still one more day of riding with a whole new bunch of riders, many of which were the top guys in this league that I had just started riding in.

I packed my gear up and once again walked hand in hand with Stacy, my bag slung over my shoulder. I was feeling pretty damn good about myself. Stacy, now completely relaxed again and was pretty happy with her boyfriend. She wasn't about to let go of me and stayed hooked to my side. We went to the hall that night for the rodeo dance. With my riding complete for the weekend I had no worries about having a couple beers with the rest of my riding buddies. I was always very careful to stay away from any alcohol the night before I rode. I didn't want that to become an excuse of why I didn't ride well the next day. We hung out with some old friends, Stacy laughed her ass off at our dumb jokes and crazy rodeo stories. We had become Myron and Stacy. We had been together long enough now to be known as a couple. We were still so young, but we were so in love with each other. Most had stopped teasing us about our young love as they realized that neither of us were going anywhere. We were together forever.

We spent the night at the farm, sleeping in late as I had nowhere else to be at any specific time. We eventually got up and headed back to the rodeo to hang out and watch the rest of the day's activities. One of the events Stacy's family entered every year was the wild horse racing. It's a bizarre event where eight teams of three would tie a rope to a wild horse that was standing in the bucking chutes. The horn would blow and every horse was turned loose at the same time. It was sheer pandemonium! People getting trampled and dragged around as they attempted to get hold of the wild animal, get a saddle on it, get one rider on its back and stay on it long enough to get across the arena. First team to accomplish this would win the prize. A few of Stacy's cousins had entered just as they do every year. It got a bit rough. One of the team members got smashed in the face. Once the horses had been cleared out, the fella with the swollen face and blood leaking from his mouth was walking around in circles as if he was lost.

"Hey what are you looking for?" asked one of the judges.

"My teef!"

Apparently, he was hoping to find his teeth in the dirt. They had been knocked out of his head when the horse cracked him in the face. We were in stitches laughing at this peculiar moment. Although he looked to be in some pain, we were pretty sure a couple cold beers would have him feeling just fine in no time.

I sat with Stacy on the fence surrounding the outdoor arena as the bull riding was set to begin. Jamie had passed his gateman job off to another volunteer and stood on the other side of Stacy, watching with us and enjoying the event. The first few riders came out and hit that hard dirt, one after another. I was starting to do the math in my head, five riders left, worst I can do is 6th place. Another rider hit the ground, 5th place. Then another. This continued until there were two riders left, both of them at the top of the league.

Well, 3rd ain't too bad, I thought to myself.

The next rider fell. One left. The last rider to go was a man I had a lot of respect for. In a sport where the biggest ego reigns supreme, this guy was very polite. Wyatt had helped me years before when I was just getting started. He was always helpful and supportive, never boastful even though he had every right to be. He was good, really good. They turned him loose, he stayed for only a short time and landed with a 'thud'. I said nothing.

Jamie looked over at me. "Well kid, looks like you won it all!"

I smiled back at him. "Yeah, I guess so!"

I was pretty sure that was the longest conversation we'd ever had. It hadn't completely sunk in yet. I had been the only one to stay on my bull at an event that Stacy's folks had been a part of organizing. I had finally had the chance to prove my worth as a bull rider. I had done what I had set out to do, and I had won the event. I was as happy as I had ever been. Failing at the finals meant nothing to me now. This was more important.

Above all else, I had started to realize that there was one thing more important to me than all of this. It was Stacy. She meant the world to me and I would have traded the title of national champion to be with her for the rest of my life.

Chapter 7

The rest of our summer was spent in the fields, working with cattle and heading to other towns for rodeos. Stacy had slowly started to become more comfortable watching me ride. She still would fuss over me if I got a little banged up, but it was in her nature to care. She was such a soft hearted person and genuinely cared about my wellbeing. I was at a bit of a loss when it came to expressing my feelings, even to her. My family was never big on talking about feelings. Stacy's was the same, but she seemed to be able to find ways to tell me how she felt and let me know what was on her mind.

She'd write a lot of it down. If a thought popped into her mind that she didn't want to forget to tell me, she would write it down and show it to me later. This was before email and text messaging was a thing. A handwritten note was all we knew. Stacy taught me to write things down. If I had something on my mind I'd struggle to find a way to express it. Stacy told me to write it down and I found it helped. It didn't have to be perfect, it didn't have to even make a lot of sense. Just put the pen to paper and let my thoughts run out onto it. We'd write each other dozens of notes and letters. The love we had for each other had grown so much and it was uncharted territory for the both of us. We both had questions and were both uncertain on how this was supposed to go. Writing to each other was a great way for us figure out what we were thinking when we weren't able to find the right words.

With summer coming to an end, Stacy was going back to high school for another year. I continued to work at the ranch, enjoying the job for the most part. It was something I could do outside, riding horses, working with the cows and fixing fences.

As the weather began to change from fall to winter, the work slowed down and there wasn't much left to do but feed cows. The owner had to let me go. There just wasn't enough work to justify me being there all day. So I headed home and started searching for another place of employment. I didn't know much of anything outside of what I had been doing. Many of my friends had started into different trades or gone off to college to get started on their chosen profession. I hadn't given anything much thought. Bull riding was all I really thought about up until I met Stacy. Now she had begun to take over the majority of my mind. Knowing this and thinking about our future, I was sure I needed to get some kind of job that could support us once she was done with school. I was certain we'd be looking to get a place of our own, although we had never discussed it. I wasn't even sure she shared the same thought, but I wanted to make sure I was prepared if she wanted to go that route.

It didn't take long before I had found a job, it was an oil field position which was what most folks worked in around Grande Prairie. You didn't need a college education to do it, you just needed to be able to work hard in all types of weather. Didn't seem like a bad deal to me. The only downfall to this job was the time away from home. I'd be gone for two weeks at a time, then home for a week. Stacy and I hadn't been away from each other that long, but I knew the money would be worth it. I was a little worried this might screw up my rodeo season but I had to do something, winning at rodeos was generally a decent payout but it was seasonal and not exactly a good career move at this point. I started the job just after the New Year and I soon discovered what it felt like to truly miss someone you loved. It was brutal for the both of us. My two weeks of work felt more like two months, the one week off felt like one day. I'd call whenever I could. She'd cry while I would do my best not to. I always thought I was pretty tough, but Stacy brought out a softer side of me I never knew existed.

We eventually started to get used to this job, the money was enough to keep me heading off to work. It also made our dates a little easier to afford. I no longer had to save every penny just to put gas in the truck and take her somewhere cheap. I loved to spoil her in any way I could, she deserved anything I could possibly give her.

The next few months were busy. I was working and Stacy was busy with school and her 4H steer. This was her last year showing for 4H. She was ready to be done with it, but wanted to have a good final year. I was saving up money where I could and trying to set some aside for a rainy day fund...or upgrades to the truck (same thing really). I had a couple broken leaf springs in the rear suspension and I needed to replace them. But in my immature mind, why put more of the same back in? Why not add more lift? Seemed like the obvious choice to me. I ordered the new lift kit and waited for a few weeks before it showed up.

My next week off of work, I picked up my parts and headed out to the farm. I had planned to get this new suspension put in the truck there. That way I could still hang out with Stacy and get my parts put in at the same time. Stacy was less than impressed with my plan. She didn't want to sit around watching me bust my knuckles while working on my truck. She wanted to get away from the farm for a little while, go off somewhere and spend some time alone. I assured her it wouldn't take long to do. I was wrong. I spent a solid 4 days cursing at rusted bolts and stubborn parts that just didn't seem to fit like they should. Finally on the fourth day I had it done and ready to drive again. It was late at night by the time I had it done and was pretty happy with how it had turned out, although it did look pretty goofy with my 'little' 35 inch mud tires and nine inches of suspension lift. I ran up to the house to tell Stacy it was done but she had gone to bed. I was pretty sure she had gone to sleep angry with me and the lack of attention I had paid to her over the past few days. I went home and prayed that she would not be mad at me the next day.

Next morning I couldn't wait to go pick her up in my now terribly tall truck. I cruised into the yard smiling ear to ear. She wandered out of the house when she heard me coming.

"What do you think?" I asked, hopeful she would share some of my enthusiasm, but I knew she was not likely to be very impressed.

"Did you really need it to be that tall?"

I took that as a rhetorical question. Obviously it was necessary or so I thought anyway. I did my best to make her forget about the last few days I had spent not paying much attention to her, but she was not having it. I had pretty much put her on the back burner while I did what I wanted to. I felt bad but I was hoping she would come around after I took her to town for a date night. She eventually warmed up to me again, but I knew she was not about to forget about this. I'd be making it up to her for a while.

A few days later I was at the farm as usual. Work had slowed down a little so I had been able to spend a few extra days with her. We were both pretty happy to get the extra days after my wrenching episode. It was getting late and I needed to head home. I jumped into my jacked up truck and headed out. I turned off the paved highway onto the dirt road leading to my parent's house. The roads had been dry for quite a while now but had started to get rough. I barreled down that dirt road, kicking up all the dust I could. I started hitting some washboard and backed off the throttle a bit, but the truck took a hard right turn. I turned into the skid, confident I could drive it out of this minor situation. The front tires dropped down into the ditch as the truck continued to skid sideways.

"Shhitttt"

I'm not sure how long I had been sitting there, but when I woke up I was completely confused as to what had happened. Nothing was as it should've been. My steering wheel was busted, the windshield was caved in and my door windows were missing. I was covered in glass and my head was throbbing. I tried to open my door but it was jammed. I was sitting upright, so I didn't understand what had caused all the damage. I was still behind the wheel in spite of not wearing my seatbelt. I looked down and realized I was sitting on my floor mat, somehow it had gone from the floor of the truck to me sitting on it. I also noticed a little green light blinking at me. It was my cell phone. I picked it up and hit the call button.

"Hello?" Debbie asked.

"Uh…I think I rolled my truck."

I don't remember if I hung up or dropped the phone, but I woke up again to my dad prying my driver's side door open and my mom yelling at me to wake up in a tone that I had not heard in her voice before. She sounded scared and I couldn't figure out why. Moments later Stacy was by my side.

"Baby are you ok? Talk to me, what happened? Look at me!" she pleaded.

Things were foggy, but I took another meat wagon ride to the hospital that night. I spent a couple days there while they assessed my third concussion. Stacy came in to see how I was doing. My head hurt and I was a bit sore but other than that I was fine.

"How bad is the truck?" I had no idea what it looked like.

"Who gives a shit about the damn truck?" Stacy half smiled at me. She knew I was ok now but she had been scared that night. I didn't know how bad it looked and I didn't remember much of the event. I did know I was lucky I hadn't been thrown from the truck. Someone was watching over me that night I guess.

Once I was cleared to leave the hospital, Stacy came with my folks to pick me up and take me home. My dad and Jamie had pulled what was left of the truck back to our house and left it in the yard. When we arrived home, I slowly walked over to the truck, it was a mess. There wasn't much left of it, the only straight piece was the tailgate and it wouldn't open. I stared at it in disbelief. Stacy wrapped her arms around me and started to cry. To me it wasn't a big deal, the truck was wrecked but I was fine, so there was nothing to cry about. But she was still upset. It could have been much worse. It could have been fatal.

Back to driving my old piece of crap truck, I guess. I still had it parked in the back field so I fired it back up and got it back on the road. I still had to get to work, I now needed money to fix the truck or replace it. I was done riding for the season so I could focus a bit more on working and spending my time off with Stacy again. We talked at length about what I should do - scrap the truck or get it rebuilt. Eventually it was decided to just have it rebuilt, new trucks were overrated and I was never a fan of them anyway. I preferred the older trucks that still had some character. We hauled it to a body shop and left it there to get a face lift. A few months later I headed back to pick it up. Every panel had to be replaced, but the finished results were stunning. It was beautiful, with a fresh coat of bright yellow paint on it. I thought about changing the colour but Stacy helped me pick it out. Even though she wasn't a big fan of it, she felt it just wouldn't be the same if it wasn't yellow again.

I had a few small things to do to finish it up and have it road worthy again, but it sure looked sharp. Even Stacy had to admit it looked pretty damn good. I got to work finishing up the little things. I was ready to park my old crappy truck and get into this shiny new version. I had also saved up a little extra coin to get a bigger set of mud tires that suited the tall lift a bit better.

Picking Stacy up from school in this truck was a much better feeling than using my other truck. She was not embarrassed to be picked up in this new ride. I was also happy that I would be able to take her to her graduation in this monster. Everyone wants to go to grad in something nice and I was glad I would get the chance to do that for her.

We cruised around town in the big beast, stopping at all the fancy dress shops looking for the perfect dress for her graduation. She eventually found one that was drop dead gorgeous, but to be honest, she could have made anything look good. Standing at 5' 7" and maybe 110lbs soaking wet, with her long wavy brown hair and eyes that were easy to get lost in, she was something to behold. She had grown into quite a woman. I felt very proud to have her on my arm. Anyone would have, but she had picked me and, for whatever reason, she was satisfied with me.

Once her graduation day came, I made sure to detail the truck completely inside and out. I put on my new black wrangler jeans, white shirt and black vest. I jumped in the truck and headed off to go get Stacy. When she walked out with her hair all done, wearing that dress and looking like a solid 11 out of 10, my jaw hit the floor. I was well aware how beautiful she was but I just couldn't have imagined how stunning she would be on this day. I felt under dressed standing beside her. We headed off together, stopping to pick up one of her friends along the way. Karley was vertically challenged, and wearing a long grad dress as well. She looked at us, then looked at the truck.

"Ok, so how the hell am I supposed to get into this thing now?"

Stacy laughed as she kicked the door open and held out her hand to pull Karley up into the truck. Dresses were not these girls regular attire. They were much more comfortable in blue jeans and it may have shown slightly while they tried to figure out the proper moves to get in and out of the truck. Stacy didn't have to worry as much, as I was all too eager to lift her in and out at every stop we had to make.

We went through the ceremony, walking arm in arm everywhere. We looked good all cleaned up. It was a drastic change from our normal everyday torn up t-shirts and muddy boots. Tons of pictures were taken before we could get going to the graduation party. My mom had wanted a specific picture, she could be a picky person and sometimes a pain to have behind a camera when you just wanted to get going. But I wasn't going to argue, we didn't get all dressed up for nothing. I supposed a few extra pictures wouldn't hurt.

"Stacy, can you sit right here on this bench?" my mom asked, patting the seat she wanted to use for the picture.

"OK, now Myron, you go stand in front of her and take her hand in yours." I wasn't sure where she was going with this but I did as I was asked.

"Now, get down on one knee." she instructed.

"Huh?" It wasn't that I didn't want to do it, but her father was standing right there. Come on mom. Way to make me feel uncomfortable.

Stacy looked up at me while sitting on the bench with a huge grin on her face.

"Come on, babe, do as your mom asked."

I knelt down on one knee and looked up into Stacy's eyes, we both burst into laughter. I think Jamie was the uncomfortable one now.

"Hey now jumping the gun here a bit don't ya think" Jamie retorted.

Stacy smiled at her dad as if to say, you're going to have to except this at some point.

I didn't dare say anything, but looking up at her at that moment had me thinking. Neither of us were old enough, but we had been together for a couple years now. I had no intentions of making any sort of life plans that didn't involve her. I couldn't deny it. Someday I was going to marry this girl.

Chapter 8

After Stacy's graduation, we went to a few rodeos, but spent most of our time together. Riding was never very far from my mind and I wanted to get to one more event before the season was up. I knew which one I wanted to go to. It had a big cash prize every day for the bull riding event. I'd ride my first bull and if I placed in the top eight I'd get another bull. If I got the top score on that bull I'd win $1,000. I wanted it.

I packed up and headed out with Stacy by my side in my shiny jacked up truck. (By this time Stacy had started to call it 'our' truck. I disagreed.) We drove a couple hours to the event and headed straight to the bucking chutes again just like normal. We met up with the regular crowd of rough stock riding friends, all of them had become accustomed to Stacy being behind the chutes with us and had learned that they didn't need to filter their language or dirty jokes around her. She usually had a better one to top theirs anyway. For such a sweet and innocent personality, she had a mouth that could make a sailor blush. Most of the guys would also take a second glance to see if she was nearby before they stripped down out of their clothes, not that it would stop them, but they might yell at her before throwing their shirts on the ground and doing their best to flex what muscles they did have. She'd just laugh and shake her head, "Nice try," she'd say. "Better put a shirt back on before the sun fries that pasty white skin." She was always quick with a reply and could easily take an ego down a notch or two.

They got my bull loaded up and I was ready to go. Stacy stood off to the side at the end of the bucking chutes so she'd have a better view of the arena. I slid down onto my bull, all set to go and nodded. He wasn't the best bull around, but after having a subpar season I needed a confidence boost. I just needed to stay on a bull long enough to get my head back into the game. He bucked and kicked, never really getting into a spin, but switching directions left to right constantly. I got a couple decent spur licks into his side, but didn't get carried away. I didn't need to get showy, I just needed to stay there for the full 8 seconds. The bull had us headed straight for where Stacy was standing. We were 20 feet away from her when the buzzer sounded. As it did, the bull jerked hard to the right, catching me off guard. My feet lost their grip and I slid off the left side, instantly getting hung up in the rope. I quickly got to my feet and pulled hard on the rope as the bull begun to spin away from me. I wasn't worried, I had been in this situation many times and knew I would be fine. With my hand still stuck and making every effort to stay on my feet the bull continued a hard spin to the right. I caught Stacy out of the corner of my eye. Her hands covering her mouth and eyes filled with fear.

I couldn't help myself, I started to laugh. I was still hung up, but the look on her face had me giggling. I reached up and yanked the tail end of my rope and was free to walk away. I strolled over beside the fence to where she was standing.

"What are you so worried about?" I said laughing while tugging at my protective vest to loosen it up.

She shook her head at me in disbelief. She couldn't believe I'd start laughing while I was hung up. She looked down at me and said, "You're freaking crazy and the biggest asshole I know."

By then I had figured out that asshole was an endearment she loved to use for me.

Staying on my first bull and scoring enough points had put me into the short go round. Now I was pumped. I had the chance to win a substantial cash prize. The bull they loaded for me was one that I had seen before, he was fast, very fast, and he was well known for his flat spins that were hard to the left. A perfect animal to score decent enough points on to win that prize. However, this bull was small, which was not a great fit for my longer legs. He was going to be hard to get a good hold of with my spurs. He was also a chute-fighting bastard, you couldn't sit down on him and slide up on your rope. You had to nod your head and jump down on him if you didn't want to get thrashed. *I've done it before*, I thought. I could do it again. The stock contractor saw me standing over top of my bull getting set to ride again.

"Hey Myron, this bull is getting worse in the chutes, once you get your rope on him you gotta be fast in there or he'll start throwing himself around before you can get out on him"

"No problem, I got this"

He slapped me on the back.

"Yeah, I know you do"

Standing up over top of the bull, my feet at the height of his back. I got my hand in my rope and held it up off his back so he didn't feel it until we tightened it up. I guided my hand down to the proper position as the slack pulled tight. Grabbing the tail end of the rope, I whipped it around the back of my riding hand, squeezed it into my grip and clenched my fist. I nodded. The gate cracked open and I jumped down as the bull exploded out of the chutes. He gave me a one jump opportunity to get myself into a good seat before he began to spin. I dug my left spur into his side and did what I could to kick my right spur forward and get set for this tornado. The bull dropped his left shoulder and charged hard into his left handed spin, away from my riding hand, making it that much more difficult to stay with him. His spin felt like a top that could grab higher gears. The snot oozed out of the bull's snout in streams of clear goo. I felt like I was falling behind the bull's maneuvers and did my best to compensate. It was to no avail, before I could get back to center I was in the dirt, right underneath this torrent of spinning hooves and hate. I was in a bad spot for sight-seeing! I rolled to my knees and made my move to get the hell out of there. As I tried to bolt away, a hoof slapped the back of my head and drove my face into the dirt. I was seeing stars but I kept rolling and clawing my way in the dirt to get away.

The bull ran off and left me in the dust. I sat on my knees spitting dirt from my mouth and held the back of my head. I was pissed at myself for not keeping up with that bull, but I wasn't going to let it ruin my day. I knew Stacy was probably losing her mind right at that moment. I picked myself up, found my rope and slowly walked back to the fence where Stacy was waiting for me and slowly climbed up. Stacy grabbed my rope from my hand and dragged it over the rails, tossing it on the ground. She grabbed my arm and looked at me with worry in her eyes.

"Are you ok, babe?"

I motioned for her to hold out her hand as I leaned over the rail. She put her hand out somewhat tentatively.

I spit my mouth guard out into her hand, covered in dirt, mud and drops of blood, smiling at her as it covered her little hand in filth.

"Nice, really nice, babe. That's disgusting"

I chuckled "I thought you might like to have that. Ugh, my head hurts."

"No shit your head hurts. Not sure if you noticed but you just got kicked in the back of the head!"

I slowly crawled over the fence and knelt down on the ground. Stacy grabbed a water bottle from my gear bag and poured it over my head. I looked up at her. She started to laugh.

"You better wipe your face off, you look like a dirt monster." She laughed.

It had been a brutally hot day, and the water she'd poured over my head felt amazing. After having my face smashed into the ground, it felt like I brought a shovel full of dirt out with me. Most of it was on my face. I attempted to wipe it off with my hand, but with the water she had poured over my head, I was just making a bigger mess. I stood up and fumbled with my shirt to get it off. Stacy pushed my hands away.

"Here let me do this, you silly boy"

I was still feeling a bit woozy. She peeled my shirt off and found the cleanest dirty spot of the fabric to wipe away the mud and dirt from my face, much to the amusement of the other riders.

"Aww, Myron. Getting a little help from the missus? Got a little boo-boo and needs a little special attention? How sweet!" They all laughed and teased.

I grinned at them. They could make all the jokes they wanted but I knew they were all jealous of my lady.

With my riding done for the weekend, and at this point, the rest of the season, we made our way back to the truck. I was feeling fine now after downing a few bottles of water and rehydrating myself. Stacy had cleaned me up and had me looking not quite so dirty. There were still a few mud streaks on the side of my face but not as dirt monster-like anymore. I tossed my bag into the box of the truck and opened the door for Stacy. She moved towards the door, paused and turned to me. She reached up with both hands around the back of my head and gently pulled me in, kissing me softly.

"I love you." She looked at me intently

"I love you more," I said back with a grin.

She didn't smile back.

"I love you most!" She wrapped her arms around me and held me as if I would have flown away had she not held me tight.

"I know you love riding, and I want to support you in any way I can. But you scare me. You laugh when you get hung up. You make jokes when you get kicked in the head. I know you're tough, but you're not bulletproof, honey. I don't want you to get hurt anymore, it hurts me to see you in pain."

She was being very sincere and this was not a time to start joking with her about it.

"I know it scares you. I know I'll have to give it up at some time, I can't do this forever. When that time comes, even if I don't want to hear it, you tell me when it's time to hang up my rope."

The words hurt me to say, but she was right. I wasn't going to keep this up for a long time and it was a young man's sport. Even though I was not old in age at 19, I had suffered a lot of injuries and they were already starting to bother me when I got out of bed in the mornings. I started riding steers at around 12 years of age. Seven years of riding rough stock can be brutal on a person's body. I had already known a few riders that had been paralyzed or killed doing what they love. I didn't want that to happen to me, but I also didn't want to give this up before I was done. We headed for home, chatting the whole way as she held my hand, skipping through songs on the CD player with her free hand. She was my favourite person to travel with. We laughed at some of the memories we had made and talked about what the future might hold. Although the back of my head still hurt, she had a way of making that pain disappear.

My job was going well. I had started to move up at work and Stacy needed a vehicle to get herself to work. I had a little money saved so I bought her a car. It was nothing special, actually far from it. A 1988 Sunbird, 2 door, I got it for $800. *Perfect for a first vehicle*, I thought. She loved it. It wasn't the fact of the car itself, but the freedom it gave her to go somewhere whenever she wanted to. She had found a job in town. Just part time, it wasn't anything substantial but she wanted to make her own money. She was always such an independent person, so much so that it would annoy me sometimes. I wanted to be able to take care of her, but she would only let that go so far before she would push back and tell me to back off.

She had been saving up to go to college but the part time pay was not going to cover the cost. She didn't say anything about it, being her stubborn self and refusing to ask for help. I knew something was bothering her since her general chattiness had slowed to barely a word.

"What's up sweet pea? You seem unhappy?"

"Nothing," she lied.

"Yeah right. I know something is wrong, you're not talking, which is bizarre for you" I cracked, trying to get a smile out of her. It didn't work.

"Shut up. That's not nice"

"Okay. Well, tell me what's happening then."

"I can't afford the books for college." She said it quietly as if she had done something wrong and didn't want to fess up to her crime.

"What? That's all? How much is it?" I was relieved to know it wasn't anything serious.

"It's like $600 for the first semester…but I don't want your damn money" she retorted.

"I don't care if you don't want it. You need it and you're going to college." I wanted her to have the opportunity to get the education she wanted and $600 didn't seem like much more than a drop in a bucket. I found a bank, pulled out the money and gave it to her.

"If you need something, just ask, please. I don't want you to go without just because you are afraid to ask." I was serious, I wanted her to succeed in her goals. If I could help her do that, I would be happy to do it.

She started to cry, I had started to get used to the fact that she was a bit of a crier. She cried when she was happy, sad, scared, angry or overwhelmed. Sometimes she cried for no reason at all. It was her soft heart that made it happen and she hated it. She was tough as nails when she had to be, but when she was with me she would let it all go and just be who she needed to be at that time. I had learned to just hold her and not speak. She didn't want my words when she cried, she just wanted to be held and know that I was there for her to lean on.

That fall she got into college. I went off to work again. I needed to start saving up some money. I had some big plans in mind but those plans called for a few decent pay cheques. I had been thinking about this for quite some time, although I had not yet filled her in on my idea. I was sure she wouldn't object.

Chapter 9

My grand plan was taking longer than I had hoped. Work was busy and the cheques had been decent, but my truck broke down and I had to get the motor rebuilt. I wasn't saving as much as I wanted. I went to a jewelry store and looked through the glass, not really knowing what exactly I was looking for specifically. I knew I needed a ring, but that's as far as my thought process had taken me.

"Can I help you find something?" The young lady behind the counter asked.

I felt incredibly out of place. Many well-dressed people stood around picking through $1500 watches, fancy diamond necklaces and many other things I knew I could not afford.

"I'm sort of looking for a ring," I said, hoping to not sound like a child.

"What kind of ring are you looking for?"

What is with all the questions? I thought to myself. I need a damn ring, something nice and something I can afford.

"The engagement kind," I answered, hoping that was enough information to get through this awkward situation.

The lady looked at me somewhat quizzically. I'm sure I had the youngest baby face of any twenty year old she'd met. I had started supervising at my job by this time and still had company men asking me if I was old enough to be on the drilling rig. I felt mature beyond my years.

She dug through the rings, bringing out many options for me to choose from. All of them very nice, but none of them really jumping out at me. She tried some more, I did my best to look at the ring before the price. I did not want the price to affect my decision of what I thought she would like best.

None of them were quite what I wanted

"I'll just look around for a bit if that's alright." I said.

"No problem. Just come get me if there is one you would like to see."

I wandered around, spying each one carefully. Nope, not this one. Nah, that one ain't quite right either. Then I saw it. Yes! That one! Underneath the glass was a ring that was perfect. It wasn't huge and it wasn't the fanciest but it was her to a tee. A gold band with one large diamond in the middle. On either side of the diamond were three more that somewhat resembled a heart. I needed that one, it had jumped out at me the instant I had laid eyes on it. There was no question it was the right one. I had not yet looked at the price tag though.

The young lady carefully took it out from under the glass and showed me the price.

"Damn! That much?" It wasn't even all that expensive, but it was far more than I had managed to save up.

"We do have a payment plan as well if that helps you"

"Oh?" I might be able to make this work after all!

"Okay, yeah, let's do that." My knees suddenly became weak. I had just said that I would purchase an engagement ring. I was planning to take a massive leap of faith. I knew I wanted to marry Stacy. I knew I loved her and wanted to make her mine forever. But this made it all too real. Am I ready for this? Holy shit! Is she ready? Get a grip man!! It's time to slide and ride cowboy. I gave the lady all the cash I had. I would be coming back a few more times before I could take that ring home.

I headed home, taking my time on the terrible winter roads. My mind was racing. Would she say yes? I'm sure she will. Why would she even say no? How should I do this? Do I get down on one knee like all the romantic movies? That seemed kinda corny to me and not my style. We are so young. Is it too soon? Oh my God, I have to ask her father for permission! My heart dropped into my stomach. We had been dating long enough that Jamie had gotten used to me being around, helping on the farm with whatever I could while trying to not be distracted by Stacy too bad. Sometimes the distraction was completely on purpose. Jamie had known that this cocky kid that had shown up at the farm one New Year's Eve a few years ago was not likely to go away now. Our conversations had progressed greatly from barely a word to sometimes as much as 3 or 4 sentences in a row! I was sure I was growing on him by now. But I had to come up with a game plan on how to ask him for his daughter's hand in marriage.

Before I could do that, I had to get back to work and put every dime I could on that ring before I could even think about going to the next terrifying step. I spent months working, waiting for my cheque to come in and then headed to the jewelry store to put another large lump sum down on that diamond ring. After a few months of stress, trying hard to get this ring paid off and keep it all a secret, I put my last few hundred dollars down on that glass showcase. I took the little white case that held the most important piece of gold I could ever buy and walked to my truck. I sat behind the wheel with the windows open, staring down at the ring with the sun glinting off the diamonds. I was excited and terrified at the same time. I knew what I had to do next.

I went home, not sure how I was going to go about this step. Stacy was working that evening and wouldn't be at home. Probably no better time than today to do it. I waited until supper was over, knowing Jamie would likely be taking a moment to relax in front of the TV after a day of farm work, and it would give me a chance to go ask this petrifying question.

I drove to the farm and walked into the house, I nodded a sheepish hello to Jamie who was in his recliner and alone in the house.

"Stacy's not home yet."

"Yeah, that's ok." I sat down on the sofa and stared at the TV, unsure of what to say next. We sat in awkward silence for what seemed like hours.

"Something on your mind?" Jamie knew it was odd for me to just show up and go sit in a room with just himself in it.

"Uh, yeah, well, you see…I was just wondering…" I stumbled over my words.

"Spit it out man." Jamie was curious now what was going on in my head

"Well, I…Do you think maybe…it would be okay if me and Stacy got married?" Holy crap! The words finally came out. I started sweating.

Jamie leaned back in his chair, looking back at the TV. He knew I was extremely uncomfortable now and was going to milk this situation for all it was worth.

"Well, she seems to be pretty happy with you, and you don't seem to be going anywhere, so I suppose it would be alright as long as she stays in college."

Was that a yes? That sounded like a yes! I'm going to take that as a yes!

"Have you asked her yet?"

"Nope." I knew I wasn't going to ask her before I had gotten permission from her father. It may have been a little bit old school but I felt like it was the right way to do things.

"Why not? You chicken?" Jamie said with a chuckle

"Yup"

Jamie started to laugh.

"Don't tell Debbie I asked you yet. I want it to be a surprise for her." Debbie was one of those ladies that loved everyone. Stacy had inherited that from her mother as well. I knew she would be happy with our engagement, so I wanted to surprise her.

I waited around until Stacy had got home from her job. We hung out, but I was not my usual self. I didn't want to ask her right there. I wanted it to be a little more special. I went home and laid in bed unable to sleep. Tomorrow would be a big day.

My lack of sleep had made me feel ill in the morning, or maybe it was the nervous knot in my stomach causing me to not feel well. It was a gorgeous day and I wanted to go pick up a gorgeous lady and head to some place nice. I got dressed, just slightly nicer than my usually torn jeans and wrinkled shirt and headed over to pick her up. Stacy was completely unaware of what this day would have in store for her. She was in a great mood and had her chattiness set to non-stop babble. I was grateful for it today as I was not sure what to say yet. We drove through the local Dairy Queen to get some ice cream, and then drove to a park with a creek running through it. It was a nice quiet spot to hang out, beautiful lush green grass and flowers beginning to bloom. We started to walk hand in hand, crossing the bridge over the creek. Stacy noticed that I hadn't been saying much all day.

"You Okay? You seem like you have something on your mind."

"Yeah, I'm fine. Just enjoying the day with you." I smiled at her half-heartedly. I was nearly ready to vomit, I was so nervous. I could feel that ring in my pocket, but I didn't know how to say the words. I looked down at the ice cream in my cup, it was half melted now. I tipped it slightly to pour out the melted portion.

Splat!

The entire cup of ice cream slid out and splattered on the wooden bridge.

"Nice, babe, real smooth." Stacy laughed at my clumsiness. With our ice cream now out of the picture, I wouldn't have to try to put it down to ask her I supposed.

We walked a few more minutes, heading up stream along the creek away from where any other people were. By now she knew for certain that something was up.

"Where the hell are we going anyways?"

"I don't know…Aww hell, I suppose this as good a place as any."

"For what?" She was now half grinning, she knew I loved to surprise her with things. I wasn't sure if she had caught on to my plan yet though.

I took her hand in mine and looked into her eyes.

"We've been together for quite a while now and I have loved every minute of it. I still think about the day we met at that horse auction. I had no idea that that day would change my life forever. I love you more than anything in this world…"

The tears rolled out of her eyes and down her cheeks; she knew what was happening.

I wiped the tears from her eyes with one hand as I pulled the ring out with the other.

"Will you marry me?"

She threw her arms around me and held me tight as she sobbed into my chest.

"Yes, of course, I will marry you."

I thought I would float off the ground with the huge weight that had just been lifted off my shoulders. I held her tight and kissed her lips. I wasn't about to let go of her. We stood there for a long time enjoying our lips being pressed against each other's, the taste of her cherry flavoured chap stick all so familiar but tasting so much sweeter now. She was going to be mine forever. And I would be hers. Nothing else could have made this moment any more special. The love I had for her could not be put into words. This was a whole new beginning for both of us.

We were both crazy with a love drunk feeling. We laughed, kissed and walked hand in hand back to the truck. I had planned to take her for dinner, but we were now eager to tell our parents. We jumped into the truck and tore off back to the farm. We flew into the driveway. Stacy jumped out and grabbed my hand, half running and dragging me behind she kicked the door open and ran in to find her mom. She found her, said nothing, but held out her hand to show off her new engagement ring that shone brightly on her tiny finger.

Debbie gasped and took Stacy's hand to get a closer look.

"Is this for real?" she asked in near disbelief.

"Well it sure as hell ain't fake," I said with a slight sneer. That ring had cost me a bundle, it better damn well be real. But that is not what Debbie was asking.

"Yes, Momma. He asked me and I said yes!"

"Oh boy, this is awesome! I'm so happy for you guys." Debbie stood up and wrapped her youngest daughter in her arms. "Woohoo now we get to plan a wedding!" Debbie said, doing a little happy dance.

I hadn't thought about that part yet. Once again I had come to the end of my entire thought process and didn't know what I had to do next. But I was happy. I was sure the planning would be a lot easier than what I had just gone through to get to this point. As far as I was concerned, my job was done, all I had to do now was show up on the right day and say some vows.

I couldn't have been more wrong.

Chapter 10

We had some time before rushing into this whole wedding idea. We wanted to enjoy calling each other our fiancé for a while anyway. The wedding would come eventually, but we wanted to take our time planning it. We didn't have much money to put into it and we were not about to ask our parents to shell out any funds for it either. One way or another we would figure out a way to do this in a big way that didn't have a large price tag.

I'd been working so much I missed my annual bull riding school that year. I was a little apprehensive about getting back on a bull, not having had the chance to get warmed up again. I convinced myself it was like riding a bike. I had done it hundreds of times before and it was all just muscle memory and mental toughness, both of which I thought I had mastered by then. I entered into my first rodeo of the year and planned to head out the next weekend to ride. My folks hadn't been out to see me ride in quite some time and since they were not working, they offered to come with us.

We took my dad's truck that day, talking the whole way about what our wedding might be like. I was a bit quieter as I was feeling a bit shaky about riding. It just didn't feel right. I hadn't practiced beforehand like I always did and it felt weird to be nervous. We finally arrived at the rodeo grounds. Stacy and I headed to the bucking chutes again while my parents headed for the grandstands. I knew the stock contractor and the bullfighters. Most of them knew Stacy now as well and treated her like one of the guys. She showed off her new ring. They laughed and shook their heads at us in disbelief. Such a young couple of kids. No one denied that we should be married, it was just unusual to see such a young couple diving into it head first.

I started to get myself ready, doing my usual stretches and warm up routine. Stacy hugged me and gave me a kiss.

"I should go find your folks and sit with them. I love you babe. You're gonna do great!" She was still my biggest fan and her words of encouragement felt good. But I didn't want to admit to her that something felt off today.

My bull was loaded into the chutes, a big SOB Brahma bull, tall with a decent set of clown stabbers on his head. Pretty typical looking bucking bull. Every bull is given a name by the contractor and this one was called Dirty Deeds. I watched as a few of the other riders took their turns. I tried to shake the nervous feeling out of my mind, get my head right. I was sure it was just the first ride jitters. I just needed to get past this one and I'd be right as rain again.

I threw my leg up over the chute panel, resting my foot on the bulls back. He flicked his tail and pawed at the ground, smashing the front of the chute box with his head. I smiled. Seeing this brought that adrenaline back into my system. It felt so good for my heart to pound with anticipation.

"I'm gonna kick your ass," I said to the bull, but was trying to convince myself of that more than anything else.

I was up next, the gate man walked up beside my chute gate.

"Alright, Myron, cowboy up son. Show us what you got."

I slid down onto this bull, he felt more my size. With his deep girth, my legs fit this bull properly. He fussed and thrashed in the chutes a bit, but I wasn't bothered. I focused on getting my rope right, set it proper, and wrap it perfect. Get up on top of that rope…nod

"Let's go boys!"

We leaped from the gate. I felt the bull's chest swell as he flexed his muscles. My rope stretched tighter in my hand as he sent us skyward. I reached forward and used every ounce of strength I had to stay forward on this powerful beast. He dropped down, his front hooves landing hard in the dirt and shoving his weight to the left. I was not focused. I was already leaning to the right. I slid down, letting my grip come loose and landed in the dirt flat on my back. Bad way to land when the bull is next to you. I couldn't get turned over quick enough. The bull turned his attention to me as soon as I had landed. I could see his huge angry head coming right for me. I kicked at his face and tried to roll out of the way.

The world went black.

I could hear someone gasping for breath, wheezing in pain.

"Hey don't move, can you hear me?"

"Get the medic!"

More darkness.

Someone's hand was in front of my face, pulling dirt away so I could breathe.

I passed out again.

I looked up and could see lights, but I couldn't move. My whole body felt numb except for the excruciating pain in the back of my neck and the right side of my ribs.

"Hey, you with me?" a medic asked, right before I blacked out again.

The next time I awoke, I could hear someone crying. The pain hadn't gone away. Now I could feel pain in my left arm as well. Man this hurt. My neck felt like it was on fire. I wiggled my toes and they moved, thank God. Okay, I wiggled my fingers, they seemed to work as well. I still couldn't move my body though.

"Hello?"

Stacy ran to my side, tears streaming down her face, she grabbed my hand and said, "Oh my God, babe, please be okay!"

"Well, that was fun." I tried smiling up at her.

"This isn't funny!" She cried harder than before. She wasn't joking either. I was in bad shape. It'd been a few years since I'd had a serious injury and this one was bad.

I was strapped down to a gurney. My head and neck were immobilized and the rest of my body was strapped down tight. My head throbbed with pain. I closed my eyes and groaned. I knew this wasn't good.

The doctor came in and wheeled me into x-ray. I closed my eyes and wished the pain would ease up. After an hour or so, the doctor came back and removed my neck brace.

"Doesn't look broken," he said. "I think you dodged a bullet today, son. I need more x-rays though and you're going to have to stand for these."

He helped me up slowly, the pain flooding even more into my head and neck now. I thought I was going to pass out again. I eventually got to my feet and eased myself to the spot he wanted me to stand.

"Okay, now I need you to hold your arms out to your side and stay still."

Yeah, you bet. I was in such rough shape, just standing still was not going to be easy. But holding my arms out as well? Good luck.

I stretched them out as far as I could and held as still as possible. The pain rushed through my body. Tears started to roll down my face. The pain was more than I had ever felt before.

"Okay, I think that's enough, you can sit down now."

I fell to the floor, the cool tile felt good on my head. But the pain in my neck was still unbelievable. I was happy that he had said it wasn't broken but with the amount of bones that I had broken in the past, I wasn't sure that his diagnosis was correct. Still, I wasn't about to ask for a second opinion. The bull had thrashed me into the dirt, stomping on my neck as I attempted to roll over. A second hoof landed on the right side of my back and slid off my protective vest into my ribs. A third had stepped on my left bicep. I looked like hell and I felt worse. But I was alive. They bandaged me up, put a neck brace on me and sent me on my way. The ride home is a little fuzzy, but the conversation had been much more somber compared to the drive out.

Stacy was upset. She had asked me years before how she would know if I was really hurt. The answer I had given her had become the truth and she did not ever want to have to go through that again. She sat behind me in the truck, reaching her hand out to hold my uninjured arm and sobbed quietly most of the way home. I didn't feel like it was that bad of a wreck. It wasn't a great one to have to go through and I knew the healing for something like this would be fairly lengthy. I didn't realize the physical healing would be far less compared to the mental side of it.

The ride home was a blur but I was happy when we finally pulled into the drive. I cleaned up as best I could and 'nurse Stacy' got to work cleaning my wounds. The back of my neck had started seeping blood again, my right rib cage and left arm were not much better. They stung like a road rash, but my neck and my throbbing concussion was my biggest concern. This was my fourth concussion, and they didn't get easier with practice. I needed to relax and get some rest. I eased into my bed and closed my eyes. Stacy laid down beside me, careful not to bump me. She didn't sleep much that night.

The next morning I woke up and felt as though I had been run over by a freight train. I could barely move. Stacy helped hoist me up onto my feet and got me dressed. I wasn't looking forward to the work we had to do. With all the calves on the ground it was time to brand and castrate them. We did this mostly by hand, it was a very physical labor. I wasn't in any shape to be doing it, but I knew my help would be appreciated. I wore a loose tank top shirt so it wouldn't rub on all my open wounds. We drove to the farm, I gently got myself out of the truck. Jamie met us in the driveway, took one look at me and burst into laughter.

"You find yourself an angry critter to run you over yesterday?"

Stacy didn't share his sense of humour. I tried to smile.

"Yeah, he didn't play well with others, but no one told me he wasn't a friendly bull" I said.

Jamie looked at my battered and beaten body.

"I got something better to patch ya up."

He started toward the house. I slowly walked behind him. Stacy stayed with me to make sure I didn't face plant on her watch. I sat down in the kitchen. The sun was already throwing a lot of heat, making my head pound. Jamie brought out a medical kit and peeled off what I had on for bandages. I knew he was trying not to laugh at my discomfort, but I couldn't appreciate his efforts. My strength was fading. He finished patching me up with a second skin bandage while giving me the rundown on how we were going to get today's work done. He knew I'd be useless at anything physical. He handed me a scalpel so I could do the castrating.

I gently walked my broken parts out to the pen where the rest of the crew was waiting on us to get started. The branding irons were already blazing away in front of the propane torch. Debbie brought out all the medical supplies and paperwork we needed to begin. I had barely assessed the situation before the first calf was on the ground. It was a bull calf. It was time to do my job. I eased myself over to it, desperately trying to be helpful, but being slower than the second coming of Christ. I knelt down, found the scalpel inside a pail of disinfectant liquid, grab a hold of the parts that needed to be removed and slowly began my cut. Jamie laughed again.

"Here, like this." He snatched the tools from my hand, whipped the parts off like a pro and walked away.

"Okay, I got it," I said as I struggled to get to my feet again.

This went on for the better part of the day. The sun was blazing hot and my wounds felt like they were on fire. The rest of the crew did their best to be patient with the cripple who held the scalpel. My speed easily added an hour to the work that shouldn't have taken that long. But I wanted to help. This was my family now, as well, and I didn't want to let them down by sitting on the side lines. Stacy was in a much better mood. Being around the cows always brought a smile to her face. She'd started to lighten up after the events of the previous day. Stacy talked to the calves, calling each one of them 'pretty little babies' while the rest of us burned hot irons into their ribs and cut their nuts out like heartless bastards.

With the calves all done, the rest of the work consisted of running the cows through the squeeze, giving shots and Ivomec to eliminate any parasites. This was far less physical, but after having finished the calves and the sun beating down on us relentlessly, I was cooked. My neck and head throbbed like an extra heartbeat. Stacy looked at me with concern and said, "Are you doing okay? You don't look so good."

"I think I need to sit down for a bit." I wandered back to the house and slowly sat down at the kitchen table.

Granny was busy cooking up a big dinner for the crew that had come out to help. She was a gentle soul who had the harshest words. "You look like a squashed up piece of shit," she cackled as she looked at me. I attempted to grin, she was the sweetest old lady I had ever met, but she had the mouth of a trucker. She waddled off to the freezer and grabbed a couple bags of frozen peas, tossing them onto the table.

"Here, throw these on yourself."

I laid one down on the table, planted my face on it, put the other one on the back of my neck and passed out.

I'm not sure how long I had sat there. When I woke up everyone was coming into the house for dinner. The work was done and the peas that I had used for a pillow were all but cooked. Even though I was glad I was able to help, I felt like I was more of a hindrance. My battered body wished I had stayed home. We spent the rest of the evening chatting and cracking jokes. Jamie used me as the brunt of most, but it was a sign that I had been accepted into this household. I was comfortable there. If it weren't for my injuries, I would've been having the time of my life. I was home and this was my family.

Chapter 11

I laid in bed for the next few days, barely able to move and only getting up when absolutely necessary. I had to go back to work soon. I wasn't about to call in with the excuse of getting trampled. Stacy stayed by my side and fussed over me like she always did, checking my bandages and cleaning my wounds. Giving me a lecture the entire time about how bull riding was a dumb sport and how I needed to come up with a better plan to stay alive. I knew she was just joking around, but when she was done with her jokes she would start to cry. My head was aching less but I still couldn't turn my neck left or right. Still, I was already trying to plan my next rodeo event. Deep down I knew I didn't want to get back on again. I also knew if I just got back on and stayed on an easy bull, I would be right back in the game as if this had never happened. I thumbed through a rodeo schedule, trying to plan ahead for when I thought I would feel well enough to ride. Stacy snatched the papers from my hand.

"No, I don't think so!" she snapped.

"What? I'll be fine in a few weeks and I want to get entered up again," I replied.

"Babe, you're not going to heal that quick from this. Just stay off for this season, we can talk about it next year."

Next year? What the hell was that supposed to mean? This is what I do. I can't stay away from the rodeo circuit long. That was just ridiculous. Give me a few weeks and I'll be ready to go again. The local rodeo her parents put on was a month away, which would be plenty of time to get healed up. Nothing was broken right? If only I had known then that my neck was actually fractured.

I headed back to work a few days later. I walked into the shop much slower than normal. The scars down my neck were not quite such a brilliant red as they had been a few days earlier, but they still looked terrible.

"What the fuck happened to you?" a co-worker asked as he grabbed my arm and turned me around to have a closer look at my neck. I winced in pain as he had grabbed the arm that was bandaged up.

"The bull riding didn't go as planned last weekend"

"No shit, man that looks brutal. You gonna be able to work?"

"I wouldn't be here if I wasn't gonna go to work"

"Well, you look like hell, but whatever, it's your call"

My boss came out, took a look at me and called me to his office.

"Look, I know you like this stupid bull riding thing you're into, but at some point you're gonna have to decide if you want to be a bull rider for half your life, or have a career for the rest of it."

I was a little pissed at this. Who did this guy think he was? I was fine, maybe I didn't look like it (or feel like it) but I wasn't missing any work, I was here and ready to go. He can't tell me what I can or cannot do when I'm on days off!

"I'm fine," I insisted, "There's nothing to worry about. It's just some scrapes and bruises." I wasn't sure who I was trying to convince, him or me.

"Well you look like crap, but I'm not going to stop you from going to work if that's what you want. But you have some decisions to make kid"

Kid? Come on now. I was an adult and could make these decisions without his input. *I'll quit when I'm goddamn good and ready,* I thought. I headed off to work and did my best not to show the pain I was in constantly. I suffered through two weeks in the field. My soreness never seemed to dissipate much. My open wounds had started to heal up pretty good towards the end of my set, but were still awful tender to the touch. If I hadn't been worried about saving up some money, I would have likely sat that set out. I wanted to buy a home for me and my soon to be bride and I wasn't going to be able to do that by sitting on my ass.

I went home for my week off, excited to see Stacy again and spend some quality time with her. She met me in the driveway as I pulled into the farmyard. She wrapped her arms around me in a hug I had begun to realize was one of the biggest comforts I could receive.

"Hey babe, how was work?" she asked.

"Painful, but I made it through." I didn't like to admit it, but I was still hurting pretty bad, I didn't have to tell her though. She could tell.

"I don't want to tell you to stop riding, but please, please, please stay off of them for this season."

I knew she was right. The way I was feeling I knew I wasn't going to be in good enough shape to ride at the local show this year. I had ridden there a few times now and didn't want to be left on the sidelines this time. But she was right, I had to take time to get healed up.

"I will take time to get healed up, I won't rush back into it"

"Promise me." She wasn't kidding around this time.

"I promise."

She hugged me again as we strolled around the yard for a while. We looked at the herd of cows and she'd point out each of hers and tell me about them. She had them named and knew how old they were. She even boasted a little about how nice her calves were this year. She was the only one that named her cows anymore, a habit that came from her years in 4H. She always picked names that came from some Beach Boys song and stuck with that theme with all of them. I was more into calling them T-bone, sirloin or burger, but I was slightly less attached to them than she was. My pain was always much less when I was with her, she had a way of healing me without even trying. Being around someone you love so deeply can make miracles happen I guess.

"Hey, what do you think of getting a place of our own?" I asked, not to cut her off of her cow stories.

"What did you have in mind?"

"Well, something affordable, close to town so it's not such a long drive for us to get to work and college for you."

"That might be okay. We will have to find something anyway unless you plan to live in my parents' house," she laughed. She knew that was not about to happen. I loved being out on the farm with her, but I wanted us to have a home of our own.

"I guess we should start searching then. I have a little saved up, but I'm not sure how much I actually need." I really was at a bit of a loss when it came to knowing much outside of riding bulls or my work. Stacy was always more detail oriented. She saved all of her receipts and filed everything according to dates and payment type. I was more of a fly by the seat of my pants kind of person. It drove her crazy.

A few weeks later, with our local rodeo weekend upon us, we headed out to the rodeo grounds to enjoy a relaxing weekend together. Stacy's sister Twila had been dating some dude who bragged about being a badass bull rider. I called bull shit on him. Jamie shared the same view. I had never met him before, and the rodeo family is a tight knit group. I was pretty sure he was a chicken shit liar. I had still packed my gear bag and dragged it along into the grounds. There was usually a few younger kids just starting out who were short on gear. I never minded helping them out if I could. I didn't get a lot of help when I started out and had made the decision to lend a hand to some of the younger generation if given the chance.

Stacy was in a good mood since I had kept my promise and hadn't entered to ride this weekend. I refused to admit I was still in rough shape, but it wasn't too hard to tell. I was not sharing her happy demeanor though, I was feeling pretty left out and out of place as I watched a lot of my friends packing their gear bags behind the chutes and getting ready to ride. It wasn't helping that Twila's boyfriend, Lenny, was flapping his gums on and on about how he wished he had entered. He was so full of shit and it was pissing me off. Jamie had been annoyed with this guy for months already. He was a boastful pain in the ass and treated Twila like crap. I stood around, trying not to be a downer on such a nice weekend. But I was being a bit of a pouty pants. One of the bull fighters, Glenn, saw me standing near the arena and walked over to say hi.

"Hey, fella, which bull did you draw today?"

"I'm not riding this weekend. I'm still healing up from a few weeks ago." Just saying it felt like a kick in the nuts.

"Ah shit, that sucks man. We have a bunch of young bulls we wanted to buck out and see if they were any good." Stock contractors will sometimes get a herd of young bulls and will get riders to try them out and see if they have any potential to be good bucking stock or if they're not suited well for the task.

"Oh? Well, I know I can't do it…but I know someone who thinks he can." Stacy looked at me somewhat puzzled. I was grinning ear to ear when she finally figured out who I was talking about.

"You're not seriously going to tell Lenny to get on one are you?" she asked, sounding almost hopeful I'd do it.

"Oh, hell yeah, I am. He's the best one around, don't ya know?" I said sarcastically.

Stacy started laughing. "Okay, well make sure to let me know if you actually convince him to do it. I don't want to miss this."

The bull fighter stood there, confused as to what was going on, so I decided to fill him in,

"Stacy's sister is dating one of them bullshitters who thinks he can ride. I don't think he's done much more than run his mouth off about it and today seems like a great day to shut him up."

Glenn laughed, "Whatever man, we just need to see if these bulls will be good or not, you send whoever you want over when we get to the end of the show."

"Oh, he'll be there," I smiled. "Don't you worry" I had a plan.

Stacy was already searching the infield to spot her sister.

"He's right there." She pointed. I could see Twila standing near her somewhat pudgy boyfriend.

"Don't be an asshole about it, though, okay? You don't need to give him an excuse to be lazier than he already is."

"Yes, dear." I wasn't planning to get him hurt, he could do that all on his own.

"Hey Lenny!" I hollered across the field, waving at him to get his attention

He waddled over to us, making sure that he had his store bought belt buckle plainly visible, which was a bit of a feat given his not so scrawny features. He was not built anything like a regular bull rider.

We were all terribly thin, flexible and wiry. He was more of a hefty and slow version of whatever he thought he was.

"Hey, what's up?"

"They have a bunch of bulls they wanna buck out and see how they perform. I'm still busted up so I can't do it, but I told them you were itching to get on since you missed your chance to enter." I played it up, hoping he would take the bait.

"Oh, well, uh, I'm not sure. It's been awhile. I don't even have any gear here."

"I got all the gear you'll need." I awaited his next excuse.

"But you ride right handed and I ride left, so I guess that's not going to work."

"I have a left handed rope as well." I had been packing one around ever since I had injured my riding arm years ago and had decided to try with my left until my right arm had healed up again. It seemed like a good thing to keep with me just in case I needed it.

"Oh, you have one? Well, that's okay, but… um, are they pretty rough? I'm rusty so I don't want to get trashed just for the sake of trying one out."

"Nah, man, they're just young. They'll likely smash around in the chutes a bit, but nothing an old hand like you can't handle, right?" I was now trying to build up his confidence just enough to reel him in.

"I'll have to ask Twila if it's okay first I guess."

I called bullshit on this too. He had never asked her for permission for anything before. He did what he wanted, when he wanted to. Twila walked up behind him while we discussed this adventure. I would do him the favour of asking her.

"Hey, Twila, you okay with Lenny trying out a few of the young bulls? The stock contractor has a few new ones he wants to try out. They won't be anything drastic, they're just babies really."

Lenny looked at Twila with some hope that she would say no.

"I don't care, go right ahead."

Oh boy, I love it when a plan comes together! This was going to be awesome. Jamie and I were about to get some gratification today, but Lenny didn't know it yet.

"Alright Lenny, let's go back and I'll get you all squared away with gear."

Lenny looked at all of us as if we had just told him he was going to be executed by firing squad. Stacy held back her emotion like a champ, but I knew she was bursting with laughter on the inside. I may not be able to ride, but I wasn't going to sit here and listen to this mouth piece all weekend long either. It was time for him to put up or shut up.

The show wound down after the main event. I grabbed Lenny and half shoved him towards the back of the chutes.

"Time to shine big fella."

Jamie had noticed us behind the chutes and looked at me perplexed. "Whatcha doin'?"

"Oh, the contractor has a few young bulls to buck out. Ol' Lenny here is gonna use my gear and get on some…or at least one." I leaned toward Jamie and lowered my voice. "Let's hope he gets on one without shitting his pants."

Jamie smiled at me like a cat that just got his fill of field mice.

"Ha, well I'll be sure to run the gate then," he said.

I laughed. "Yeah, just make sure he nods before you bust him loose this time, would ya?"

"You were ready dammit" Jamie snarled.

"Yeah, but I never nodded my head!" I snapped back. This had become our favourite thing to argue about.

"Well, you stayed on him, didn't ya? And, as I recall you ended up winning."

"Yeah, yeah, but that ain't the point." We laughed at each other's retort.

"Just make sure you get twinkle toes over there suited up and ready," Jamie said as he nodded over to Lenny, who was now doing his best impersonation of a bull rider behind the chutes.

The young bulls were loaded up. I picked out the nicest looking little red bull. Such a fine looking young animal, I was sure he was full of potential.

"Hey Lenny, you're getting on this one."

"Why that one?" Lenny asked hoping for something…less like a bull I guess.

"He'll be fine, don't worry about it." I already had my left handed rope slid down the side of the bull and was getting it pre-set for him. Jamie was standing to my side helping me out.

"You think he's gonna get on?"

"Well, if he doesn't, he's never gonna live it down as long as the two of us are around," I replied, then turned to Lenny. "Alright Lenny, you're all set. I can pull rope for ya and Jamie is gonna run the gate, we got Glenn out in the arena, he's your bull fighter. You got this." I did my best to pump him up so he wouldn't give up and foil my master plan.

He slowly strolled over, his lip over flowing with chewing tobacco and shaking like a leaf on a tree.

"Don't worry about it, he ain't nothing. You'll ride him just fine." I slapped Lenny on the back as he climbed over the chutes and eased onto the young bulls back. The bull was unaccustomed to this scenario and thrashed wildly. I quickly grabbed hold of my protective vest that Lenny was wearing, which appeared to be bursting at the seams. I didn't actually want him to get hurt, I wasn't a complete asshole. I just wanted him to shut up about the bull riding talk when I knew he wasn't one of us.

He slowly warmed up the rosin in the rope, appearing to be very out of practice…or maybe like it was his first time. He got his hand in the rope and I started to pull it tight. I could see the brim of his hat shaking now; he was either pinging with adrenaline, or scared shitless. Either way, I was enjoying myself. I pulled the rope one more time and handed him the tail end so he could wrap his hand. He eventually got himself set, while I kept a hand on him to make sure he didn't get thrown into the front of the box as the bull fussed impatiently to get out of his prison.

Jamie stood with his hand on the latch, grinning. We had both been waiting for this for a long time.

Lenny slid up.

"Ok boys!" He yelled out so loud he nearly startled the poor young bull. Jamie swung the gate open. The bull stepped out and with the ferocity and grace of a gazelle, he jogged out of the chutes. Lenny slid all of his weight to the side and hit the ground with a heavy thud.

I looked at Glenn. "I don't think that bull is gonna be much good to ya."

Glenn shook his head at me, smiling.

Jamie chuckled and turned away as Lenny picked himself up off the ground.

Meanwhile, Stacy and Twila had been sitting on the fence watching this all take place. Stacy being the person she was, teased her sister about her so called bull rider. Twila was a little unimpressed with how this had all turned out, but she had been entertained nonetheless. The entertainment had been a good distraction for me. I was in a slightly better mood now, but it would be short lived. I was having a bit of a hard time even being at a rodeo that I could not ride at. It was depressing.

Chapter 12

Stacy and I had started to make some wedding plans. It wouldn't be long before our big day. I wasn't getting too involved in the planning just yet. I'd give her my input whenever she would ask me about certain colours or designs for cards, etc., but I was busy searching through ads for a house that would work for us. It didn't need to be anything fancy, neither of us were raised like that. I eventually found a few that would be worth a look. I called up a realtor and made the appointment. We walked through at least four different houses. All of them looked okay but nothing really said this is the one. We went home and continued to search for something that was more us. I wanted to know without a doubt that the one we picked was the one that was meant for us.

A week later we had found a few more that we liked and went back to town for a look. Same deal over and over. There was nothing wrong with the homes, they just didn't feel right to us. The last house we looked at was different, though. It felt clean, warm and inviting. It was in a decent neighbourhood, in a small community just outside of town. I would be much closer to my work and Stacy wouldn't have such a long drive to get to her work and college. It didn't have a big yard but three bedrooms and two bathrooms seemed like more than enough for us. I put what money I had saved as a down payment and made the deal. We were going to have our first home!! Stacy was thrilled.

Snow was still on the ground when we were finally able to get possession of the home, but we didn't feel the chill too much as we moved what few things we had. We had no table, no chairs and hardly any dishes. It seemed very bare and empty, but it took us no time to move in. We had a mattress on the floor of our room and nothing else for furniture. But we were completely happy with our new home. I was a little worried about the mortgage payments. I hated having to make payments on anything and would do whatever I had to pay things off as soon as possible. With Stacy going to college and working part time, I had no intentions of using what little money she was making to help pay for things for the house. She had enough on her plate as it was.

We slowly found some used furniture to put in the house, one small piece at a time. We were learning what life was like being away from the farm and with each other all the time. It seemed very surreal at the start, but what a treat it was to come home to see Stacy every time I got off of work. We both knew how to cook a mean mac 'n' cheese, but that was about all we really knew. We both faced a steep learning curve as to how to do some things to make our lives easier and live with each other's habits.

Stacy found it terribly lonely when I would leave for work. She was all alone in this little house and she wasn't very comfortable with it. She cried a lot when I was gone, even though I called her multiple times each day just to hear her voice. It just wasn't the same as me being there with her. She would spend some weekends at the farm while I was gone to work just to get away from the loneliness that had become our home. She enjoyed having the added freedom the house had given us, but being all by herself wasn't healthy for her mind.

Our wedding date was coming up fast now and we had to get things looked after. There are a lot of traditions when it comes to getting married, none of which either of us planned to follow. When it came to picking out her dress, she didn't want to go with anyone but me. I was happy with that. After all it was our wedding and not anyone else's. Being on a tight budget made finding the right one fairly difficult. She must have tried on twenty dresses while I sat near the change room patiently waiting to see her walk out in them one after the other. She looked stunning in every one of them, but it was never the dress I was looking at. Stacy would snap her fingers at me.

"Hey, eyes on the dress silly. What about this one?"

"I like them all. What do you think?" I knew we would know which one was the perfect dress once she put it on. But nothing had really been any better than the previous one.

"Nah, I don't know. It's nice but I don't think this is the one."

I was being as patient as I could. To be honest I really didn't mind doing this. It was fun seeing her come out in all these fancy outfits, but I wasn't about to admit it. We shuffled through more dresses that were hanging in the store until we came across one last dress. It was simple, not full of flare, but it was very classy.

"Hey, this one looks pretty." Stacy pulled it from the rack and took it to the change room. It seemed like it took forever for her to get it on. One of the ladies was trying to pin it up. Stacy was a tiny lady and most of the dresses were a few sizes too big. She walked out to give me the tour.

"Oh, hell yeah! That's the one! I love it!" It was perfect for her.

Stacy had a few tears to wipe away after seeing my reaction to this dress. Our love story was about to take the next step. We purchased the dress which was less money than we had expected it to be. This one seemed so much nicer than the rest, but the cost did not reflect that. I was happy to have been there to pick it out, even though it was not what tradition says you're supposed to do. We didn't care, and this was for us. We strolled down to a jewelry store to search for a wedding band for myself and the matching wedding ring to go with Stacy's engagement ring. Any old band would be fine with me, I didn't really care what it looked like. Stacy took over the search as she didn't want me to end up with a cheap piece of tin that was bent in the shape of a ring. She found one that was fitting for the both of us and we found her wedding ring to go with her beautiful engagement ring. We were pretty much set. Or so we thought.

The location Stacy had picked for the wedding was far superior to anything I would have come up with. She wanted it to be outdoors, in a private place that didn't cost much, but had a great view. She convinced me to take a drive to the cattle lease one day, we would go there from time to time to enjoy the peacefulness of this place, so it wasn't uncommon for her to want to go there for the day. We drove out, parked the truck and started walking.

"Right here! This is where I want to do it." Stacy held her arms out in the direction of her grand plan.

We were on a hill that overlooked the river below, surrounded by trees on both sides, but this area was clear and covered with lush green grass during the summer months. I couldn't think of a more perfect place than this for our wedding. She was right, this is where it had to be. We had spent a lot of time here before. Winter months had us coming here to spend time with family while tobogganing and cooking hotdogs over a warm fire, summer months we would ride horses through to check on the cows and the condition of the fence lines and fall would have us hiking through in full camouflage, searching for elk or deer during the hunting season.

"This is my favourite place." Stacy smiled as she took in the view. I couldn't agree more, this place was perfect.

Stacy quickly called her dad to see if it would work to do the wedding there.

"Hmm, well, yeah, I suppose that would be alright. It'll take a fair bit of work, though. The cows will need to be moved and fenced off, grass cut. The trail in would have to be in better shape for folks coming in. You'll need some sort of power source for the speakers. The ground isn't all that level, so you'll have to figure out something for chairs." Jamie hammered out a ton of questions and Stacy had an answer for each one.

"The cows can go to the bottom side of the lease. We can use grandpa's pull-behind mower to cut the grass. The trail just needs a bit of sand and gravel. We can use a generator for power and set it down the hill a ways so we can't hear it running and I want to use square bales covered with horse blankets to sit on." It seemed as though she had been thinking about this for a while. The work began shortly after.

One detail Stacy asked me to look after was the music. We listened to music constantly, driving or just hanging out at home there would always be music playing of some sort. We listened to every genre and era of music that was out there. Stacy loved it all but she was partial to country, of course. I spent many hours trying to figure out which song to use for each part of the wedding. I would play different songs for her to see what her reaction was. Some she loved, some she was not fond of and I would scratch those off the list. I had one picked out for our walk back down the rows of people as husband and wife, but I told her she was not allowed to know which one it was.

"What do you mean I don't get to know?"

"Nope, not telling ya. It's a surprise." I smiled at her.

"It better not be a dumb song, 'cause if it is I'm gonna trip you on our walk back down the aisle." She was not completely impressed with my idea. She loved my surprises, but wasn't sure about this one. She was very suspicious of what I was up to. I laughed at her aggressive tone.

"You wouldn't do that, would you?"

"Just don't be a jerk." Stacy laughed at me. She knew I was not about to make a mockery of our wedding day with some song that she hated, but she wanted this to be perfect. I wouldn't let her down.

The plans were all starting to come together. This was starting to look like it would be a spectacular wedding that suited us very well. We were only days away now.

The night before our big day, my groomsmen and I stayed at the farm. We had a couple beers, but I wasn't up for a runaway. I was nervous as hell and it was a different type of nervousness that felt foreign to me. With all the bulls I had ridden, being in some wrecks and going through the torment of asking her father to have Stacy's hand in marriage, you would think a person would be used to this. But I was feeling ill. I knew it wasn't cold feet, of that I was certain. I wanted to marry her in the worst way. I was just second guessing how the day would play out. I'm sure she was doing the same that night, but just as I had done in the past, I tried not to dwell on it too much. Sometimes the best thing to do is take that leap without thinking about the outcome.

I woke up to birds chirping in the farmyard. The sun was already up and it was feeling very warm. I slowly rolled out of bed. My neck still felt stiff in the mornings. I tried to eat but didn't get much down. It was a habit I had formed from riding for so many years. Eating a big meal when my stomach was nervous with anticipation, just to climb on a bull and have that huge rush of adrenaline would usually end up in vomiting when my ride was over. Toast and water--breakfast of champions who were nearly ill with thoughts of what the day would hold.

We loaded our horses and headed to the lease early to get some things set up. We saddled up and road down to the bottom where my guys and I would be riding up from when the wedding started. I looked at Kyle, a friend I had since we were in elementary school, his face was cherry red.

"You alright there, Kyle?" I was nervous, but he looked like he might faint.

"Yeah I think so. I just never really rode horses much growing up, and it's hot out here."

Myself, Travis and Stacy's brother Trenton, my other groomsmen, all looked at each other and burst into laughter. We had grown up with these animals. It was nothing we were even remotely concerned about. But Kyle was not in the same boat as us.

"You'll be fine. That horse will just follow the rest of us up. You have nothing to worry about." My laughter started to die off as I looked at my watch. Ten minutes to show time.

We waited for what seemed like forever as I continued to keep an eye on the time. I did not want to start off late and have the ladies arrive before us. Stacy would never let me forget it if that happened. My watch finally landed on 1pm.

"Ok, I guess we might as well get going." I grabbed hold of the horse that Kyle was riding to give him a chance to get settled in. Then I swung up onto my horse and looked at the guys with a nervous grin.

"All right, follow me," I said as I turned my horse towards the base of the hill and slowly rode up. As we made it closer to the top I could see the crowd of people all sitting on the bales, taking pictures of the beautiful scenery and waiting for this special day to take place. Once at the top, we slid off and tied our horses to a hitching rail that we had prepared the week before. Some folks were still mingling around and chatting, my mother included. I gave her a bit of a dirty look that said hey, stop chatting and go sit down. We gotta get going. She laughed at my unhappy face.

"I'm going, I'm going. Stop rushing me." She scowled.

We stood there impatiently waiting for the cue to start the ceremony. The girls were fashionably late, just as they should be. But it was only a few minutes before I could see it, an original stage coach from the late 1800s was being pulled by a team of horses, driven by Murray who was a mountain of a man and a close family friend. Stacy's cousin Allan rode shotgun, both men holding rifles. Inside that stage coach were three of Stacy's best friends and the woman who I was about to marry. I walked up the aisle with my mom and dad at my side, hugged them and turned to go stand front and center.

I watched as each bridesmaid was assisted out of the stage couch by my groomsmen and slowly made their way to the front arm in arm. With everyone now at the front, it was the moment I had been waiting for. Stacy appeared from the door of the coach. I had seen the dress before, but with the sunlight shining down on her and her hair done so beautifully, I nearly started to cry. My uncle Paul stood by my side and put a hand on my shoulder. He was there to lead the ceremony and marry us.

"You're ok, just enjoy this," he said, trying to encourage me.

Jamie helped her out of the coach while Debbie looked after Stacy's long dress as she stepped down to the ground. They walked with her down the aisle slowly while the song, (Everything I Do) I Do It For You by Bryan Adams played.

Stacy came to the front and took my hands in hers. She stared into my eyes and Paul began the ceremony. Neither of us ever recalled exactly what was said throughout the sermon. Apparently, it was a long winded one, but we didn't notice. We were both lost in each other's eyes the entire time. We said our vows, we placed a ring on each other's finger. I held her close and kissed her lips for, from what I was told after, was far too long. After the papers were signed, we were introduced as husband and wife. A song came to life over the speakers. Stacy shot a quick look at me, I smiled back at her.

Sold (The Grundy County Auction Incident) started to play. It was a song that everyone asked if we had heard before once they learned that we had met at an auction.

Stacy burst into laughter and shook her head. She squeezed my arm as we walked down the aisle together. The crowds of people stood up laughing and cheering at my song choice. There was never a song that fit so perfectly for our story.

We took hundreds of pictures and spent a lot of time laughing and goofing off much to the annoyance of the people behind the cameras. But eventually we settled down enough to get some fantastic shots. Once we were wrapped up, I picked Stacy up in my arms and put her into our chariot--a bright yellow, jacked up truck. The day had gone perfectly. It could not have been planned any better and best of all, Stacy was now my wife. She had made me the happiest man on earth that day.

We headed to the hall where we had gone so many times before to attend local dances and rodeo parties. The room was packed full of people. We ate, we drank and said some speeches, mine being slightly unprepared…or maybe not at all. I was never into writing out a speech. I just walked up and said what I felt like. Stacy shook her head again but smiled because she knew there were just some things she was never going to be able to change about me. But she wouldn't have it any other way, we knew each other's flaws very well, and we loved each other for them. It's what made us who we were.

The day turned to night, and with it being late June, that meant it was getting late. The party was hopping, but Stacy and I were anxious to head to our hotel for the night. We said our goodbyes and made our way to the truck, I lifted her in again. I had become quite good at this by now and enjoyed doing it. She was happy I didn't drop her on the ground. We laughed about the day's events all the way to town, it had been such a perfect day.

I walked into the hotel to get checked in, gave the clerk my name and she began to type.

"I have a honeymoon suite booked for you guys?"

"Yep, that's the one."

"Um, can I see some ID please?"

Seemed strange to me, but no problem. I dug my driver's licence out and handed it to the clerk.

"Oh, okay, that's fine. I just wanted to check…you guys look so young, I wasn't expecting to…"

She fumbled over her words a bit, trying not to say something that I was sure she was thinking. We were young, by most standards we were too young.

"Here is a bottle of champagne. Congratulations."

Stacy and I both laughed and headed off to our room. The day had been amazing, the night would be no different. We had been in love for years and the passion we had for each other would continue to grow, starting with tonight.

Chapter 13

The next morning, we put on our normal everyday clothes and put our wedding attire away. We really enjoyed being all dressed up, but it was back to faded blue jeans and t-shirts for us. We headed back to my folks place to open gifts with family and friends. I wasn't real excited about this, I wanted to hit the road and start our honeymoon. But it was the one tradition we were both going to give in to. The rest of our families were looking forward to it anyhow.

The yard was full of vehicles by the time we got there. A group of my friends were mingling around, apparently staying away from everyone else.

"Hey, fellas, how was the rest of the night?" I asked, even though I had a bit of an idea how it had gone judging by the way they looked and smelled. They were ragged, some still wearing an article of clothing from the day before. Standing downwind from them was a bad idea. The hot sun assisted in draining the booze from their pores.

"Ugh, man, I feel like a train wreck." Kelly sat in his truck with the door open, but the air conditioning on full blast.

"Uh-oh...I gotta..." He ran around to the back of the truck and yakked out his stomach contents.

Stacy couldn't help but laugh. "Looks like you guys had a good time," she snickered. "I'm glad we left when we did!"

"Yeah, what the hell was up with that?" Wayne asked. He had been a friend of mine since elementary school. "We were just getting started!"

"Wayne, what the hell do you think was up with that?" I asked, hoping he would read between the lines.

"Oh…yeah, right. Never mind"

Stacy smacked me on the arm "Hey, we are at your parents place. No dirty talk."

All my high school friends had known Stacy for almost as long as I had. She had become one of the boys and was always greeted as such. Everyone loved her although they all thought she may have been half crazy for getting married to me at such a young age. These guys were all still busy working during the week and partying all weekend while we were more focused on getting on with our adult lives as a husband and wife.

We sat down in the shade behind my folk's house and started to go through cards and gifts. My mom had the bright idea to pass the cards around so everyone could read them. All of my friend's eyes got real big. I opened one:

Congratulations
Wishing you all the best…
And a honeymoon that leaves
You walking funny for a week!

"KYLE!" My mom gasped, completely mortified.

"Hey, in my defence, I didn't know everyone was gonna be reading these." Kyles face was bright red with embarrassment.

Stacy nearly fell out of her chair with tears of laughter streaming down her face. There was no better group of friends. She loved them all like brothers.

We didn't stay long. I wanted to hit the road and get our honeymoon started. While many newlyweds would go to beautiful beaches and other tropical countries, we weren't anywhere near being able to afford something like that. I left my mud truck behind and grabbed my dad's Chevy. We stopped by Stacy's grandpas house and hooked up to his holiday trailer. We were headed to the mountains for a week.

It was a 6 hour drive to get to Jasper National Park in the Rocky Mountains. Since we hadn't slept much last night or the past week really, it didn't take long before we were looking for a place to park for the night. We found a small campground and I set up the trailer just enough to allow us to sleep comfortably. Stacy curled up next to me and put her head on my shoulder.

"I love you," I said as I kissed her forehead.

"I love you more." She smiled up at me.

"I love you most." I closed my eyes and fell into a deep sleep.

After sleeping for nearly 12 hours we were full of energy. Our holiday was waiting for us! Driving another few hours we arrived at our destination and set up camp as best we could. This would be home for the next week. I had picked up a few pamphlets that had all the info about the national park we were in and what there was to see and do. Stacy circled all the things that did not cost anything, or very little. She was a planner and needed to know what sights we were going to see on each specific day. I was more the type to just go out and find these places without any sort of plan. That was not about to happen while Stacy was there to do it her way. I wasn't about to argue.

We hiked up every trail, found every waterfall and glacier. Everything was small in cost but huge in beauty. The mountains were incredible. Stacy and I had always been outdoors people, the crisp air and scent of pine trees made us feel very relaxed. During the evenings we'd sit by the fire and talk about our future plans, our careers, and maybe kids at some point. It had been awhile since my wreck and the resulting broken neck. I was still hurting a bit from it, but it felt like it was slowly getting better. I was missing my sport and mentioned it to Stacy. "I still want to get back on. I'll take some time off, but maybe next year I can get back to riding."

Stacy looked somber. She was not enthused by my comment.

"I don't know, babe. I don't want to tell you to quit something that you love. Only you can make that decision. But I hope whatever you decide, you think about us first."

Her words hit me like a ton of bricks. She was right, I was being selfish. I still wanted to ride but where was I planning for it to take me? It wasn't just about me anymore, she was a part of my future now more than ever. My decisions needed to be more focused on us rather than just myself. I dropped the subject and didn't bring it back up again. I wasn't looking to spoil the mood with a depressing conversation. We headed to bed, looking forward to another day of hiking in the mountains.

After getting showered up at the facility in the campground, I braided Stacy's hair for her. She was shocked to learn that I knew how to do this, but she was less impressed when I told her I learned how to do it with a horse's tail. I didn't understand what the big deal was, I thought it was funny. We walked hand in hand back towards our camp, as we drew closer I noticed a truck parked in the camp.

"Who the hell would park their damn truck in our camp? What a dick move…" But that truck looked familiar to me.

Stacy looked at me. "Is that…?"

"Heeyyy what's up guys!? We felt bad for missing the wedding so we figured we would crash your honeymoon instead!"

It was Richie and Sherri. I had known Richie for a few years through my work and Sherri worked with Stacy. They had met through us and had become friends. Both of them were unable to make the wedding day and had been up since 4am to make the drive here. We weren't surprised at all that they would pull something like this. They were very spur of the moment people and were a ton of fun to hang out with. We all piled into my dad's Chevy and headed up the mountain. It was going to be a fun day! All of us took turns taking pictures of each other, laughing and cracking all the dirty jokes we could come up with. The day ended with some pan fried beer steaks over the fire and a case of Corona to wash it down. Richie and Sherri crashed in the holiday trailer with us and were gone again by early morning. We had a few days left to spend together before we had to go home and get back to reality. I have seen some couples struggle with being alone together for extended periods of time and end up getting bored with each other and run out of things to talk about. That was never an issue for us. We spent the next couple days discussing everything from our house to friends and family, baby names, future plans and when that ran out we always talked about the memories we had made. The day we met, the first dance, first kiss and all the rodeo adventures. It is cliché to say it, but she was truly my best friend.

After seeing all there really was to see without spending what seemed like a small fortune, we decided to head home a day early. It would give us a chance to get settled at home and relax in our house for one day before we had to get back to work. We fuelled up and headed for home, cranking some classic rock most of the way. We nearly made it the entire way before we ran out of diesel. We only had 3 miles to go before I could make it to the next gas station, I had made a gamble, I was wrong and Stacy made sure that I knew that.

"I told you to fill up," she teased.

"Yes, dear."

"I warned you," she continued.

"Yes, you did."

"I was right." She smiled.

"I know, you were right, I was wrong." I replied, hoping to satisfy her urge to be correct.

She shook her fist at me and did a victory dance.

"Well, just keep saying that and we will be fine." She laughed.

I looked at her with annoyance, she smiled at me. We laughed hysterically. It wouldn't be a typical day for us without laughing about something. We unpacked all of our camping gear, everything smelling of campfire cologne and began preparing for what would become our normal, everyday life.

Stacy went back to her job, college had wrapped up for her for the time being and she was now working full time at a work and western wear store. After being back to work for a few weeks, she came home one night to tell me a new girl had started. Sarah had much the same background as Stacy did. She was raised on a farm, but instead of cattle and horses, they had sheep. Stacy teased her constantly about being a sheep herder, something cow people will do. They hit it off and were soon hanging out regularly. It was good for Stacy. She had been feeling a little lost after our move to a place that was not surrounded by fields and herds of cattle. Having a friend to hang out with while I was gone to work was what she needed.

I, on the other hand, wasn't so sure about this new friend of hers. They were close in age, but with Stacy being married and Sarah still ready to go out and party, I wasn't sure that it was a good fit. I didn't want to complain. I knew I was going to be gone a lot of the time and I couldn't expect Stacy to just sit at home and be lonely. Sarah would eventually grow on me and become a part of our family. She may have been a bit on the crazy side but that just meant she fit in that much better.

I had been flying out nearly every time I went to work. I was working near Medicine Hat on a project setting casing in the ground on a few drilling rigs. It was a good experience for me. The work was busy and I needed the funds. In the back of my mind I was still thinking of riding the following year. Although the thought of it was constant, my drive to actually do it had begun to fade. I just assumed it was due to my wreck. It happens to a lot of guys. A bad injury can mess with your head and ruin your courage to ride again. I knew I would just have to get on one more time and it would all be back to normal. I still felt like my focus was not all that strong, though, and my thoughts of riding would eventually turn back to Stacy and what she had told me on our honeymoon. I didn't want to make a decision that could be detrimental to our relationship. Not that she would have left me if I returned to riding, but I had been very lucky last time. Next time I might not be so lucky. Maybe it was all just nerves doing the talking in my head.

During the long winter months I had been sent north of home to work on another project. It seemed like my summers were spent south and the winters were spent further north. It was tough on my Stacy. The house was very quiet when I was gone, but we called each other several times each day just to see how things were going and to tell each other we loved one another one more time. I had called her one morning as I was leaving for work and we chatted for a short time. I drove for a couple hours to the drilling rig, but just as I got there, I was asked to turn around and leave. A man had just lost his life on the drill floor. My stomach turned. Stacy called me as I was turning around.

"Hey, babe, how is the job going?"

I wasn't sure what to say. I never kept any information from her.

"I'm, uh, turning around and heading back, I guess," I said, hesitantly.

"What? Why? What's wrong?" she asked.

"Some poor fella just lost his life on the rig."

Stacy started to cry. We had been away from each other so much and the thought of something like that happening to me was never far from her mind. I always seemed to be around things like this and Stacy knew how dangerous it could be. She was a bit of a worrier, and though her heart was in the right place I was always careful. Or so I assumed.

Chapter 14

Spring was starting to come around and work was easing up. The slower pace finally had me home more often than not, which made Stacy and I much happier. We missed each other so much while I was gone and my days off never seemed to be enough. But we didn't have to worry about that for the moment. We filled every evening with date nights, cruising around town in the beast of a truck that I…or we…still had or curled up together watching movies. It was during one of those movies that I asked one last time

"There's a rodeo coming up close to home. I was thinking of entering. Are you okay with that?"

Stacy didn't say anything. Her silence spoke volumes, telling me what I didn't want to hear. I wanted to try again, just one more time. I didn't want my last ride to have been a disaster. It didn't feel right to quit on a bad note.

She finally turned toward me and said, "You really don't want to give it up, do you?"

"Do I ever just 'give up'?"

"No, but how long are we going to do this for? I'm not trying to tell you to not do it; I'm trying to tell you to think before you just jump back on again."

I wasn't overly happy with her reply, but what did I expect her to say? 'Oh yes, please, go get on more bulls and get hurt. That would be so much fun for me.'

"I just don't want to throw it all away because I got hurt. I don't want to go out like that"

"I get that, but are you willing to just throw everything we have away for one more ride?"

I glared at her. That ticked me off. It felt like she had no faith in my riding anymore. She'd seen me ride and win several times before. I'd only really been hurt badly a couple times. Now she didn't want to support me anymore? It didn't seem fair.

"Just give me another fucking chance! I can do this again, I know I can. Don't tell me I can't do it!" I yelled. I instantly regretted raising my voice. I knew she was just worried about me.

"Just do whatever the fuck you want then! Don't worry about me. I'll be fine without you here if you get killed." She stormed off to our room in tears and slammed the door.

My heart sank into my stomach. What had I just said to her? My words had come out too strong. I wasn't mad at her at all, she had every right to be concerned. It's not like I could guarantee an injury-free ride. That's not how the sport worked. It was a gamble every time I nodded my head and I knew that. My anger hadn't been directed at her intentionally. In a way I was mad at myself. I knew better than to get back on after months of not riding, especially without going to my regular school to hone my skills before the season started. That had been a bad move on my part and the results spoke for themselves. But no one ever wants to end their time in a sport they love on a bad note. However, if I had had a great season, I wouldn't even be thinking about hanging up my spurs for good. How does anyone ever decide to give up? How would I make this final decision? What would I do with my energy and insatiable desire for that extreme rush of adrenaline?

I waited for an hour before I even dared to go open our bedroom door. I knew she was like a vicious animal when she was angry, but I had to talk to her. I had to let her know what was on my mind and I needed to know what was on hers. I crept in quietly. Stacy was laying on the bed, still sobbing. I slid in beside her, wrapping my arms around her gently.

"I'm sorry, I didn't mean for that to come out so harshly. I'm not mad at you. I get it."

"Do you? Do you really get it" Stacy was still pissed.

"I think I do?" Now I wasn't so sure.

"Do you know what it feels like for the dust to clear and see your fiancé laying there completely lifeless? I rushed out to find you unresponsive and saw the blood running down your neck. I was terrified. I had no idea if you'd ever wake up."

I was taken back by her response. We hadn't talked much about that day. She had kept her true feelings to herself on the subject. Although we had been together for a few years, we still had a lot to learn about each other.

"No, but I…" I tried to explain my point, but she needed to tell her side first, apparently.

"No you don't. You don't know what it feels like to be completely helpless while you wait to find out if you will be alone for the rest of your life."

I kept quiet now, better to not dig myself in any deeper than I already had. She had never told me how she really felt about that day. I assumed she was okay and knew I'd want to ride again. I also made the assumption she had no worries about it. My thoughts were all based on my own selfishness.

"I'm sorry," I whispered. What else could I say? I wanted to ride, but not at any cost. I had written a letter to her years ago about this. I had told her that if I had to choose between her or riding, I would choose her every time. She still had that letter hidden away somewhere. That moment had finally come and I didn't want to make the decision now. If she would've told me to not ride, I would stop. But she wouldn't say the words. I laid my head down. There was no point in continuing my argument. She was right…again. Stacy rolled over and pushed her face into my chest.

"I don't want to see you get hurt again, but I don't want to tell you to stop. I can't tell you to stop doing something you love." She paused, waiting for my response. I had nothing to say. "Promise me you won't get hurt?"

I thought for a moment, questions flooding my mind. But again I responded selfishly.

"I promise." What a dumb thing to say. How could I promise something I had little control over? I had some control on whether I got hurt or not that came from years of learning things the hard way.

But some things were not in my control. How could I make a promise like that? I pushed the thought out of my mind.

"I love you," Stacy whispered.

"I love you too."

It had been our first really big fight since our wedding. I was guilty of being a selfish asshole who wanted to make a decision that only involved something I loved and didn't take into consideration how she felt about it. I slept very little that night. Visions of riding the perfect bull danced in my head, but were suddenly changed to a girl I had met by chance and fallen deeply in love with. I was tormented all night with the choice I had to make.

The next morning Stacy got up early and left for work, I had the day off and didn't have much planned. I sat and thought for hours about what to do. Today was the entry day. If I was going to do it, I had to call in before the entries closed. I pulled my gear bag out into the kitchen and unzipped it, releasing a pungent odor that only a rodeo arena could bring. The smell sent a chill up my spine. I had missed it so much. A small shot of adrenaline shot through my chest. I picked up the phone and dialed the number. I had to do it, even if it was only this time.

Stacy came home that evening and stopped in her tracks, "What the hell is that smell?" she gasped.

She walked into the kitchen and saw my gear spread out on the floor.

"You entered?" she asked.

"Yeah, I called an hour ago. They don't have many riders, so it won't be a big show," I said, trying to convince myself it was a good idea.

"Okay, I hope it goes well for you." She was trying to sound encouraging, but her tone was not convincing.

Stacy was pretty quiet for the rest of the day. I didn't know what else to say to her. I was damn sure she wasn't enthused with my decision, but I had already made my mind up. I just wanted one more chance.

We both had the next day off of work and hadn't made any plans. Life had been busy and we just wanted to do nothing for a day. We hung out, listened to music and cleaned up the house. The sting from our recent fight had dissipated, but Stacy still seemed to be on edge. I made sure to not bring up the subject. I knew she didn't want to hear any more about it anyway. The phone rang later that evening. Stacy answered it and handed it to me.

"Hello?"

"Hey, Myron, we only had a hand full of rough stock riders enter yesterday. The stock contractor said he wasn't going to bring any if we didn't have a full show, so we are cancelling the rough stock events"

"What? So I can't ride?"

"No, sorry, not at this one."

I slammed the phone down. I was pissed.

"Everything alright there, hulk?" Stacy teased.

"They cancelled the rough stock. I can't ride next weekend."

"Oh? I'm sorry, babe." She sounded relieved. I would never admit it and I hated to feel it, but I was somewhat relieved as well. I knew I was done, but I didn't want to say it. I shoved my gear back into my bag in anger, zipped it up and threw the bag outside, slamming the door shut. I sat down on the couch and starred at the TV. Stacy said nothing, knowing I was disappointed, but she had no idea I was feeling the slightest bit of relief. I wasn't about to tell her either.

"I just wanted one more chance."

"I know you did, honey. It's okay. Maybe you can enter in the next one."

"No, I'm done. I give up." I was so defeated.

"Are you sure? I don't want to go through this again."

"I'm done."

Stacy kissed me on the cheek

"I love you."

She always tickled the corner of my mouth when I wouldn't smile. I couldn't help it. I tried hard but I couldn't keep it away. I grinned at her.

"I love you more."

"You lie. You know I love you most and don't you ever forget it."

She was happy. I knew the call had come for a reason. I took it as a sign that I needed to quit for good, but that didn't mean I was happy about it. I was crushed. I had put my heart and soul into this. I thought about it constantly. I dreamt about it, talked about it, ate, slept and drank it. Bull riding was who I was and what I was known for. Who was I without it? I was nothing, or at least that's how I felt. I had failed to leave the sport on a high note. My last ride had been a complete disaster. What was I supposed to do now? I wasn't about to take up calf roping; that would just add insult to injury. I was lost. I was also not looking at the bigger picture.

Beside me lay a woman who had complete trust in me, who felt safe when I was around her. She had put her entire future in my hands and here I was thinking about nothing but myself. I sat there staring at nothing while my head reeled and hers lay on my lap. She seemed to be at complete ease now. I felt so guilty for being so selfish. Every decision I had been making on the subject had only involved myself, again. Maybe it was a good thing I was going to give it up now. Obviously my decision making skills needed some work. My focus needed to change from what I wanted to do to what she needed. She didn't need to be left all alone or with a husband who was crippled. She didn't deserve that at all. I loved her more than anything and she loved me the same. She would not say the words outright because she didn't want me to resent her for not being able to ride anymore. I could never blame her for anything except letting me get away with this for a little too long.

I glanced down at her and began to say something, but I stopped myself. She was fast asleep and looked so peaceful. I laid my head back and closed my eyes, a slight streak of pain shot through my neck.

"Yeah, maybe it is the right time to move on." I smiled to myself. Dammit, she was right again.

Chapter 15

A few months had passed by. I was still dealing with the pain from my neck injury. It never really seemed to go away. I was constantly taking pain medications, which did not bode well for my stomach. Stacy had expressed concern about it numerous times but, being as stubborn as I am, I just tried to deal with it. Eventually I had to give in, though. I couldn't deal with this pain forever. I found a sports medicine doctor in town and made an appointment for the next day. When I arrived I was greeted with the usual paperwork to fill out. I always grinned when I had to fill out the part about previous injuries; there was never enough room for me to write everything down. I filled it in then flipped the page over and continued on the back side. A few moments later the doctor called me in and began reading through my charts.

"Okay, let's start with you lying face down on the bed please," she instructed.

I stood up slowly, feeling that pinch in my neck as I stood and laid face down as she had requested. I was so uncomfortable in that position, I gripped my fists as I lay there waiting to see what she would do. She noticed my discomfort and adjusted my head slightly. She started gently pressing down my spinal cord, stopping in one specific spot and slowly moving her thumb over the vertebrae. She stopped and picked up my papers reading through them again.

"So, how long ago did you break your neck? You didn't write that on here."

Her question took me by surprise. "Sorry? What was that?" I asked.

"You have a vertebrae in your neck that has been fractured and healed over. I can feel it, but you don't have it written down in your history here," she replied as she looked over the charts once more.

"Um, well, I can tell you when it happened, but I didn't know it had been broken."

I told the doctor the story of my bull riding wreck from the previous season. How much pain I had been in and how it had never really felt right since that day. She listened to my story and shook her head in disbelief.

"So you walked around with a fractured vertebrae, branding calves, riding horses and working in the oil field. I would say you are very lucky. You should've been in a neck brace for a month. But you are here now so we will get you started on some physical therapy to get the strength and mobility back, which will reduce your pain."

The doctor set me up with a program of exercises and stretches to start with. It would take some time but now I had a plan to get back to normal. I left the office and sat in my truck looking over the instructions I had received. My mind went back to that day, remembering bits and pieces of the wreck and the pain that followed. My heart ached to get back on and ride again. Maybe this would be what I needed to do so that I could get the chance to ride again? I thought to myself. But then the vision of Stacy crying when I woke up in the hospital after the wreck, the fight we had over me wanting to ride again and the things she had said to me came back. For as much as I wanted to have the chance to ride again, I knew in my heart that it was never going to happen. There were other things in my world that needed me more than the rodeo arena. Stacy needed me and I needed her. I shook my head and chuckled to myself knowing she would be giving me the I told you so speech when I got home and told her what the doctor had discovered.

Stacy understood I had given up something that had defined who I was. What she would never understand completely is the effect it had on my mind. I had all this energy built up and I didn't know where to put it. I craved that adrenaline rush like a junkie craves their next hit of poison. I sat around most of the summer, unsure of what to do with myself. Sometimes I would take my mud truck out for a drive on my own while Stacy was at work. Usually that would take me down some trail in the woods, sometimes I'd get stuck. Being out late and coming home with a broken truck became the new normal. I was battling depression and hadn't figured out a way to clear my head in a productive way.

I couldn't watch bull riding anymore and I didn't want to go to any rodeos. I hated seeing guys I knew out there doing what I wanted to. Truth be told, though, my heart just wasn't in it anymore and I had no business getting involved in a sport that takes a ton of heart and determination. . I had to be fully invested in it or not at all. I never blamed Stacy for my move to not ride, she never told me I had to quit. I had to do that myself, but she was happy she didn't have to worry about me getting hurt again. The depression I had fallen into was something neither of us saw coming, though. My usual positive demeanor had changed and I was becoming a person who was very negative and unmotivated to do anything. I tried to keep it to myself, but a lot of times I would end up starting arguments over nothing, causing Stacy to feel alienated by this person she didn't seem to know anymore.

I had started to spend a fair amount of time messing around with my truck. It was broken half the time from my random drives off into the woods. I'd try to fix it back up, sometimes making small upgrades as I went. The time spent with wrenches in my hand seemed to ease the depression for a little while. Word had gotten around about some kind of mud bog event in town coming up. I got some more information about it and decided I'd go check it out. I had some decent sized mud tires, differential locks and a weak V8 engine but what the hell? I had nothing better to do anyway.

It was the first event of its kind I knew of. Nothing too serious, just a pit dug down a few feet and filled with a bunch of clay based mud. Stacy ended of getting roped into helping…a lot. She was timing the trucks, recording the runs, figuring out the score, keeping each class organized. She was doing the job of five people all at once, but she was having a blast. She always wanted to help out with whatever she could. I entered my truck and tried it out, made it almost nowhere and was stuck. I watched a few other big trucks run through and absolutely annihilate the mud hole. They were pretty impressive, and the engines in those trucks were far superior to what I was running. I was starting to get a warm tingly feeling inside. Being born with a very healthy competitive side, anything I got involved in would end up becoming some kind of competition. I did enjoy working on my truck and doing what I could to make it faster or stronger. It was much safer than riding, but it just didn't have the same rush.

After the event, Stacy jumped up into the truck with me, both of us were peppered with mud. It had been a good day. She had been able to be involved rather than just sitting on the side lines for a change. It still felt weird to me, though. It wasn't the crowd I was used to and the adrenaline wasn't there. I wasn't even close to being competitive. It didn't take any sort of endurance or strength to do. It was fun, but just not the same.

A few weeks later I had met up with a friend in town. We were standing in the parking lot by my truck BS'ing when a fella pulled up beside us.

"Hey, I'll give you five hundred dollars to come pull my buddy out of the mud tomorrow."

"Five hundred buck!? Done!" I headed home and told Stacy all about the fortune I was going to make the next day. I got up in the morning, packed any sort of tow straps and gear I thought I might need and made my way out to meet up with this guy. I headed south of town across the river to an old cut line in the woods. After making a few turns I found his buddy's bone stock Chevy down a muddy cut line. I locked the hubs in and idled up beside the truck. It was a fair ways off the road and would not have been accessible for a regular 4x4. I hooked up my winch to straighten him out first, then backed up and yanked him out all the way to the road. The driver shook my hand and gave me the cash. It wasn't even noon yet so I thought it would be a wasted day if I didn't go find some more trails to explore. I found some fresh mud holes and tore them up, I was having a blast but it didn't last long. It ended when I had two dented fenders and a broken front driveshaft. I limped my poor truck back into town, stopping in to see Stacy at work. I barely had my foot in the door…

"What the hell did you do?" She asked with one hand on her hip and not looking impressed.

"Huh? What do you mean?"

"I know that look on your face, don't play games with me. What did you break?"

Well shit, can't a guy get away with a little bit of shenanigans without getting in trouble anymore? Nope, not with Stacy. She could read me like a book. She knew when I was up to something.

"Well, I made $500 this morning!"

"Uh huh, and then?"

"I broke a few things."

"Of course you did. How bad?"

"Just a driveshaft."

"And?"

"...some fenders." She never cared all that much about the parts underneath the body but whenever I put a new dent in that very pretty truck, she would get slightly angry with me.

"Can you not just go play without wrecking nice things?"

"Uh, have we met? I'm pretty good at breaking things."

"Yeah, like your neck?" Stacy sent a cheap shot my way and I took it on the chin like a champ. Her sense of humour was always very sharp

and she was the best at knocking down my ego when it was needed. Although I was pretty sure it was always in check.

Stacy laughed at me and shook her head. "What am I ever going to do with you?"

She was happy I was out doing something I seemed to enjoy rather than moping around the house and whining about missing the ride. Tearing up those mud holes was something that was slowly taking the place of what had once defined my life. I headed for home and started replacing broken parts again a pattern I seemed to repeat consistently. Drive around, get bored, head to the woods, come out with broken pieces, fix it and repeat. It wasn't always cheap but it was much easier to fix broken parts on a truck than it was to heal broken bones and Stacy really did love driving around in that truck.

I had a company truck at my disposal and for any longer drives I would use it, but it was a boring truck. If it was a reasonable option though, we took the beast. Why wouldn't we? It looked good, and was a helluva lot more fun to drive…until the cops started pulling us over for almost every little thing.

I was heading to pick Stacy up one day for a lunch date. I was just making the last turn when the red and blues lit up behind me. I could see her shop but didn't quite make it before I got busted. I sat and chatted with the officer for a bit, being as polite as I possibly could and, for the first time, got off with a warning. Meanwhile, Sarah, who had been outside and saw me get pulled over, made sure to throw me under the bus.

"I think Myron is gonna be a few minutes late picking you up. He's out back with a cop behind him." Sarah laughed.

"Again?"

They were laughing at me when I arrived.

"How much was the ticket this time?" Stacy asked.

"Ha, what ticket? I got a warning this time!"

"Well, that's a first and likely your last." We headed off for our usual lunch date in style, doing my best to drive like Jesus would.

Our lives had seemed to become a little simpler and laid back as I slowly started to pull out of my depression. I talked to her a lot about it, something I would do with no one else. She was the one person I could just let it all out to and she would listen to me babble on about stuff that mattered to me. Guys are never the type to talk about how they're feeling unless it's some sort of physical ailment. But with her, I was completely comfortable. She would sympathize with me. She understood my side and would express hers. We didn't always see eye to eye, but we could always find some place in the middle that would work for us. So many people end up in one sided relationships, where one person suffers while the other gets everything they want. I started to realize we were headed down that path over the issue of me riding. I may have given it up, but it was worth it because she was worth it.

I had begun to lose touch with the guys I rode with. Once you're not involved with the sport you eventually move on to other things. It's just the way life goes sometimes. But we had started to meet new people through four-wheeling and mud bog events. They weren't the type I was accustomed to, some of them were awful rough around the edges, but they all had big hearts. Many of them would become more like family to us. We spent a lot of late nights wrenching, getting stuck or heading out to get someone else out of a jam. I found a comradery I never had while riding. We were all competitive but not so much that we weren't willing to help each other out. Sometimes you were unable to get near the truck if it broke, there were already more than enough hands on it.

Stacy was a little uncomfortable driving the truck because she claimed to not know how to drive a standard. I called bullshit. I had seen her drive the finicky, old grain truck down the road and that was a piece of crap, hard to find the right gear in. But I wanted her to be able to be comfortable driving it if she wanted to so I started making plans to do an automatic transmission swap and make it that way.

That swap would quickly snowball into a complete big block build, ridiculous amounts of wrench time and headaches. But I had suddenly been sucked into something I loved to do. Instead of endless chatter about the next rodeo, it had changed to which camshaft I thought would be best, how much power it should make and what brand of pistons to use. Stacy just listened as she always did, smiling at my excitement, but possibly slightly annoyed with my constant talk about something she didn't share quite the same enthusiasm for.

She was about to drop something on me that would change my world forever, something no man is ever prepared for.

Chapter 16

I had been working quite a bit, but for the past few months it had been around home. What a treat it was to go out to work and be able to go back home at the end of the day. The hours of an oil field service worker were weird and I would come home at random times, but it was still home. I had already started my big block build and automatic transmission swap. My mind was buzzing with ideas and not one to ever keep anything from Stacy, she had heard every detail whether she wanted to or not. I was heading home from the shop late one evening when she called me.

"Hey babe, where are you now?"

"Almost home. Be there in about five minutes."

"Ok...I have a surprise for you." Stacy sounded different, not in a bad way, but whatever it was, it was big.

"Sweet! I love surprises!"

"I'm pregnant"

"What! Are you serious? You're not messing with me are you?"

We had been wanting to start our family for months now. Stacy, being the type of person who wanted instant results, had grown impatient and had all but given up by this time. I on the other hand was perfectly happy with just practicing...practice makes perfect right? But I had been hoping for this as well. Although I had little to no experience with babies and would have a lot to learn in short order, I wanted to have babies soon.

"I'm not joking. We're going to have a baby!"

I screeched into the yard, ran into the house and scooped her up in my arms, spinning her around. I couldn't believe it. We were going to have a baby! She was going to be the mother of my baby! I was going to be a father…Holy shit, I was going to be a Dad! The excitement and happiness we both felt was something I can't put into words. I wasn't sure if I was ready, but I don't think any man is ever truly ready to become a dad. It's something that happens by taking a leap of faith and doing your best. Sliding up and nodding your head. Once the gate swings open you just do your best to be in control of what's coming your way and try to be one step ahead.

My instincts instantly took me to the over-protective spouse status. I treated her like she was made of glass. If she was tired I would get her a blanket and lay her down. Hungry? Craving something? I would drive around town until I found it. Stacy laughed at my sudden change, but just let it happen. And why not? She was getting care like she had never seen before, no need to spoil a good thing! She hadn't even begun to grow a baby belly yet and I was helping her into the truck, making sure she had hold of my arm if we were walking so she had me to hang onto if she tripped. At some point Stacy's independent side kicked in again.

"Ok babe, I love you but I'm not broken. I got this. You don't have to worry so much."

"Um, ok babe. I love you too, but you're carrying our baby, just accept this and let me do my thing."

Stacy giggled at my insistence. I loved to do things for her, but now it felt so much more important than before. I knew she would be an incredible mother and I was hoping to be able to keep up to her standards as a father. She had the soft touch and words, at least when she wasn't cussing, that is. I wasn't uncomfortable with babies, I just didn't know much about them. But I was determined to figure it out. We read books, listened to everyone's advice and heard all the stories about who did what and how this never worked and this was what you had to do. We took everything in stride and did our best to sort through all the info.

Stacy had terrible morning sickness right from day one. I had a strong stomach but I was never good with vomit. It takes a special person to be fine with it, and I am not that person. She had mastered it though. She had been driving into town one day, heading to work in her Grand Prix (which her and Sarah had nicknamed the Big Prick) when she felt like she was about to get sick. She was in a bad place to pull over and didn't want to puke on herself, so she found an empty soda bottle, spun the lid off and spewed into it. She screwed the lid back in and tossed it out the window, feeling a little guilty for littering and hoping some poor 4H kid didn't end up picking it up during their annual highway cleanup.

Knowing I didn't have the stomach for this subject, she had to call to tell me a story.

"Hey babe, guess what I just did!"

She promptly told me every detail while I gagged over the phone. Gross! But then I had to wonder, how is that even possible? Simple physics says that it shouldn't work. I stopped myself from asking for more details. I had heard more than enough already.

I cleaned out one of the spare rooms in our house. Stacy found a crib and hundreds of baby accessories she thought would be needed. I would leave for work and Sarah would come to the house to help sort out how the jig saw puzzle of a crib went together and keep Stacy company. They were both super excited and had become very close friends, sisters not by blood but by choice. I was a bit more at ease knowing that she could rely on Sarah if she needed help with anything while I was gone. Everyone needs one friend who will be there when they're needed.

A few months passed and my engine build progressed, as did our babies growth. Stacy's folks had passed on their duties as rodeo organizers to the next generation of folks who wanted to do it and were now setting up a mud race event in the same area. I scrambled to get my truck together again so we could go try it out. I busted my knuckles while Jamie and my dad helped me get it put together last minute. Once we had it running, I got my five-month pregnant wife hoisted up into the truck and took it for its first cruise. We had built a 468ci big block with 500 horse power. It was a huge improvement from the basically stock small block we had originally. The small block had hung in there and never really let me down, but it was time to go bigger. Now it had an automatic transmission so Stacy could drive it whenever she wanted. She had driven it before but only with me there to coach her along through the gears in the old 4 speed. I was excited she would be able to take it now without fear of stalling the truck at a light. I hadn't considered the fact it was about two feet too tall for a pregnant lady to get into on her own. The summer was brutally hot that year and her craving was always for slushy's, but even with the heat that seemed to be so unbearable for her while she carried our baby, she still would choose the jacked up truck with no air conditioning. Windows down, stereo cranked up, she was happiest that way. The truck had become a part of who we were just as riding had been a part of who I was.

With the baby getting closer, Stacy had decided she wasn't comfortable with the car she had been driving and wanted to get a truck. This suited me just fine as I hated cars during the winter anyhow. We headed into town and started searching for the right one. After many test drives, we picked a brand new Dodge Powerwagon 4 door truck. It was still sitting in the show room when the paperwork was complete so they opened up the huge glass doors and we drove it out and headed home. Stacy was proud as a peacock driving around in her new truck and felt much safer and more confident that this would suit her needs better during the long winter months. By this time she was on her fourth vehicle. I had bought her first car in which she had a fender bender and it was written off. The insurance money covered a super clean 1980 C10 Chevy truck she adored and had received her fair share of tickets with. We sold that when we started thinking about babies and I found her the Grand Prix, aka the 'Big Prick'. But after going through one nasty winter with it, she was not comfortable driving a car and I agreed. With the new Dodge, we were feeling somewhat prepared for our baby to come.

As summer slowly creeped away and fall was just around the corner, we were both becoming impatient. Stacy started reading up on all the old wives tails of what could bring on labor. She tried them all, numerous times. For the record, they are all fake as far as we were concerned. I would lay in bed beside her, unable to sleep, I would lay my hand on her belly to feel the baby move around and kick. It had been a fascinating experience. I thought constantly on what this child would grow up to be and if I would be a good father. I had so many questions about how things would turn out. I knew Stacy would be an incredible mother. That was never in question. The love she had for everyone would be multiplied several times for her own child. She would be there for every special moment of this baby's life, every bump and bruise, first word, first step and I was worried I would miss so much with my job. I wasn't sure I was ready for this. But finally, one early morning Stacy woke.

"Honey, wake up."

"No, it's too early."

"Babe, I think it's time."

I slowly opened my eyes, not quite understanding what that was supposed to mean. Then it clicked. I leaped out of bed and ran around the house like a man possessed, grabbing all of the bags that we had packed for this event. Stacy sat down in the kitchen watching the show and giggling between contractions. She sat with a bowl of cereal, slowly eating some breakfast and just as it had been for the last nine months, she set down her bowl and waddled off to the bathroom to throw it all back up. Poor girl had not had it easy the entire time. I loaded everything into the truck and turned to run back in to get my bride, who was already making her way down the front steps. I ran and grabbed her arm to help her down.

She laughed as she watched me lose my mind. "It's okay Babe, I've got this. I'm not broken, I'm just going to have a baby."

A smile crept over my face. This was going to happen! We headed to the hospital, got checked in and walked into the maternity ward where I was gut punched by the noise of women screaming bloody murder!

"Oh my God, what's going on?"

Stacy laughed at my sudden shell shock. I had been gone when Stacy did the tour of the ward a few months earlier, so I was not mentally prepared for the pandemonium that seemed to be going on. It was a busy day for babies and the place was full of pain and agony.

They put us in a labour room with a bed. Stacy was calm as could be, where I, on the other hand, was white as a ghost. We waited for an hour before the doctor came to check on Stacy's progress. She was in labor, but it didn't seem to be very far along yet. We were asked to go for a walk and come back in a few hours. We found some coffee, walked around, stopping every few minutes until her contractions would ease up. Getting back into the ward again, the nurses decided she could get into the bed and begin the prep for this baby to come meet the world. She had been having terrible pains in her back during the contractions and I would push my fist into her back to help ease some of the pain, which only helped slightly. She got up and into the shower to have the water pressure massage her back. Her contractions grew stronger and more frequent. I convinced her to get out as I was sure the baby would just fall out, and I didn't want that to happen. She stepped out and sat down on a chair. She grabbed onto me as another pain shot through her. She leaned forward towards me, and I assumed it was to lean on me. No. She bit down hard on my shoulder and did not release me until the contraction had passed. I screamed in pain just as she did.

"Oh, my god…this hurts so bad…I'm so sorry." She laughed between deep breathes.

"You did that on purpose!"

"You did this to me! Suck it up, Sally, it was barely a nibble," she laughed.

I examined what was left of my shoulder. Still intact, but with a definite impression even a dentist could have found useful. I helped her back into the bed. It had been hours now and I wanted it to be over. I couldn't imagine how she was dealing with the pain. She was the toughest girl I knew, but all I wanted to do was take her pain away. I felt so helpless. The doctor finally came back. Stacy's water hadn't broke yet, so the doctor broke it to help speed this along. By this time my mom had arrived and was in the room to help me put pressure on Stacy's back to try and ease some of her pain. A nurse came back to examine her progress.

"Okay, Stacy, this baby is coming now. The doctor is busy with another lady who is being a drama queen. We are going to do this together."

"Push!"

Stacy started to scream.

"Don't you scream, I know you're tougher than that!" the nurse bellowed.

Stacy glared at the nurse, bit down hard and proceeded to push without making a sound. I was floored. I had been through some bad shit. I had felt some intense pain, but my wife was now delivering a baby, tears rolling down her face and not making a sound. They had given her morphine, but it did not take effect. She was doing this with nothing but pure grit. The baby slowly began to emerge.

"Dad, get ready to cut that cord," the nurse warned

"Huh?" I had to do what?

"Cut the cord, you bastard!" Stacy yelled one last time as she gave a final push.

Our baby was in this world. I grabbed the scissors and cut the cord. I looked down at a life we had created, but something wasn't right, the baby wasn't breathing. The nurses quickly whisked the baby away and started working. I looked back at Stacy. The pain was gone, she was covered in sweat and exhausted but I had never been so proud of her. She was amazing. I looked over at my mom who was now sitting in a chair and not looking so good.

"Mom, you okay?" And then she fainted. We helped her into the next bed and let her rest. She had seen the baby not breathing and it scared her.

The nurses had worked fast and got our baby breathing. She had gone from purple and not looking good to pink and crying. What a fantastic sound, but holy crap that kid had some lungs on her!

"Here you go, my dear, your new baby girl." They brought her to Stacy wrapped in a blanket. I did my best to keep my tears from rolling out of my eyes. She was so beautiful. Halle Mae was born September 23, 2006. She was long and lightweight, much like her parents. I kissed Stacy on the forehead. I had just witnessed the miracle of life. The instant feeling of love for my own child washed over me; I had never felt anything like it before. The love a person has for their spouse is incredibly deep and unconditional, but the love for your child is different, and it is indescribable.

The nausea that had plagued Stacy for the past nine months had instantly gone away, and she was now starving. Our families had come in to meet the next generation, each taking a turn to hold her for a few minutes before passing her to the next person.

We got a private room that night. Halle slept soundly beside the bed, wrapped up tightly. I laid down beside Stacy and held her close. I had witnessed the sheer determination and strength of a woman I had been in love with since we were just kids and I was there to see her bring a new life into this world. My baby was beautiful, my Stacy was beautiful. I loved her so much, I thought I could never love her more than I already had, but this had changed things. My heart pounded as

I held her, I had found a depth of love I had never known existed.

Chapter 17

After a few rough nights in the hospital, we were finally cleared to go home. I packed everything down to the truck and pulled it up to the front doors. I ran back up and adjusted the safety harness of the car seat for this tiny human. I took my baby in one hand and held Stacy's hand with the other as we walked out. I got Halle locked in and ready for her first trip home. As we left the hospital I felt myself become extremely alert to our surroundings. Everyone seemed to be driving at 90 mph while I was driving 20 clicks under the speed limit down every road, eyes up and scanning for threats.

"Babe, what are you doing?" Stacy asked.

"These sons of bitches are driving like mad men!"

"Uh, no, they're doing the speed limit. You're the one driving weird." She laughed.

"Don't care. They're being unreasonable. I have to get us home safely." I was on high alert, my protective nature in overdrive. Stacy just laughed at me and let me be who I was at the moment. We got home after what felt like an hour long drive, but was only maybe twenty minutes. I got my girls into the house and brought all the bags in. Once settled, Stacy sat on the couch holding Halle in her arms.

"She's so gorgeous. I'm sure everyone says that about their baby, but she's perfect." Stacy admired the work we had done creating this new life. She was right though, the nurse had made the same comment before we left. I took a couple weeks off work so I could stay home and get my little family settled into our new normal life. Halle was fussy most nights and we didn't get much sleep. We had no idea how this parenting thing was supposed to go. I learned to change diapers, clean up baby puke and burp her after she ate. All things I was new to. I was also new to the feeling of having a baby in my arms, screaming her face off and eventually falling asleep while I carried her around the house while I talked to her softly until her eyes closed. It was new to me, it was new to Stacy and hard for the both of us. Anyone who says the first baby was easy either had a baby who slept through the first year of their life or they had someone else there to do the hard work and brutal hours.

I was hoping I'd be close to home when I went back to work, but it didn't always work out that way. Being away while the love of my life stayed at home with our baby girl was heartbreaking for me. I wanted to be home with them so terribly bad but I had to provide for them as well. I couldn't have both and it wasn't fun. I usually didn't mind heading out and being gone for a while, the money was good and getting home after a long set was always a huge treat. But now I struggled. Stacy was at home doing her best to figure this new mom thing out and I was not always there to help. She was such an independent lady, though. Sometimes too independent. She wouldn't ask for help when she was in desperate need of it. Our mothers would both do everything they could to be there, offer advice and lend a hand when Stacy was exhausted, but she would have none of it. In her mind, needing help with your baby was a sign of weakness and she was not weak.

Her insistence on doing things on her own while I was gone ended up putting her on edge when I did get home. She'd have Halle on a schedule. Then I would come home and mess it all up and she would have to start over when I left. It frustrated her and would come out in anger sometimes. I didn't realize what I was doing was undoing everything she had accomplished while I was gone. I did my best to help cook, clean and take care of the baby when I could. I wanted to give Stacy a chance to rest. But I was still nervous to be alone with my daughter for any length of time. What if something went wrong? What do I do?

Halle was a few months old and wasn't feeling well, but Stacy needed to head to town. I said I would stay home and look after Halle to give Stacy a chance to get out of the house for a bit on her own. I sat with Halle in my lap. She slept but I could tell she was uncomfortable. She was running a fever that was nearing a dangerous temperature, but not yet high enough to take her in to see a doctor. Stacy said if the baby reached 102 degrees, I needed to call her right away. I sat there with a thermometer in my hand, checking her every few minutes while putting cold wash clothes on her head to try and cool her down. I wanted to pick her up and hold her close but she didn't need the extra body heat. Stacy had been gone for a half hour when her temperature suddenly spiked to 104°. I panicked. I tried calling Stacy constantly, texting, anything. But she didn't answer. I stripped Halle out of her pajamas and put more cold cloths on her, doing everything I could think of. Her temperature eventually dropped enough so I wasn't so scared. Stacy arrived shortly after. The minute she walked through the doors, I freaked out on her.

"You said to call. You said if her temp got higher to call, I called! You didn't answer your god damn phone!"

Stacy ran over and checked on Halle. Her temperature was down below 100° now.

"Babe she's fine. I didn't hear my phone, I'm sorry. But you got this, look she's fine! You did good!"

I was still pacing the house I didn't have a vehicle at home or I would have taken her to the doctor. I did the only thing I knew to do. Halle had barely even woke up for a few minutes while I scrambled to cool her off.

"Honey, calm down. You did the right thing. You're fine and she's fine. You did awesome." She grabbed my hand and pulled me in. I couldn't take my eyes off of Halle. I was so worried and unsure of what else to do to make it better for her. She laid on her blanket, fast asleep as if nothing had happened. Stacy's mood had relaxed so much with the short trip she had taken to town. She needed it, I felt bad for yelling at her when she walked in the door. She didn't deserve that.

"I'm sorry I freaked out on you. I just didn't know what to do," I said.

"Yes you did. Her fever is down more now than it was before. You did fine, honey."

With our busy winter season coming up, the work load had ramped up with it. I was gone again. I was often on the roads when they weren't safe to travel. I thought about my girls constantly and missed them so much. When I did get home again, Halle would cry for her mama every time I picked her up to play with her. I was a stranger. Stacy reassured me it was just a phase, it would be fine. I played with Halle on the floor until she was comfortable with me again. We would be best buds by the time I would head back to work and then leave Stacy with a baby girl looking for her daddy. It was a brutal cycle that continued until it became normal for us all.

After a few months I noticed a change in Stacy. It was gradual, but noticeable. She wasn't as cheerful as she normal. She was on edge a lot of the time and I couldn't figure out why. I would try to talk with her but she wasn't up for conversation. I passed it off to just being exhausted. She had all the house work on her shoulders as well as taking care of a very fussy baby. She didn't get much sleep and just didn't feel like herself anymore. She still had some good days, but being tied down and not free to do what she wanted when she wanted was a drain on her.

Spring finally came. Being able to be outside in the sun shine was a welcome feeling after the long winter cooped up indoors. I was able to be home more and Halle had become my best buddy. She had learned to crawl in the first few months, was standing at six months and walking at nine months. It was bizarre to watch her try so hard to get up on her feet, get angry when she fell and get right back up and keep trying. We learned very quickly she had been born with Stacy's sassy attitude. I thought it was hilarious, but it drove Stacy crazy. She would get so angry at Halle's stubbornness, but it was like watching Stacy argue with herself sometimes.

We did a ton of stuff with our little girl in tow, we herded cows with her strapped to the front rack of the quad, took her to mud race events where I had to keep her from eating the mud off of the truck. Anything we had to do, she came along and we figured out how to juggle thing to make it work. Usually. But Stacy was feeling the burden most of the time. She didn't feel like helping with the mud events anymore. She didn't want to hang out with the crowd as much. I was a little worried about her, she just wasn't the person I had met years ago.

My mom had tried so hard to be there to help Stacy with everything, so much so that it slowly began to drive a wedge between them. My mother had wanted her mother in law to be there to help her and have a good relationship with her but never got her wish. She had tried so hard to be that person for Stacy, but Stacy was not up for it. Her independence was so strong, she would get angry. To Stacy it felt like my mom was over stepping her boundaries and it started to cause issues between us. I loved my mom and appreciated all the help she would offer, but Stacy was the type if she was drowning in a river she would not reach for an out-stretched hand to help her out. She was too stubborn to admit when she needed help. She had lost touch with a lot of her friends and avoided family sometimes.

The one friend Stacy had grown very close to was Sarah, who often stayed at our house. She was going to college and the room she was renting was a ways from town so she would crash at our house and keep my girls company while I was out working. She was also a no BS girl. If you were being an asshole, she was probably going to tell you. It was good for Stacy to have someone like that around. Halle loved her Aunty Sarah, she was a second mother to our little girl.

But even with some positive friends around Stacy to help her out, there was still something not right. Something was off and we couldn't get passed it. We were struggling in our marriage. She was not the girl I had fallen in love with and I was not the person she had met on a random day in November years ago. We seemed to fight constantly. Doors got slammed, and words got said that could not be unspoken. She slapped me once for saying what was on my mind, but my mouth had not chosen the proper words to express it. We were in a bad place, in danger of having everything fall apart.

The quiet times together that we had loved so much had become tense and uncomfortable, I would do everything I could to get her to smile, make her feel loved but I just couldn't seem to get it right. She appreciated my efforts but it never lasted long and we were fighting again.

Halle was nearly 2 years old when things reached a turning point. Which way it would go, I was not sure, but I was tired of fighting and Stacy was tired of trying. We had to either figure this out or we were about done with the whole shitty situation.

We finally had to straight up talk about it. We had to decide which direction we wanted to go. I didn't want to give up, I still loved her so much. But I needed to know what she needed to make this life happy again. She said I was not the same person she had met either; I was more tense and agitated. I didn't want to talk as much and was not communicating with her like I usually did. We both had a lot of work ahead of us if we were going to pull out of this slump. Neither of us wanted to say the word, but we both knew what the other option was.

Our issues did not start over night and they weren't going to get fixed overnight either. This was going to take a solid effort from both of us. If one of us backed off, it would mean the end of something that meant the most to us. I have never been an advocate for divorce unless abuse of some sort is present. That was never the case with us, we may have not been getting along with each other, but deep down we still had the desire to be together and were both stubborn enough to keep trying. We had seen many relationships fall apart due to one or the other just not caring enough to try to make it work. I could never understand how people could give up so easily, or why they would even bother being together in the first place. If both people have their hearts in the right place and are willing to fight to stay with the person they love, it will always work out. You just have to keep trying. Not every day will seem like you made progress. Some days felt like a step backwards but we picked back up and tried again.

My supportive nature and complete openness that Stacy had known me for had been distant at best. Stacy had been overwhelmed with the huge life change of becoming a mother and being left on her own much of the time while I went away to work. We both were guilty of not communicating. We didn't have conversations that would last for hours anymore.

Summer passed by before we knew it and snow was on the ground again. We were still working on our fragile relationship, but I had something in mind that I needed to do. I hadn't done it in a long time and was way overdue. Halle had just turned two, Stacy was back to work and trying to juggle a full time job while still being a mother to our baby girl. One evening she came home and I had made plans for us. I needed to take her out on a date and it had to be this day and no other. She came home tired and not really in the mood. She just wanted to go to bed, but I insisted this had to happen.

I took her out for dinner, I held her hand and looked her in the eyes nervously. I had to tell her something I had been thinking about since things had started to go bad.

"Today is a day we have always remembered as something that meant the most to us, something that would forever change our lives," I said as I reached for her hand.

Stacy looked somewhat puzzled. Our focus had gone so far off track we had forgotten some of the simplest things in our lives.

"Eight years ago today I went to a horse auction that I did not want to go to. I met a girl I would fall in love with. We would grow up together and learn what it meant to truly be a soul mate. I would ask her to marry me even though we were far too young by most standards. We learned each other's quirks and weird habits. You taught me how to write when I couldn't figure out how to speak the words…"

Stacy stopped me, her eyes got big and she realized what day it was.

"Its November 21st…I've never forgot this day before," she said.

She seemed a little upset with herself; she never forgot that date. We had both been guilty of forgetting our wedding anniversary, but that day just seemed more profound. Our story had been so fairy-tale like, so uncommon and it all started on that day.

"I know I haven't been able to talk to you like I used to. I don't always know how to come up with the words. Sometimes I try but you don't seem to want to listen to me," I explained. I was hoping she wouldn't want to start a fight over my words.

"I want to listen, but I'm tired. I'm working, Halle doesn't always sleep through the night, and you're gone all the time. I'm exhausted. And don't tell me to ask our parents for help, I want to do it my way."

"Okay, well let's start with something a bit simpler. Do you still love me?" I asked. It was time to just lay it all out on the table.

"Yes, I still love you, but I don't always feel like you love me back," Stacy replied.

The thought hadn't even crossed my mind, but it had crossed hers.

"I still love you so much. If I didn't love you I wouldn't be sitting here in front of you on the anniversary of the day we met and fighting to keep our love alive."

Stacy looked down and whispered, "It just doesn't always feel like you do."

"I know, it's the same for me. But I do love you." I said as I squeezed her hand.

"I Love you too."

It was going to take a long time, we had a lot of damage to repair. We had lost sight of what had really brought us together in the first place. We had to start from the beginning, get back to the basics. I had to find what it was about her that made my heart race every time I saw her. She had to figure out what it was about me that made her want to stay by my side for the rest of her life. We had both vowed that this would be until death do us part, and we both meant it.

Chapter 18

We spent months trying to get our relationship back to the bliss it had once been. We still fought but we learned to fight it out until we worked it out. It made for many long nights and early mornings. We would sometimes only get a couple hours sleep before we had to get up and head to work. Doing it this way was huge for us, we would not go to bed angry with each other. Some nights we would have to take a few minutes to cool off and think, then start talking it out again. It was a long painful process. Many tears were shed and a lot of truth came out that was hard to say and hard to hear. What seemed to fall to pieces in about one year seemed to take twice as long to repair. Being stubborn enough to not give up on each other was what eventually brought us back together and made us stronger than before.

We were both guilty of not communicating. I had been selfish, sometimes just doing what I wanted to do when I was home and not stopping to see if Stacy needed me for anything first. I would take off and go do stuff with some of my friends while she would sit at home with Halle. She would never tell me when she was upset or needed anything and she stressed about money constantly. We never had joint bank accounts and she never really wanted that, but she would also never ask me if she needed something. She put everyone else first, which is usually a good trait in a person until it drains them and they become unhappy. She needed to do some things for herself that made her happy and I needed to be there to help make sure that happened. The more we tried, the better things got and eventually we started to see the light at the end of the tunnel.

The love we had once had for each other had taken a terrible hit. Our trust and respect for each other had been lacking but now things were improving. At some point along the way we surpassed what had been a great relationship and entered into something so much deeper. Without noticing it we pulled out of the darkness and into a light that shone much brighter than ever before. We had found the love we once had and improved on it. We could talk things out much easier. I knew how she felt because she would tell me. She knew what I was thinking, usually before I told her, because our communication skills had been pretty much perfected. We also began to see a change in Halle. One thing most people don't ever consider is how their relationship with their spouse can have such a huge effect on the kids. They are more in tune to what is going on in the house than anyone would expect them to be. They may not be able to understand the words but they understand the feelings very well. Halle was more goofy and silly now, she would run around the house laughing and giggling. We were happy and it showed in her attitude as well.

We struggled to find a good day home for Halle. There were many available, but finding one that made us comfortable was not easy. We continued to search, go for interviews and then start searching again. Finally one afternoon we walked into a home that felt good. We met Aimie, spending about an hour chatting with her while we watched a few other kids run around the house playing. She had rules, a no bullshit attitude but a love for these kids. Our decision was made. Halle was excited and both Stacy and I felt comfortable with this lady watching over her while we worked. It was a huge weight off of Stacy's shoulders as well. We had been through some terrible places that just plopped the kids in front of a TV and expected to get paid top dollar for it. Aimie and her husband, Jeremy, had seen struggles in their lives as well. Their son had gone through cancer as a toddler, but battled through it and was in good health now. They also had a younger daughter who was a couple years older than Halle. The two of them would grow to me like sisters. This family would end up becoming a part of ours.

I started planning the next engine build for the mud truck. I decided with the attention the cops had started to pay this rig, it was better to take it off the streets and turn it into a full race truck. We had become quite involved in the sport by this time and it was growing every year. I had an insatiable desire to go faster every time I ran it at an event. The faster it went, the more adrenaline I would get. It was nowhere near what I would get from riding but I couldn't ride anymore so this was my next best option. I found an engine builder that specialized in race engines and began the process all over again. I wanted to be the fastest in our area. The engine would go from a 468ci big block ford motor that made about 500 horse power and be transformed into a 532ci race engine that made just over 800hp.

My constant chatter about engine parts annoyed Stacy sometimes and she wasn't completely thrilled we would not be driving it on the street anymore, though she understood why I was doing it. It did make her happy to see me so driven to be good at something I loved to do again. Stacy had started a new job at a plumbing and heating wholesale shop as a receptionist. She quickly grew to love the people she worked with. Many times I would think that it was odd that she didn't really have her own thing she loved to do. Some people play golf, travel or watch sports. But Stacy wasn't into any of that, her thing was people. She loved to talk with old friends and make new ones. She was such a social person and such an easy person to get along with. Even some of the hard ass contractors that no one else wanted to deal with at her work would end up having a soft spot for her. The way she would greet you with a warm smile and one of her famous hugs turned even the biggest jerk into someone who would go out of his way to stop in just to say hi and chat for a few minutes. She had the innate ability to remember their kid's names, when their birthdays were and what they had done last summer. It was her caring side that would draw people to her. She was shy at heart but genuinely cared about the people around her.

I on the other hand was a bit more brash. I had little tolerance for anyone who was being a jerk to others. I'd make sure they knew they were being an asshole. I respected those who treated others with respect, but could be a bit short fused sometimes when someone was acting a fool. Heaven forbid if someone said something to my lady that was rude. I would be right up in their face, instantly angry. Stacy would pull me back, laughing and tell me to chill out. I was never a fighter but I would never let anyone talk down to her. I had developed a reputation of being a little intimidating, which was never my plan. I did love to hang out with people and have a good time, lend a hand when I was able to and give a listening ear if someone was going through some rough times. It's who we ended up being. Stacy was loved by everyone in the first few minutes of meeting her and I was loved by the ones that took the time to get to know me. Together we had become the married couple that had set the bar for what true love was supposed to look like.

My engine build was nearing completion and I was getting excited about it. Updates on the dyno test came in constantly on my phone. Stacy and I decided to head out for a weekend away together. As we headed down the road I received a call that no one wants to hear. A friend of ours had drowned in the river but he hadn't been found yet. My heart sunk to my stomach. Jason had been a mud racing friend and had gone to school with Stacy. He had a young son who would now grow up without a father. I held Stacy's hand for the rest of the drive, our hearts both aching with the thought of his families grief. We made the best of our long overdue getaway. A couple months later Stacy called me from work, bawling her eyes out.

"Randy died on the weekend."

Randy had been a co-worker of hers. He was one of those guys everyone loved. He had an incredible presence when he walked into a room full of people and an infectious sense of humour. He would have everyone laughing with his crazy stories of wild parties and adventures with friends while riding his custom chopper all over the country. He had died in a tragic accident while out riding ATVs with his family. Stacy was crushed. I felt terrible for her. The shop was very somber as his absence had made it feel so empty now.

A month later another friend of Stacy's was killed on the highway by a semi-truck. I wasn't sure what was going on but that summer had been depressing. We were losing friends in all directions and everyone was tip-toeing around their daily lives as if we were under attack and needed to watch every step carefully.

Stacy talked about it constantly and I was having a hard time with it. I had learned to remain positive in every situation, or as best I could anyway. Stacy dwelled on some of these hard times and couldn't seem to get away from the negativity. She was going on and on about how much this sucked and what a terrible year it had been. I cut her off.

"Stacy, I know this has been a shit year. No one wants to see their friends die, especially in such tragic circumstances, but we can't continue to sulk at home. They all lived their lives to the fullest and would want us to do the same."

She sat quietly for a moment before she replied.

"I know, you're right. I need to get out of this gross feeling. I just feel like a dark cloud is hanging over our family of friends." She was saying words I had been feeling as well, but we both knew we had to get up and continue loving each other and those who were in our lives. Life is precious and far too short to stay down for any length of time.

We had just finished our conversation when my phone rang. It was Ashley. Her family had become a part of ours through mud racing. Her husband, Jeff, was one of the best guys to have with you when you broke down. Jeff and his dad, Ray, were incredible at sorting out tough problems and coming up with a solution that would work long enough for you to finish the race.

"Hey Ash, what's up?" I asked.

Ashley was sobbing over the phone.

"Ray was killed on his bike. He was hit by a truck," she said through her tears.

"Oh my God, NO!"

Stacy looked up at me as tears started to build in my eyes.

"What's wrong? What happened?"

I hung up the phone and looked at Stacy. I couldn't believe this was happening.

"Ray is gone." I hung my head and started to cry. I will never understand why this was happening. We had lost four friends in the matter of a few months. I hugged Stacy tightly as we both wept.

"I love you. I need you to know that you mean the world to me. If anything ever happened to me I want you to know you are the best thing that ever came into my life," I whispered.

Stacy nodded her head in my chest as she cried.

"I love you too. If something ever happened to me I need to know that you will keep living. Don't stop living. You have to keep going and know I have always loved you."

It had been a brutal summer. I wanted it to be over. We needed something amazing to come into our lives that would blow this dark cloud away from us.

I had been slowly moving up in position at work. As I moved up my time at home had increased somewhat. This had been good for us. I had spent years in the field and was looking forward to having a better home life. After everything that had happened, I felt I needed to be around more than ever before. I still went out to work fairly often but I would only be gone for a couple days instead of weeks.

I was heading home one evening when Stacy called me, which was odd. I had just messaged her to let her know I would be home in a few minutes from the shop.

"Where are you now?" she asked.

"I'm nearly home, woman. What's going on?" I was laughing, I could hear excitement in her voice.

"I'm pregnant"

"Serious?!"

Stacy was laughing with excitement now. We had just recently discussed the idea of having another baby. We had worked out our issues in our relationship. We were in a good place with each other. It felt like the right time to bring another life into this world…but that had only been a few weeks ago! I drove into the driveway and ran into the house, meeting her at the door. I wrapped my arms around her and kissed her as Halle ran into the room yelling "Daddy, daddy, daddy!" I felt her little arms wrap around my leg. I picked her up and squished her between me and her mama.

"You're gonna be a big sister!" I said as I hugged that little ball of energy.

Halle had been wanting a sibling to play with and had expressed this to us numerous times.

"I'm gonna be a big sista? When? Tomorrow?" she asked innocently.

"No, sweetie, not tomorrow, but in a few months," I chuckled.

"How long is that?"

"Probably in spring some time. The snow has to come and then melt away first." I explained.

"That's a long time, Daddy"

"The baby will be here before you know it, sweet pea," I answered.

We hung out around the house, music turned up as usual. I grabbed Stacy's hand and danced with her in the living room. We never got the chance to dance together much anymore. I was hyper with the news. Stacy was glowing with excitement and trying her best to not start crying, which didn't last long. She soon had tears streaking her face to go with her huge smile. The girl I had met so long ago was now standing in front of me looking as if she hadn't aged a day past twenty. Her natural beauty still took my breath away. My heart skipped just as it had when she had first kissed me at that high school dance. This is what love really felt like.

Chapter 19

We prepared our home once more for the new addition. Every room in the house would be used now and it would likely feel complete and a little full at times. It seemed like the second round was easier for both of us. This pregnancy was not nearly as hard on Stacy as the first one had been. She was more relaxed and laid back about everything. It was incredible to see such a calmness in her now. Halle, on other hand, was impatient. She wanted to be the big sister in the worst way. I was happy the timing would have this baby arriving during the spring when work was slow. I'd be less likely to be working away from home.

We pushed through the winter months again, knowing that Christmas would be the last one with only three of us. By this time next year we would have another little monster crawling around the house. Other than having some terrible heartburn throughout this pregnancy, Stacy was in fine health and felt good the whole time.

Early one morning Stacy woke me up again to tell me it was time to go. I felt calmer this time around. I called Twila to come to the house and stay with Halle, who was still fast asleep. I got things packed up into the truck and we were ready. Stacy had jumped into the shower, the contractions were fairly strong and the water pressure had helped last time. I stood in the bathroom talking to her and timing her contractions.

"Honey, we really should get going. I'm not much of a doctor and I don't wanna deliver this one myself," I said, trying not to sound rushed.

Another contraction started and I looked at my phone, 2:53a.m.

"I think we have time babe, remember last time? They made us wait forever before we got a room? I don't want to do that again." Stacy said confidently.

The next contraction started and I looked at my phone. 2:55a.m.

"Get out now! You are 2 minutes apart and I am not delivering a baby! Move your ass!" I yelled.

"Alright, alright. Calm down. I'm getting out, jeez."

I rushed around, now starting to feel more panic.

"Get dressed! Come on, we gotta haul ass!"

"Babe, we are FINE, my water hasn't even broke yet." Stacy replied, still not moving as quickly as I would've liked her to.

"Nope, don't care. Move it. I don't wanna risk it."

I finally got her out the door and headed to the hospital. When Halle was born it had only been forty-five minutes from the time they broke her water until the time she was born. That didn't allow much time to get into the hospital if her water broke now. We got checked in and got a delivery room right away.

"Hey, things are going better this time!" I said with a grin.

Stacy looked at me with an expression I had seen nearly every day with the first pregnancy. I grabbed a bowl, she yakked in it and laid back in pain.

"I need some ice. Please go get some for me," she begged.

"Okay, be right back." I got up to leave.

"Wait where are you going?" she asked, almost sounding angry.

"Uh, ice? I thought? No?"

"No, don't leave. I don't want you to leave," Stacy pleaded.

"Okay." I sat back down beside her.

"No, I do need the ice. Go get it quickly, please."
"Woman, I love you but make up your damn mind. You want ice? Cause if you do I have to walk out of this room for about five seconds."

"Yes, yes go get ice, dammit. What are you waiting for" she begged.

I snickered to myself, and got up to go get Princess Demanding her ice. It was better than her attempting to tear my shoulder off with her teeth like last time.

I grabbed a cup, filled it with the ice and handed it to her. She popped some into her mouth and started chewing on it. Her contractions were coming hard and fast now.

"Oh my God, this is taking forever," she complained.

"Forever? Shit, we just got here. I haven't even taken my jacket of yet!"

"Stop being funny, it's not funny...oh shit my water just broke!"

I ran out to find the nurses. They called her doctor and came running into the room with me. The doctor arrived moments later and in 10 minutes Stacy brought another fresh face into the world. Layla Faith came out so fast her poor little head and face was bruised up pretty bad. But she was breathing and healthy, I could ask for nothing more.

I leaned over to Stacy, who had just barely broke a sweat through this ordeal, kissed her forehead and whispered, "That was a little close don't ya think?"

Stacy laughed at me. If I hadn't insisted on her getting out of the shower when I did, I would have had a mess to clean up in the truck. So many poor women end up being in labor for hours, sometimes even days. Not my wife, this all happened within a few hours; she wasn't

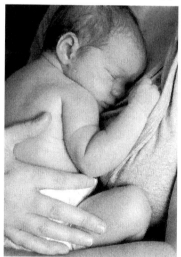

messing around. I was pretty convinced if we ever decided to have a third, I would need a catcher's mitt and a back stop. One good sneeze...things could happen.

The nurse cleaned Layla up, weighed her and brought her back, they set her down in Stacy's arms. I sat in awe. God they were beautiful together. Layla was already starting to close her eyes again, it had been a rough ride for her and at such a high rate of speed. We got mama and baby settled into a room and I started calling family and friends to tell them the news. But I really wanted to go get Halle and tell her in person. She would be awake by now and wondering what was going on. I made sure my girls were in good shape and headed home.

"Daddy!" She was always so excited to see me come in the door, sometimes a bit too excited. She had broken my nose once. As I bent down to pick this bouncy little girl up she jumped up and head butted me. I leaned over slightly less and picked her up.

"Guess what?! You, my dear, have a new baby sister!"

"Not a baby brother?" Halle inquired.

"Nope. Now daddy is completely outnumbered! Do you want to go meet her?"

"Yeah Will mommy be there?" Her innocent questions made me laugh.

"Yes, sweetie, I'm sure mommy is waiting there for us."

We headed back into the hospital to find Stacy feeding the baby. She seemed like such a content child right from the start. Halle hopped up on the bed beside her mother, excited to see what was going on. I sat down and stared at them. My entire life was sitting on that bed in front of me. Halle was goofing off and trying to help her mom while still trying to get a better look at her little sister. Stacy was fussing with the baby who was still trying to eat while wrangling Halle and keeping her from falling off the bed or onto the baby. I laughed at the site. It was awesome. I got up to get the bouncing blonde one off the bed and give Mama some room.

Once the baby had her fill, Stacy wrapped her up tightly and brought her over to Halle to set her in her little arms. Halle sat there grinning and admiring her tiny fingers. She talked to her quietly for a few minutes and sang the only song she knew, the ABC's. She was pretty proud of herself and happy to finally be a big sister.

Sarah stopped in for a few minutes to see Layla and give us all hugs before she was headed off for vacation. She ended up being the only visitor that day. Stacy and Layla needed some rest so we left them alone for a while. The next morning I headed back to the hospital with some books and things for Stacy to do while the nurses fussed over the baby for a day. I walked in to greet them but Stacy was dressed and on her feet.

"Grab the baby and let's go," she said.

I was puzzled "Go where? I brought you things to read and coffee."

"No, I got shit to do. I'm fine. Baby's fine. I don't wanna sit around here all day. Let's go home. I have a few stops to make in town before we leave."

"What the hell woman? Get your ass back in that bed, you need some rest!"

"I'm fine, please carry the baby to the truck, I have stuff to do, let's go!" she insisted.

Ugh, Princess Demanding was not one to argue with. I went down and got the truck situated, ran back up and carried the baby, this time trying to keep up with Stacy as we walked out. She was a woman on a mission! No one else besides Sarah had gotten the opportunity to come see the baby in the hospital yet. We had been there for just over 24 hours and she was already tired of it all. But Layla was calm and relaxed, not fussing at all. Stacy was in good shape as well, so I guess there really was no reason to stay. Off we went, making a few stops in town and heading for home. Once home we brought the girls and all the bags inside, I put Layla down in her crib while she slept and Stacy started on laundry.

I pleaded with Stacy. "Would you please sit down? Not sure if you noticed but you just popped out a kid. You need to rest."

"Are you gonna do the laundry?" She asked, sounding very annoyed.

I stood up. "Well, of course, I will"

"Uh no. I've seen you do it. You do it wrong. I got this."

I loved her and her stubborn ways. She was something else. Who has a kid and goes home to start doing laundry? Stacy does. She was the busiest and most determined mother I had ever met. She could multi-task like no other and balance all of life's twists and turns. A baby in one arm, one kid wrapped around a leg, phone in one ear held with her shoulder while she cooked with the other hand and still had that smile on her face the entire time. She was the most amazing person I had ever met.

We took Layla to her first mud race in Fort Nelson, B.C. when she was only 2 weeks old. I was not sure if it was a good idea, but Stacy was completely confident that she would be fine. Jamie and Debbie were heading up as well. Jamie had started racing in his Suzuki Samurai that we had fitted with a 12A rotary engine from a Mazda RX7 and it was a crowd favourite everywhere we went. Stacy kept the girls well away from the noise and enjoyed the show with her mom while Jamie and I raced. The girls were both being brought up around high revving engines that would have likely been better suited for an asphalt drag car, but since we are country people, mud is what we did. I had done well all day with my runs and was going into the final heat, but I had noticed the end of the mud pit had gone from a gentle exit ramp to more of a ski jump. Trucks were coming out the end and slamming into the exit as if it were a brick wall and jumping the truck out with a bang.

My last run was for all the marbles. I had qualified for the finals with my first runs. Now it would be the fastest single pass that won. I sized up the ski jump and thought maybe I could just ease off towards the end before hitting that wall…That thought passed. Yeah not my style. I lined up my truck, pulled my five-point harness tight and pressed the trans brake button to hold the truck on the start line. I slammed the gas pedal to the floor and let go of the trans brake, 1st, 2nd, 3rd gear and never lifted off the gas. The truck dipped down slightly and slammed into that exit ramp. Then it pitched into the air. Everyone nearby got a good view of the underside of the truck before I came crashing down hard. My neck pinched instantly with a shooting pain. I gathered my thoughts and came to a stop. The landing had been brutal. I crawled out of the truck to have a look around the front end to see if it still existed. Yup, still intact. The crowd had loved it, lots of cheers and high fives everywhere. I, however, was not feeling so good. My neck was killing me.

Stacy caught up with me while I packed up my tools and got ready to head for home.

"Jeez, babe, didn't want to slow down before that jump or what?"

I gave her a look of confusion. I didn't need to answer her.

"Yeah, yeah. I know, not your style to say whoa in a mud hole. How's your neck now?" she asked.

"Terrible sore. I may need to invest in a proper neck brace of some sort," I replied as I rubbed my fragile neck.

She laughed at me while digging in her purse for some pain medication. I took my first prize cash, loaded up the truck and headed for home. Layla had traveled very well for her first trip. We decided, since Stacy was home with the kids and I was working, we would hit a few more events during the summer. It gave Stacy a chance to get out and enjoy herself, chatting with everyone and showing off our new baby girl. I got the chance to race more and travel with my family. It was a terribly busy summer, but a ton of fun. I had found something that, while maybe not on the same level as bull riding, had become something I was fully invested in and my family could be with me the whole time.

Layla was very attached to her mama, not always happy to be with me, but that was ok. She needed her mother more than me right now. I would eventually start to grow on her and soon we were best buds. Halle played with her and tried to help her mom out with whatever she could, which did not always work out in Halle's favour. Stacy was changing the baby's diaper on a table one morning. Halle came to see how this was done, but was standing in a dangerous place. Stacy pushed Layla's legs up to her chest, Layla grunted and covered Halle in…well, we had some cleaning to do. Halle was not concerned that it was in her hair and on her arm, but it was on her dress and she was not impressed. Stacy and I were completely useless to help her as we could not compose ourselves. I was dying of laughter. I wiped the tears from my eyes and held my stomach muscles until I could gather myself up long enough to go get a wet cloth and clean up my helpful little girl.

Chapter 20

Stacy decided she wanted to try and stay at home with our girls rather than going back to work. I was all for it. I liked the idea of our girls being home with their mom and coming home to them every day after work. But it started to bother Stacy that she was not (in her words) contributing to the household. She wanted to earn her own money again and get more of her independence back. I wasn't going to argue with her. She needed to do what she felt would make her happy. A few weeks later she went back to her old job full of the people she loved to work with. It was exhausting for her to be working full time and looking after the girls while I was gone, but my job was changing as well, so I would be home almost every night. I had taken a position as a team lead, so I would not be in the field as much anymore. I liked the field, but my family was way more important. It also took some of the work load off of Stacy's shoulders since I could help her out a lot more. Now I could have supper ready for her when she got home for a change!

But before she went back to work, I took her on a way overdue vacation to Playa del Carmen, Mexico. She had been by my side for so many years and we had never traveled outside of the country yet. She deserved it, after everything we had been through together we owed it to ourselves. We left the girls with their grandparents. I had a hard time driving out of the yard when we were leaving. Stacy assured me that they'd be just fine. We both missed them terribly but it was ten days of some of the happiest memories we had ever made. Some couples get bored with each other on a vacation like that, but we were never that way. I loved to talk to her…or maybe listen to her is the better way of putting it. We had many adventures and new experiences together.

I continued to race through the summers, racking up as many trophies and top prize money as I could. Replacing broken parts and trying to make the truck faster had become who I was. My new position at work had been going well, I had an awesome team to work with who had all become more like family to me. I had known many of them for over twelve years and worked beside them in some of the worst conditions. The company we worked for did not do Christmas parties so I decided I would throw my own. These guys all deserved it. I set everything up and let everyone know where it was going to happen. The night started off fun as usual, lots of dirty jokes, good food and a few drinks. Stacy being the trooper that she was, stayed sober and kept a close eye on all of us to make sure we didn't get into trouble.

The night was nearly over. Stacy headed out to the truck to start it up and get some heat into it before we drove a few guys back to their homes. I stood outside of the bar with a few of them while they smoked and chatted. Off to my right a few guys were having a bit of an argument, which turned into some fists flying. Mark (who was one of our supervisors) decided he had to go get a closer view of the match, but I stayed away. I didn't need to get involved. Soon he came running back with a swollen cheek. Mark's operator, Rocky, jumped in and they both ran back into the fray. This had started to turn into a bit of a shit show. There were now thirty or more people out in the parking lot beating on each other. I still stayed out…until I witnessed a young lady get punched.

Oh I don't think so! I ran towards the lady and picked her up.

"Are you ok?" I asked. She was crying, but the crowd was still fighting so I pushed her in a general direction that was safer. As I turned around to find out where my guys were, I got smacked in the cheek bone by some random person. I squeezed my fist and jacked him in the jaw. He fell backwards. *Great, here we go,* I thought. But the dude got up and took off. I found Mark and pulled him out. Then we found Rocky who was bleeding from a gash on his head. But there had been four of us when this all started…Where the hell was our lead operator Paul? Then I saw him, stumbling around the corner of the parking lot, blood pouring down his face.

"Oh shit, Paul, what happened? Are you alright?" I asked. Paul was a combat veteran and was one of the most laid back guys I had ever met, but he was not calm now. He was pissed!

"Right after you guys ran in I got jumped by a few others," he managed to say.

I grabbed Paul by the arm. "Shit. Alright, let's get you guys to the truck."

Just then the cops started rolling in. Paul being in a not so chipper mood anymore started lipping them off for showing up when the fight had already ended.

"Nice of you idiots to show up fashionably late. Couldn't get your donuts quick enough to be here to do your fucking job or what?" Paul jeered.

The cops started making their way towards us, they seemed upset with Paul's attitude.

"You wanna go to jail, sir?" one cop asked sternly.

Oh, hell no! This wasn't happening tonight. I grabbed Paul by the collar and started dragging him away.

"I got him officer. He's just upset. I'll get him out of here," I said as I did my best to drag my beat up buddies towards the truck.

"Yeah, you better. He might need some stitches. Take him and that other fella to the hospital."

This whole time Stacy had been sitting in the truck, wondering what was taking us so long. When the cop cars drove in, she knew for sure we had been up to no good. She was standing outside of the truck glaring at me as I dragged Paul towards the truck.

"What the fuck happened?" Stacy asked as she examined our injuries.

I tried not to laugh as I explained, "Things got a little western. We gotta take these fellas to the hospital."

"You assholes! I gotta work in the morning!" Stacy was anything but happy with us. She got us all to the hospital. I helped get the guys inside and told Stacy to head for home. I would catch a cab later. It was already 4 a.m. and she was supposed to be at work for 8 a.m. "Sorry babe, my bad."

Once I had the guys squared away, I called a cab and went home. What a night! Not what I had planned exactly, but it was memorable if nothing else.

Stacy called me at ten in the morning, not in a cheerful mood.

"I need coffee, and I need a damn sandwich," she ordered, followed by the sound of a phone getting slammed down.

I guess that means I have to get up. I was not feeling too good, but I wasn't going to let her down. I picked up what she requested and slowly wandered into her work.

"Sorry, honey. I love you," I said with a sheepish grin

"You better damn well love me. I expect supper when I get home too."

There was nothing else I could say except for, "Yes, dear."

I went home and made dinner. I was slightly in the dog house now. She laughed about it after she got some rest. Bunch of grown ass men acting like some junior high kids in a school yard dust up. I headed back into work on our first day of rotation, the rest of my team strolling in shortly after, black eyes, split lips, stitches. Then my boss came around the corner…I had some explaining to do.

Stacy decided it was payback time when we went to her Christmas party. She never did drink much, except for that night. I did my duty and made sure she didn't hurt herself. I found a small pail and set it in her lap for the ride home. If memory served me right it would be needed in… Three, two, one, yup, there she goes. Now I do not have a strong stomach for vomit, not at all. It was thirty degrees below and I had my face out of the window driving home. Yuck! Neither of us were ever really big on going out to clubs, big drinking parties and such. We were more social people that liked to hang out and chat with those around us, so this was not a common scene for either of us, but we were there together, looking after one another just like we always did.

That spring I took an opportunity to go work out of country for a while. Our work had really dropped off around home and I wanted to save up some money and set it aside for us. I got on the plane and left my family behind. Layla didn't understand what was going on, she hadn't grasped the concept on how talking to me on the phone was supposed to go yet. But after being gone for a couple weeks I got a call from Stacy.

"Hey babe, Layla would like to talk to you." She passed the phone to my little monster.

She was bawling. "Daddy you need to come home right now. I need you to snuggle me to sleep. I don't want you to be gone anymore I miss you too much!"

I was speechless. She had never said more than a couple simple words to me on the phone before. I felt her pain through the phone and my heart broke listening to her cry. I felt terrible and I couldn't talk her down. She left the phone with her mom as she ran off crying to her room.

"She'll be fine, babe. Don't worry about us. Just come home safe okay? I love you."

"I love you too." I hung up and took a few minutes to gather my thoughts and get back to work. Layla had not grown up knowing me to be gone for any length of time. I had not thought about that when I took this position. The day I finally flew home, I walked into the airport just in time to see two little girls running as fast as they could towards me. They tackled me and we all went crashing to the floor. I was so happy to see them and I had the feeling they had missed me. I looked up to see my gorgeous wife smiling down at us and laughing.

"Welcome home, babe. I think they missed you!"

I stood back up, one munchkin wrapped around each leg, wrapped Stacy up in my arms and kissed her.

"God, I missed you guys," I said. It is absolutely true that absence makes the heart grow fonder. Stacy took a couple days off work and we barely left the house. It had been a long time since we had been away from each other for that long. We were like a couple of young adults, just married and madly in love.

One morning Stacy said, "So I'm glad you made some decent money for us."

"Yeah me to. We should be able to set some aside and work up a down payment for a bigger house." I knew we were starting to outgrow our little house.

Stacy smiled at me, she was up to something.

"…or…Disneyland?" she exclaimed.

"Huh?"

Stacy laughed. "Yeah we are going to Disneyland in a couple months. I've wanted to go all my life and I want to take the girls there."

"Oh, um, well, is now the right time? Maybe we should wait until Layla is a bit older?" I asked, I hadn't expected this.

"No, it's already booked. We are going." She grinned at me waiting for my reaction, which was as expected.

"Yes, dear," I answered, knowing I couldn't argue with her decision.

Stacy had always been a huge Disney fan. She knew all the characters and story lines. I knew very little. But we would go in the fall. I have never been comfortable in crowds and I was not a fan of rollercoaster rides, which amused Stacy. A former bull rider and now the pilot of one of the fastest mud race trucks in our area and I had a fear of rollercoasters. Halle on the other hand was just barely tall enough to go on every single one of them. Stacy went with her against her will while I rode the merry-go-round with Layla numerous times. It was more suited to the both of us. It had been a dream for all of them to go. It wasn't my first choice but I wouldn't have changed it if I could. Seeing the smiles on all their faces was better than anything I could have come up with. My legs burned as I carried a backpack full of water bottles, sunscreen, extra hats and all the trinkets they found, not to mention carrying one kid or the other when their legs got tired. But it was an amazing trip for all of us.

Layla had just started grade one that year and was very excited to be going to school just like her big sister. Halle had become that protective older sibling just like I had hoped. Even though they fought at home relentlessly, they still stuck by each other's side when they were away from their parents.

We went through a winter that wasn't as busy as normal. Our whole team was a bit worried about what the future would hold. I was sure there would be huge layoffs and we would lose a lot of really seasoned employees. I had to make list after list of names to be cut if it came to that. I hated it. I didn't want to see anyone go. They were all experienced and very knowledgeable in our line of work. But one morning our team was brought into a conference room. I knew things were going to be rough for a few of these guys after this day. We sat down as the CEO stood up in front of us. He gave a bit of a speech telling us what we already knew, the work had slowed and they had to make some decisions.

"Unfortunately, gentlemen, we are closing this base. There will be no options to transfer."

What? After over fourteen years with this company we were all suddenly out of a job? This is bad, really bad. What about all our families that relied on us to provide for them? It was a company decision. Yeah, yeah, that doesn't make it any better.

I called Stacy with the terrible news, I handed in the keys to my company truck and got a ride home. This group of guys had become family to me and we all just got kicked out the door and thrown to the wind. I was devastated and worried. It's the only type of work I had ever really known. I never did go to college or trade school. I had nothing to fall back on. They gave us a fairly decent payout, which was good for us but it would be months before I found another job. We had already booked and paid for another vacation to Mexico, so we packed up and left for ten days. We would have time to sort everything out when we got home.

A month later I found a job working for a former co-worker from years ago. It wasn't what we were used to as far as pay and work schedule, but it was a blessing to have found a job. It would be many more months before most of the others found work.

Stacy had put the weight of the world on her shoulders while I was out of a job. She was tired but would work extra days whenever she could. I did my best to make sure everything around home was in tip top shape. Stacy had enough stress on her mind, and she didn't need more when she came home. My plan for a bigger house was just going to have to wait a little longer now. She deserved better and I felt guilty for not providing that for her yet.

Chapter 21

My new job was pretty simple and a helluva lot less stressful. It was enough to pay the bills, which was the main thing. We didn't have much debt and I always did my best to keep it that way. Stacy still worried about it constantly, but there was always food on the table and clothes on our backs. She also worried about the area I worked in. It was not far from home, but I had to drive a dangerous stretch of highway to get there and she worried about it. Every evening I would come back home, give her a big hug and tell her I loved her. We were never strapped for cash but it was usually fairly tight. She didn't make a lot at her job, but she loved the people and that is sometimes better than getting a huge cheque every month.

I had worked at my new job for just over a year when I had a bad wreck that ended up breaking my knee in three places. I thought I was done with broken bones, but I guess I was wrong. Making a quick transition from a ladder towards the truck to shut it down, I twisted my knee hard enough that it buckled and snapped. I hit the dirt and laid there hoping that it wasn't as bad as it felt. I was a long ways into the mountains and luckily I had a radio to call for help. Getting helped up and finding a ride from another worker, I quickly called Stacy to let her know before my cell service cut out. Stacy met me in town and got me to the hospital where we sat for hours waiting to see a doctor. After x-rays, CT scans and an MRI they determined I was going to need surgery. The specialist was gone for a couple weeks, though, so I had to sit around with a busted knee for a while. What really drove me crazy (besides my knee being broken) was a big race was coming up in five days. I didn't want to miss it.

I sat at home sulking for a couple days, trying to figure out how I could make it work. How could I get in the truck and still race? The knee was already broken so it's not like it could get any worse. I called a couple friends to come over and help me while Stacy was at work. We set a small three-step ladder beside the truck. I hobbled over to it and, by grabbing onto the roll cage and hoisting myself up, I managed to wiggle myself into the truck. I had to remove my right shoe because I couldn't bend my knee enough to get it onto the gas pedal. But I was in! I worked the throttle a few times and decided this would work just fine. I sent Stacy a video of the truck running with me in it. She was not as excited about it as I was, calling me to give me hell and try to convince me to not race.

With the help of my race family, I loaded everything up and we headed out that weekend. I had been chasing the record run for years now and was hoping to get it done, broken knee or not. By this time I was running another new motor, this one being a 600ci Ford with alcohol injection that made 1100hp. It was a bit of a handful to run, but it was pretty fast and great at breaking parts. I pulled up to the line on the first day, unsure of how much this was going to hurt. I flattened the throttle when the green light flickered on. The pain shot through my knee, but I stayed on it until the end. I returned back to the start line for my second pass, this time doing my best not to tense up and I repeated the run with a little less pain. Both were good runs but not record breaking yet.

The next day was brutally cold for August. The engine was unhappy with the weather until I managed to get enough heat into it. Stacy had been asking me to swap the spark plugs in the motor before I did my runs but being on crutches on slippery ground, I decided against it. I fumbled my way back into my seat and strapped in again, lined up in my lane and laid on the throttle again. This time the truck leaped upwards and hydroplaned across the top. I returned for my next pass, hoping to repeat that same run, and lined up in the next lane. I was about halfway through when the engine shut off and died. But it didn't matter, I had already broke the record on the first pass that day! After the racing was done, I carefully sat down on the front tires with the front sheet metal pulled off the truck and started working on the engine to sort out the problem…Stacy was right, again, I should have swapped out the spark plugs. She would not let me live that one down.

My surgery finally came a couple weeks later. I got wheeled into the operating room just as I had numerous times before. I got put to sleep again and the doctor went to work repairing the damage. When I woke up after the two long hour surgery I was in excruciating pain. They went back and forth between morphine and fentanyl until I was maxed out on dosage.

A nurse walked up beside me and asked, "Have you ever done acid before?"

"Kind of a weird question, but, no, I have not." I was not in a mood for dumb questions.

"Okay, well I'm giving you a dose of Ketamine, so you're about to go for a ride. Night, night." He said as he injected the drug into my I.V.

The pain meds hit my veins and I was out like a light and having the weirdest dreams I have ever had. When I woke up again I was in a regular room. Stacy came up to see how I was doing and laughed at my spaced out look.

"They give you something good this time?" she asked.

"Yeah, I think he called it Ketamine?"

Stacy burst out laughing. "They gave you horse tranquilizer?"

"Sure, yeah I guess so," I replied.

She found a wheelchair and spun me out to her car. I spent the next month on the couch, dog on one side, and a tray of snacks and beverages on the other. Stacy would prepare everything for me each morning before she left for work. She was amazingly caring. Normally she was a tough-love kind of lady when it came to personal injury, but this time she was pretty soft hearted.

Since I had so much extra time on my hands now, I started searching through ads for bigger houses. I started sending the ads to her while she was at work and we settled on one we both thought would work for us. It was in a much better neighbourhood, had a huge yard and a garage big enough to put two full size trucks in. I was sold, Stacy was as well…almost.

"So you're going to do what? Hire a mover? 'Cause you're gonna be useless for help." she pointed out.

I knew we would be able to get enough help from friends and family given my predicament. We started packing and cleaning up our house, getting everything shuffled off into a storage unit. The possession dates did not line up very well so we spent one week at my parents place. By the time the deal had gone through for all of this, we were into the winter months again. It was brutally cold when we were finally able to get into our new home, but we made it in just before Christmas. I was happy that I could finally give Stacy a home she wanted and the extra room for our family felt awesome. We were not in the house for more than a week before she was picking out paint colours and getting ready to remodel the basement for the girls. I insisted she wait until after Christmas before she could start painting. Stacy was always big on this season. She decorated everything, including the dog much to her dismay. This year had such a good feeling, our family had made the move possible. The new house quickly felt like our home, our forever home.

Shortly after the holiday season, Stacy started busting her ass repainting every room in the basement and remodeling the bathroom for the girls. She was so determined to make this house look the way she wanted. She would get home from work, throw on some paint clothes and head back downstairs to get more colour on the walls. We bickered constantly about the en suite bathroom upstairs, she wanted to rip it all out and change everything.

I, on the other hand, was against the idea completely. That would cost thousands and I was not about to do that anytime soon. She made a list of what she wanted done to it anyways, just in case I changed my mind.

With my knee healed up somewhat, I was able to get back to work. I had a terrible time trying to walk in snow and driving did not feel good on rough roads, but it slowly got better. This job had been good to us when I had lost my long term employment, but I had also lost a regular work schedule and a salary that was hard to beat. I didn't want to leave this job all that bad, but I received a call one evening from Halliburton, which had been our main competition at my last job. They were offering me a field position with them. I hadn't been in a field position for a few years. It would mean being gone from home a bit more again, but the money and schedule made it a viable option. I talked it over with Stacy. She wasn't excited about the time away from home again, but the pros outweighed the cons so I took the job. It would turn out to be one of my better decisions.

Shortly after I started my new job, a friend of ours was finally getting married. I was never one to get excited for a wedding, but this one was different. I had known Jeff since high school and a lot of our old friends were going to be there for this. When Jeff came to our wedding so many years ago, he had dressed up so well that I was concerned I may have been a little underdressed. For the first time in my life I decided to go get an actual tie and not the clip on style either! Stacy and I hadn't had a weekend away for far too long and we were thrilled to be going. We headed south to Edmonton and met up with friends we had not seen in ages. We all looked incredibly sharp in our suits, ties and shiny shoes. Stacy had bought a beautiful dress and high heels to match; I couldn't keep my eyes off of her. She never ceased to amaze me with how she could light up any room with just a smile and her warm greeting to everyone. So full of life and laughter. It had been a long time since I was able to dance with her, tonight would be my chance. My knee complained the entire time but I held her tight and did my best to keep up with her. My heart had been feeling like it was falling more in love with this woman constantly over the past few years. She had been by my side through so many crazy adventures and made so many incredible memories with me. I was proud to have her as my better half.

We headed back home and got back to life. The incredible weekend had recharged us in a way that made us feel like goofy teenagers again. We sent each other goofy text messages, most of them very dirty, but it was our way of making each other smile while we were away from each other.

I had started to slow down a little bit with racing. We stayed more local and didn't travel much anymore, but we were both okay with that. I was content to just be with her doing whatever made us happy. She was still my biggest fan and support team when I did race, though, always snapping pictures and selfies of us. She made every other husband around jealous of what we had. An undeniable happiness.

I finished off the race season with a broken camshaft. I pulled the engine and sent it back to my engine builder for some upgrades. My not so little girls helped me pull some wrenches and get things cleaned up. We pushed the race truck into the corner of the garage and began working on Stacy's new hot-rod that I had bought for her. She loved old school trucks and I had found a 1975 F-100 short box street truck for her that was about to get some upgrades. She picked out colours, wheels and helped me sort out what she wanted for an engine. I was excited to be building this one for her to drive around when the days were sunny and warm.

Our lives felt so comfortable now, the house, my new job, which was paying well and making Stacy feel more at ease. Our girls were settled into their new school and happy to be making new friends. I was pretty sure this is what it meant to be living the good life!

Hunting season had come around again, so I had been spending my days off trudging through the snow in miserable cold weather near the farm with Jamie and Stacy's brother, Trenton. On the weekends, I would take Stacy and the girls with me instead. The girls enjoyed the outdoors and Stacy loved to be with us. We never really found much to hunt, but that wasn't really the point anyway. I drove them down into the cattle lease one afternoon and pulled up to the spot where we had been married. There was a few inches of snow on the ground, so the girls leaped out of the truck and ran for the hill we would go tobogganing on every year.

Stacy gazed out over our wedding location and said, "It still looks so beautiful out here, even in the winter."

I looked out over the terrain, taking it all in.

"This is still my favourite place," she said as she looked back at me and smiled.

We looked out for a while, enjoying the quiet peacefulness. Well, almost quiet. The girls came charging back to the truck saying they were cold. We laughed at them and did our best to get the snow brushed off of them before we headed for home. I had one more day of hunting to do the next day anyway.

Next day I headed back out with Jamie and Trenton. It took us all day, but I did finally get my elk. I let Stacy know I'd be home a little late, which was always code for getting an animal. She sent me a smiley face emoji; she knew what was coming. We cut out the tenderloins and I headed home with them. I was going to make a special dinner for us! Next evening Stacy came home to a dry rubbed and perfectly grilled tenderloin with all the sides she could imagine.

"Wow, babe, I'm impressed! You've outdone yourself today," she said with excitement as delicious aromas filled the kitchen.

"You know why right?" I asked, already guessing what her answer would be.

"Of course I do, silly. Eighteen years ago today we met at a horse auction!" She pushed me against the counter and kissed me. She was still giving me goose bumps after all these years together.

We spent the rest of the evening cuddled up on the couch, listening to music like we did so often. She played a song for me she had found called Grave by Thomas Rhett.

"This song is so beautiful," she said as the words tugged at our hearts.

I hadn't heard it before, but it was incredible. As it played, a sudden dread shot through my mind. Everything had been so perfect for so long. Maybe too perfect? I quickly pushed the thought from my mind and enjoyed my time with the woman of my dreams. We both had to get to bed, I was going back on shift the next morning. Stacy held my hand as she walked towards our room, softly closing the door behind us.

Next morning we ate breakfast, chatted like usual, and spent a little too much time hugging and kissing goodbye. We were both running a bit late but that was normal for us. We never rushed out of the house. I kissed her one more time and said, "I love you."

She smiled at me and came in close. "I love you more."

"I love you most." I kissed her and ran out the door to head to work.

I was in a morning meeting when Jenni from Stacy's work texted me to ask where Stacy was. She wasn't at work yet. That was odd, she left right after I did. I tried to call her but it went straight to voicemail. Something was wrong and I knew it. I ran out of the building and started tearing down the road to our house hoping to find her there, maybe sick or something. She wasn't home. I called the police as I sped down the route she took to her work. I told them my wife was missing and wanted to know if they had any accidents to report that she may have been involved in. The police officer paused and said no. He lied. I looked up and could see the flashing lights. I hung up my phone and screeched to a halt in front of a cop car. I could see her car, I could see a semi-truck jack-knifed near it. I jumped out and started running towards her vehicle when a cop grabbed me.

"Where do you think you're going?" he demanded.

"THAT'S MY WIFES CAR!" I screamed with my heart pounding in my chest.

I couldn't believe what I was seeing. This couldn't be real.

"Wait here." He walked back and got on his radio.

I stood there praying "God please let her be okay, don't let her be hurt, I need her to be okay."

Another police officer rolled up in his car and got out.

"Are you Myron Krahn? Husband of Stacy Krahn?

"Yes, is she okay?" I begged and pleaded with God that she would be okay. She had to be ok.

"Myron your wife was in an accident and she was killed."

My heart stopped.

Chapter 22

"NO!" I screamed. "YOU'RE LYING. PLEASE TELL ME YOU'RE LYING! THIS CAN'T BE REAL. OH MY GOD, STACY! NO, PLEASE COME BACK, YOU CAN'T BE GONE, NOT LIKE THIS."

My heart had stopped, my mind raced. Was this really happening to me? This isn't how this is supposed to go! I love her too much for her to be gone like this. I stared at her car in disbelief, the tears flowing from my eyes. I had just seen her, we had just kissed and said our goodbye like we did every morning. How can this be happening now? It can't be happening, this can't be real.

"I'm so sorry sir. Please, come sit in the car and stay warm." The officer was polite, but his words felt cold.

I was in shock. My head throbbed. I looked back at her car again. I couldn't see the front driver side of her vehicle, but I could imagine how bad it was from how the rest of it looked. I didn't know what had happened. There was a semi-truck on the road by her vehicle as well, but I had so many questions. The one that rolled through my head over and over: Why her? It was never supposed to be this way. I was the risk taker, I had been the bull rider, the one that got in wrecks, broke bones, rolled trucks and had so many rides in the back of an ambulance. This was supposed to happen to me, not her! She was too perfect to be gone so suddenly. And so tragically.

"Sir, when you're ready, I'm going to need some contact information from you." The cop had his job to do. This was likely a somewhat regular occurrence for him.

"I need to call someone. Can I call my mom?" I said, shaking uncontrollably.

"Yes, of course. You let me know when I can get the information from you."

I picked up my phone and stared at it. Anytime anything ever happened, Stacy was always my first call. But now what? Who do I need to call? What do I say?

My mom worked at the funeral home in town. I called the office.

"Hello," a lady answered.

"I need to speak to Trudy. It's an emergency!" I said frantically.

"Myron, you need to call this number. Your mom is looking for you," the lady instructed.

Looking for me? For what? It hadn't dawned on me that they had already brought Stacy to the funeral home. My mom already knew what had happened. I dialed the number I had been given.

"Mom? SHE'S GONE!" I sobbed uncontrollably into the phone.

"Where are you?" Mom asked.

"I'm at the scene of the accident. SHE'S GONE, WHY HER!?" I wailed.

"Oh my God. I'm so sorry. I tried to find you before you found out this way. We'll come get you, just stay there." My mom was usually the most emotional person, but she was solid as a rock at that moment.

I had to call someone else. I had to break another person's heart. I had to call out to the farm. I dialed the number, the phone only rang one time.

"Hello?" Debbie answered.

"Mom?" I was bawling, I didn't want to say it.

"Yeah?" Her voice filling with concern instantly.

"Stacy was in an accident."

"NO!"

"She didn't make it."

"NOOO, OH MY GOD MYRON NO. STACY, PLEASE NO!" I could hear her heart break over the phone, I heard Jamie come into the room and ask, "What? What's wrong? What's going on?"

"Stacy's gone," Debbie sobbed.

"Oh my God" Jamie had just lost his little girl. The little pain in ass kid that never heeded to his authority very well, the one that loved him so dearly, was now gone.

"Where are you?" Debbie asked.

"I'm here where the accident happened. I have to go home. I need my girls." I wanted to hold them so bad right then, but I knew what I had to tell them would break their hearts into a million pieces. I had to be the one to tell them. I had to call my dad, I had to call Aunt Diane. I had to call Sarah. I didn't want to call anyone anymore. But those people deserved to know and they needed to hear it from me. I called each one. Every time I said it, another piece of my soul ripped a part.

"Sir, can I get your cell number please?" the officer asked. "I have a team coming to pick you up. They will take you home and we'll arrange to have your truck picked up."

I needed to get away from there. I needed to get to my girls. I needed to wake up from this nightmare I was having. A van finally pulled up. Two women were sent to take me home. They held out their hands to help me out of the police car and got me into the van. They laid a blanket on me and we started making the drive home.

We pulled up to my house and my mom was waiting in the driveway. She rushed towards me and wrapped her arms around me. Through her tears she said, "I'm sorry. They brought her in right after her accident. I didn't want to tell you over the phone. I tried to find you but couldn't get there fast enough. I'm sorry you had to find out that way."

I didn't have the words to say it wasn't her fault. I would still wake up from this nightmare. I wanted to roll over to Stacy and hug her while she played with my hair and continued to read her book. She'd comfort me back to sleep, back to happier dreams. Then I would wake up and kiss her forehead again and tell her I love her. Our happily ever after would continue on just as it had for so many years. But I wasn't sure if I was going to wake up from this one anymore.

"Mom, I need to get my girls." The school had already been informed. I had called them already.

"Okay. Is it okay if I come with you?" Mom asked.

"Yes, please do." This was going to be the worst one, and I didn't know how I was supposed to say something like this to my kids. How do you tell two sweet little girls their mother was gone and was never coming back?

I walked into the office on shaky knees. The ladies all looked as if they had been crying already. They ushered us into a conference room where I sat and waited for my girls to arrive. My heart pounded in my chest. But I felt so empty.

My girls came around the corner and entered the room. They both had big smiles on their faces just like they would whenever they would see me or Stacy there to pick them up. But their smiles quickly faded when they saw my face. I took their hands in mine. Oh God, how do I say this to them? I looked into their innocent eyes.

"Girls, I don't know how to say this," I whispered, "but mommy was in an accident and she passed away." I didn't know if there was a better or worse way to tell them this hurtful news.

They both screamed in heart breaking sadness. Tears streamed from their eyes as they wrapped themselves around me, both crying out for their mom to come home. My heart shattered again. I didn't know how much I could take, this was so much pain all at once.

In that moment, as I held my girls and cried uncontrollably, I felt my soul die. I was no longer the man I had been for so many years. That person was now gone. I was lost.

Layla looked up at me and cried, "Dad, please tell me this is just a bad dream."

I could barely speak, "I'm so sorry, honey, I wish I could," I said holding them tighter.

They each sat on my lap with their faces buried into my neck. The tears they had shed were streaking down my skin. I looked up to the ceiling, my thoughts raging. God, what the hell is wrong with you? Can't you see what has happened? How can this be any part of your bigger plan?

We sat and cried for a few minutes. I didn't want to move, but we had to get them home. I picked Layla up and carried her. Halle grabbed my hand and squeezed it as she followed me out. We got back to the house, went inside and sat down on the couch. The girls curled up one on each side and sobbed relentlessly. I had cried so much that I just stared at the floor, unable to do anything. I couldn't hear. Everything around me was blurred. My chest hurt.

People started coming to the house, bringing all sorts of necessities and trying to hug me and the girls. I saw no faces, I recognized no voices. I felt only pain. Hours had passed and still I sat holding my girls. The house was packed full of people and yet I still heard no one or recognized any faces. My world had become dark, cold and empty. I couldn't move, I didn't want to move. I wanted to die. I was supposed to be dead, not Stacy. She was the angel that lived on this earth. My girls needed her to raise them to be beautiful young ladies. They could go on without me, but how can this possibly work without her here to love these girls like she did? I loved them dearly, but a mother's love is irreplaceable. How do I raise them without a mother? Why do I have to do this alone? Why did it have to be her? It isn't fair.

Friends and family came in. I would stare at them and try to figure out who they were. Even though they had been some of our closest friends, I could not recognize them anymore. I couldn't remember anyone's names. I just wanted to fly away and never come back. But I had two girls who needed me now more than ever. They had gone downstairs to play with some friends who had come over to distract them from the shock.

"Hi, Daddy!" Layla looked up at me smiling, but her smile was only half there. It was missing that innocent sparkle now. She was trying so hard to play and have fun with her friends, but her mind was elsewhere. Halle sat on the floor in her room looking through pictures she had drawn for her mom.

"Dad, I did this one for her on Mother's Day this spring." She held it up for me to see, trying to smile while she held her art work up.

"It's beautiful, honey. Your mom always loved everything you kids made for her." I knelt down and hugged her head. "She still loves you."

"I know, Dad, I love her too."

I got up to go check on the other kids. They were now in Layla's room. Layla was by her art desk scratching away at something with a pencil.

"What are you working on, sweetie?" I asked. She was always colouring something. She turned to me with a sadness in her eyes I had not seen yet.

"I made this for you and mommy on Friday, but I forgot to give it to her. You can have it now." She fell to the floor and held her face in her hands as she cried.

I looked at what she had given me. A half crumpled envelope with a paper shoved inside. The front of the envelope was written: To mommy and daddy, but she had scratched mommy out. My heart broke again. Tears welling up in my eyes, I opened the paper that was inside. 'My mommy and daddy are the best perins ever. Love Layla' I knew she meant to write 'parents'. I sat down beside her on the floor and hugged her.

"Daddy, I didn't get to give it to mommy, now she doesn't know I really loved her."

I sobbed uncontrollably. "Baby, your momma knew very well that you loved her. You said it to each other every day. Do you know that she loved you very much?" She nodded her head trying to get control of her tears. "Well, in the same way that you know she loved you, she knew you loved her too."

"But, Daddy, I don't think I said it to her this morning before she left." I didn't know what to say. Stacy never left the house without saying she loved them or me. We over used it and it never grew old for any of us.

"Honey, your mom never left the house without saying she loved you and you always said it back, I know you did. You might not be able to remember it right now but you will someday."

"Okay. Daddy," she whispered, trusting that I was right. She looked at me again and said, "Daddy?"

"Yes, sweetie?"

"I love you." She stood up and wrapped herself around me and we cried together.

I have no idea what time people were there until, but it was late into the night. From that day on my memory had been destroyed. I could not remember if I ate or if I slept. I didn't know why I was standing in the closet or what I was just about to write on a piece of paper. Everything was a mess. I needed something to feel close to her, something that had memories of us, something that belonged to her.

In the days that followed many people came to the house, not many that I can remember. The funeral home had transported Stacy to the city for the medical examiners to do their job. I still did not understand how or why this had happened. At this time I only knew that she had been hit by a semi-truck. That was the only thing I knew for certain. I could not sleep or eat, there were too many terrible things going through my mind for any of that. I knew I had a lot of decisions to make in the next few days. I was sure that going through pictures and putting them together for her tribute video would be helpful for me. I was wrong. As I opened one old photo album after another, or scrolled through all the pictures on her laptop, my heart just broke more. We had been through so much together. Now it was gone and there wasn't a damn thing I could do about it. I slammed the laptop closed and cried.

Someone came to my side and put a hand on my shoulder.

"I want to put these pictures together, but I can't do it, it hurts so bad to see everything we had and know that it's gone." I didn't lift my head from my hands to see who was with me. I had never cried so much in my life. It had started to affect my voice which had become a rough and gravely version of what had once been my normal speech. It sounded foreign to me, everything around me had become strange. The laptop was taken from me. I heard Sarah talking in the kitchen about the pictures and some ideas she had. I laid down alone and cried.

Sarah was heading to the yard where they had stored Stacy's car to pick up any belongings from her vehicle. She asked if there was anything I could think of that I wanted.

"I need her phone. That's the only thing in her car that means anything to me right now. Everything is on there and I need to have it." I knew her phone had so many memories, messages and her own touches that would make me feel just a little bit closer to her right now.

Sarah left with her husband Jason. They were gone for a couple hours when she finally called me.

"Hey, there, do you need anything from town?" Sarah asked.

"No, I just need her phone." I couldn't wait to hold it in my hands.

"Honey, I don't know how to tell you this. We found her phone on the floor of her car, it was broke into two pieces. I'm really sorry but it's not fixable."

My heart shattered all over again. The one thing she always had with her, the way we communicated constantly. All those pictures and messages, all the notes she kept that would remind me of her. Gone. I paced the house. I couldn't stand this pain, it never eased up. It only grew worse. I went to our room and glanced around. I didn't know what I was looking for but I needed something, anything of hers that meant something to both of us. Tears flowed from my eyes and blurred my vision as I started to open a drawer on the book shelf. I had been through this drawer many times already in the last couple days, but this time when I opened it there was a small piece of paper folded up sitting on top of everything else. It was old and water stained. I carefully opened each fold. My heart nearly stopped when I had it opened. It was a letter she had written to me sixteen years ago. I sat on the floor and studied every word she had written. I read it over and over. I was in disbelief that I had found this letter now. I couldn't help but wonder how it got there or why I hadn't found it sooner. Every word sounded so innocent in my head, so incredibly sweet and loving. I picked myself up off the floor and walked out to the kitchen where Jamie and Debbie were visiting with people.

"What did you find, Myron? Debbie asked, obviously curious by the look on my face.

I managed a half smile when I looked up from the tattered paper. "I found this letter she wrote me, she was still in high school and I had just started working in the oil field. It has some water damage but I can still read every word."

I passed it to Debbie. She covered her mouth with her hand as she read the note her teenage daughter had written to a boy she loved. If the situation had been different and Stacy was still here, I would never have shown that letter to anyone else. But now everyone needed to know how much we loved each other and how that love had started.

Chapter 23

I sat at my kitchen table surrounded by family and friends. There were a lot of decisions to make and most had to be decided by me. Every question asked I could not help but want to turn to Stacy and ask, "What do you think?" But she was not there. Her opinion had always mattered to me, even for the smallest of details. Now I had no choice but to go with what I hoped she would like. Just another layer of loneliness for me to deal with. It was getting later in the day and I wasn't even sure what day it was anymore or how long it had been since the accident. Time had no meaning now, nothing really had as much meaning as it had before. I sat deep in thought on how people get so wrapped up in politics, rumours and what was happening in some other far off place. None of that was relevant now, a difference of opinion was not worth the breath it would take to disagree. There was no time to tip toe around words to come out with the truth about how I felt about things anymore. Life can be completely wasted by getting caught up in the things you can't change or gossip that has no bearing on the direction your life will go.

Eventually Sarah and the guys came back to the house, she dug through a bag full of things she had picked up in town.

"I have something for you." She continued to rummage. "I don't know how they did it, but they were able to fix her phone for you."

My heart nearly leaped out of my chest as Sarah passed a phone to me. It wasn't the same case Stacy had. It was slow to react and glitched a little, but in my hand was something that belonged to her.

"They were able to put it back together. They had to put on a new screen as well. But you can't take it out of that case or it will fall apart," Sarah explained.

I starred at it and my heart had a fleeting moment of joy. But tears welled up in my eyes again as I thought of how horrific the crash must have been for her phone to be so smashed when it had already been in a case. The thought of the impact that must have occurred. I got up and went to my bed and I sat and cried. The thought of the accident, the violent impact and the stomach turning sound of the crash flowed through my mind. On the bed was the knee high boots she had been wearing that day, it was the only article of clothing that I was given. Everything else had been destroyed. The toe of the left boot was crushed and creased, I ran my fingers over the damage. The tears rolled down my face as a dagger turned deep in my chest. Why is this happening to me? Why did this happen to her? I buried my head in my hands and cried, I felt a hand on my back and heard a small voice.

"Dad? Are you ok?"

It was Halle. I looked up at her. She looked as if she had grown and aged, her face more mature and less innocent than it had been days before. I hugged her tight and did my best to pull back my tears.

"Yes, baby, I'm ok. I just miss your mom."

Tears filled her eyes at the sight of me in so much emotional pain. This was not fair for my daughters. They should never have to go through this at such a young age.

I needed to do something to help me through this pain. I couldn't express how I felt through speech or actions very well. After finding that letter and reading it over and over, I found a pen and a note book. I stared at it, not knowing what to write. Then I remembered something she had said to me sixteen years ago.

"Just put your pen to the paper and start writing a thought, a question or a feeling. The rest will follow."

I wrote until my hand cramped up and hurt. Then I shook it off and kept writing. I had so much to say, but could not speak the words. I had so many questions, but I knew they would go unanswered. I had so many thoughts and terrible feelings, but no way to express them except to write them out. I continued to write until I felt as though I had come to the end of my current thought. When I was done I flipped back to the first page and read through it. I was never very good in English class and had barely passed it in school. I wasn't sure where the words had come from but every word had meaning and depth. I set it aside, I would need to read this again but next time would be in front of many people.

Sarah had given me and the girls each a journal to write in. My frantic notes looked terrible. I picked up the new journal and rewrote everything in a more legible fashion. Halle had noticed me writing. I explained to her what I was doing and that it seemed to help me. She immediately followed my example and began writing in her book. I tried to explain it to Layla as well, but she didn't open her book. She was in rough shape and I couldn't get her to stop crying. I held her tight as she cried for her mom, asking why she couldn't see her anymore, asking why this is happening to us and why she had to go. I did not have the answers for her. I felt completely helpless as I held her. I didn't know what else to do.

The girls had both received many teddy bears and soft blankets from a lot of people, I wrapped Layla up in one of the blankets and laid her down on the couch with a few teddy bears. She laid there quietly, not saying a word. I let her be, hoping she might sleep.

My mom had told me the medical examiners were done and they were sending Stacy back to the funeral home.

"Myron, the ladies were wondering if you would be able to pick something out for Stacy to wear. They would like to get her cleaned up nicely so you can go in and see her."

I knew this moment was coming, I just did not want it to happen now. This was supposed to happen many years from now. But I got up and walked into the closet, I pulled out a few of her favourite dresses and laid them on the bed. I flipped through each one, remembering the last time she had worn each of them and what the occasion had been. I could only choose one though and I picked up the dress and brought it to my mom.

"This is the one she wore the last time we danced together. I would like to see her in this and I will wear the same thing I wore that day."

Mom gazed over the dress "I think that will be perfect. Does she have a favourite shawl or something to put over her shoulders?"

I thought that was weird, she would never wear a shawl with this dress. The confused look on my face caught my mom's attention.

"The ladies asked to have one, just in case they needed it to cover her arms."

Now I knew why she needed it. The damage I had seen on her boots, the destroyed phone… how could she not be bruised? I went back to the closet and found her favourite shawl.

It was Friday now, my mind was caught between the feeling it had just happened and that it had been months already. The house was still a buzz of activity, but we still had many things to prepare. My mom had set a time for us to go to the funeral home and pick out some cards and sort out more details. The girls stayed with Sarah at home while we went into town. I walked into a room with caskets and urns on display, all of them very well crafted. There were small necklaces, memorial candles and plaques on the walls. So many to choose from, but yet again, the choice was mine alone. Stacy was not there to tell me what she liked best. I was overwhelmed with the feeling of utter loneliness again. I eventually picked out what I thought she would have chosen, the cards were picked out but the poem that would be printed inside I left up to Debbie and Jamie. They had lost their daughter in this tragedy and I felt they should have a hand in some of this as well. For as brutally difficult as this was for me, I knew it had to be done and I wasn't going to leave this up to anyone else. No decision was easy to make, but this needed to be as perfect as I could make it. She had been the perfect soulmate for me, the perfect mother for our girls and a perfect friend to hundreds of others.

After a few hours we were able to head home, my head was pounding from the constant crying and all the decisions that had to be made. I was exhausted, I had not slept for three days now. Once home, I hugged my girls, the few hours had felt like an eternity for me to be away from them. I needed to sleep. Tomorrow would be the first day I would see her for what would become one of the last times.

I laid in bed hoping sleep would take me away to a happier place, but it was useless. I tossed and turned. I closed my eyes only to see her crumpled car. I sat up in bed with my heart pounding, not sure what to do. Many evenings we would sit and listen to music together. I still needed to pick out some songs for her tribute video. I opened my phone and scanned through songs. My face drained of all colour when I came across the last song she had played for me. I pressed play and listened to the words of Grave by Thomas Rhett. I burst into tears as each chord tugged at my heartstrings. How could I have ever known this last song would have such a profound meaning now? Did she know this day was coming somehow? At this point, while listening to that song I sure felt as if she had somehow known this was going to happen. We had just got our first life insurance policy, we had just moved into a new home that was much better suited for our family. I had just moved into a job that supported us better, so many little things had just recently fallen into place. My mind raced through thoughts as the tears continued to flow from my eyes. God this hurts so bad, I had never felt pain like this before.

I wrote down a few song names on a scrap piece of paper to give to Sarah later on. I got up and paced the house, unable to sleep and too tired to eat. I was lost. My thoughts turned to what I would see in the coming hours. I knew the time was coming when I would walk into a chapel by myself and see a casket with my bride laying in it. My heart ached as it pounded in my chest. I went back to my room and began writing again, filling page after page of memories, tormented thoughts and grief. I laid back and eventually closed my eyes.

I could smell freshly brewed coffee lofting throughout the house, but I didn't open my eyes. I could hear people speaking quietly to each other, but I didn't want to move. If I opened my eyes I would have to face this day. I told myself to get up. I didn't budge. I heard the distinct, light footsteps of Layla's feet in the kitchen. She said something quietly that I couldn't hear, but I heard her say Daddy. GET UP! I told myself. I slowly rolled over and set my feet on the floor. I didn't want to go on, but my girls needed me to. I stood up and walked to the kitchen to get some much needed coffee and a hug from my kids. After getting some food into the kids and choking down what I could, I headed downstairs to talk to the girls in private. I needed to explain to them what today would bring.

"Okay, girls, so we are going to go to the funeral home today. There will be a few people there, but we will be going in on our own to sit with mommy for a while."

Layla's eyes lit up.

"We get to go see mommy?!" Her excitement caught me off guard. Shit, she didn't understand what this meant.

"Layla, honey, mommy will be laying in what is called a casket. She will look very beautiful. She will look like she is sleeping peacefully, but she will not be able to speak to us. But we can talk to her, and I think she can still hear us." My heart crushed in pain as Layla started to cry again. Dammit God, can you not see what is happening to my girls? This is not fucking fair to them. *You can burn my soul in hell for all I care, but they do not deserve this at all,* I thought to myself.

"So Mommy is still not going to come home with us?" Layla sobbed.

I hated having to tell her the cold hard truth. "No, honey. I'm so sorry you have to go through this."

I pulled Halle in close to us and hugged them both.

"I'm so sorry you girls have to feel this pain. I'm so sorry you have to grow up without your mom to hold you. I never meant for your lives to turn out this way. I never wanted you to ever feel this kind of pain." My voice cracked. The gravely tone had become my voice from the constant crying.

Layla looked up at me. "Daddy, I'm scared to see Mommy." Her eyes so innocent and filled with pain. I didn't know how to tell them I was scared as well. I was terrified. The last time I had seen Stacy, she was kissing me goodbye. It was the last time I would ever look into her gorgeous eyes.

"You don't have to be scared, okay girls? We can take our time. I will go in first by myself and sit with her for a while. Then I will bring you in and we will sit together. I wrote some notes for her that I want to read to her, you can do the same if you want to."

"No, I don't want to write," Layla said. She still had not opened her journal at all. Halle had filled a few pages by now. At the age of 11 she understood the situation far better than her younger sister.

We spent a few more moments together before we dried our tears and headed back upstairs. Family and friends still gathered in our home, many I didn't really recognize. My brain felt as though it was under attack with grief, I could not remember any details or names and time was still irrelevant. We eventually got cleaned up and ready for the trip into town. I was anxious to see my wife but terrified of how I would feel. I rode in the back of my mom's car with my girls, my head down the entire way. I clutched a stack of journals and a tattered old letter I wanted to read to her.

We walked into the funeral home. I hung up our coats and entered a waiting room. The funeral director put his hand on my shoulder and welcomed me. I sat my girls down with their grandparents and kissed them.

"Girls, stay here, and I will be back in a little while okay?" They nodded at me. They looked about as nervous as I felt. I walked to the chapel doors and paused. Once I entered this room there was no turning back. I took a deep breath as the director opened the door for me. I stepped in and stopped, the doors shut behind me. God I've been praying for strength. It hasn't come yet. Now would be a pretty damn good time, I prayed. I slowly turned my gaze to the front of the room. There was soft music playing through the speakers, the smell of fresh flowers wisped through the air. I slowly walked up to the casket. There she was.

She looked stunning. She looked so peaceful. Yet I could see that she had been terribly broken in the crash. I knew every inch of her body, every blemish and curve. I knew how her neck would lay as she slept, how her arms, so slender, would gently rest by her sides. They had done an amazing job bringing her beauty to the forefront, but I knew she had suffered many injuries. I reached out and touched her wedding ring, the one I had placed on her finger years ago. Her hands so soft but cold to the touch. My knees weakened. I sat down and let the tears pour from my eyes. It was real. This was no longer a dream and I could not escape what had become my reality. I looked back up to her, wishing this was not true. I slowly opened the fragile letter, a tear dropped onto the paper. I never could have guessed something innocently written so many years ago would one day be in my hands as I sat by her side crying and wishing she wasn't gone.

After reading the letter to her and taking my time to sit alone with her, I got up to go get my girls. It was their turn to suffer more. I hated this. I walked out to meet them, held their hands and told them how beautiful she looked. Layla was still scared so I picked her up in my arms as we walked in together. As the girls came close to their mother, Halle burst into more tears.

Layla gazed down at her momma and said, "Daddy, she looks like she's sleeping."

"Yes, honey, she does. She looks so peaceful, doesn't she?" I said, hoping it would bring her some comfort.

I sat down in a chair beside the casket and began to talk to Stacy. Layla sat on my lap trying to understand what was going on. I opened my journal and read a few of the notes I had written. I played a few songs for her I had picked out to use in her tribute video. Halle opened her journal as well and spoke to her mom. She told her how much she loved her and how she wished she would come back. Layla slowly got to her feet and picked up her journal; I had brought it along just in case. She opened it to the first page, pressed a pen to the paper and started writing. I smiled at her as she wrote and drew pictures of angels and hearts. My two young girls were forced to mature well before their time. They both appeared to age right before my eyes. We sat for a while, taking our time and sharing memories with each other. Layla continued to flip pages and write. It felt amazing to see her open up just a little in that moment.

Chapter 24

Eventually, we opened the door for the rest of the family. They each took time to shuffle past her. Everyone cried when they saw her beautiful face, many came over to hug me and the girls. Again my mind failed me, faces and voices unrecognizable as they gave us their deepest condolences. We stayed for a while until everyone had a chance to see her, but soon it was time to leave and go back to the home that had been my safe place and had now become so cold and empty.

I walked back to Stacy's side, I leaned down and whispered to her, "I'll see you again soon baby. I love you."

I reached across her and laid my hand gently on her arm. I hadn't touched her yet except for her hand. I felt how swollen her upper arm was, a shot of pain flew into my chest. The shawl I had picked out was covering her arms. I had suspected she was in rough shape but feeling her arm now I knew it was worse than I could ever imagine. I wiped the tears from my eyes and turned to leave. Halle was in front of me as I turned around.

"Dad, can I hug mommy before we leave?"

"Yes, of course, honey. Just be gentle okay." I hoped she wouldn't notice what I had.

She walked up and gently laid her head on her mom's chest, tears rolled off her nose.

"I love you mom."

She turned away and grabbed my hand. I held Layla in my arm as we walked out together.

174

The next morning Sarah got up early and ran a recon mission around town to find some dresses for the girls. She texted me pictures to choose from. I wanted to avoid spending too much time in town. I didn't want to run into anyone who might want to talk. Sarah did the hard part of searching several stores. I finally told her which ones I liked and, unfortunately, they were at the mall. She drove to our house and picked us up. *Maybe this will be okay,* I thought. It would be good for us to get out of the house for a little while. I hoped it would ease the sadness even if it just lasted an hour.

Christmas was only a month away so the mall was packed. My heart began to pound in my chest as we pulled into the crowded parking lot. I held Halle and Layla's hand as we made our way to the store. I kept my head down to avoid eye contact. I didn't want anyone to stop me and offer condolences. The girls tried on a few dresses and picked out their favourites. We had to find Layla a pair of shoes before we could escape. Thankfully, Halle's feet had grown enough she could wear her mom's shoes and she'd found a pair she wanted to wear.

We made our way back out of the busy mall. Again I kept my head down and walked fast to distance myself anyone who wanted to stop and talk. Once we were back in the vehicle my pulse rate finally began to slow down. I was never a big fan of crowds, but this was unusual for me. The anxiousness and uncomfortable heart pounding was new to me. As soon as we made it home I sat down and closed my eyes. I was so tired. The mental exhaustion was brutal. How does anyone ever survive this? I needed to try and rest. The next day would be the public viewing. I just wanted to go back and sit with Stacy. Being able to see her and talk to her made me feel like my world wasn't so shattered. Stacy's dog, Bella, had noticed something was wrong too. She paced around the house constantly. She never rested or seemed to sleep.

My mom noticed and said, "You know, we do set things up for other people so their dogs can come in and see their owners. It does seem to help sometimes."

I thought about it while I scratched Bella behind her ears, maybe it was worth a try.

"Yeah, it's worth a shot, I guess. I don't know how she will react but we should try."

I went to bed, not to sleep, because that just didn't seem to happen. I sat down and started writing some more thoughts down. My words would sometimes turn to memories and stories, other times they would become angry and scribbled. I could flip through the pages I had filled and know what my heart was writing without reading the words. Some pages were neatly written, soft pen strokes from one word to the next. Some pages would be written in anger, water spots from tears blotching the ink and the pen nearly tearing the paper where I smashed it into the book. But I continued writing still. It seemed to help me transfer some of the pain onto the paper. So many of those words will never be read by another's eyes, no one's ears will hear those words. Those are for me.

Another tormenting night passed and we headed back in for the public viewing. This time the dog came along. Would she understand and be able to say goodbye to her loving owner? Stacy begged me to buy Bella when she was just eight weeks old. So many pictures in Stacy's phone had been of her and her dog. She loved to put weird hats on Bella and take silly pictures with her. Bella hated the hats, but loved the attention.

I walked into the chapel with Bella on her leash. She sniffed the floor and every person who came near. Wagging her tail with excitement, so many new faces to see for her. The directors put Stacy's casket into a private room just adjacent to the chapel. They lowered her casket to the floor and told me I could take Bella in when I was ready. I slowly walked in and the girls came in behind me. Bella saw Stacy's face and spun around on her leash with excitement, pulling hard to get to her. I held her back until she calmed down long enough to understand that something was different about her. I slowly released my grip. Bella walked up to Stacy's side, sniffing her arms and neck. She paced around the casket smelling every inch of it. Once she came back to Stacy's side she pressed her nose against her cheek, gave a gentle lick and sat down on the floor. Her tail had stopped wagging and her ears drooped low. I felt she knew this woman who loved to cuddle this dog in bed while she read her books was no longer going to be home to do that.

I lead her back out and sat in a chair wiping away tears. Suddenly Bella jerked hard on the leash, whimpering and trying to get back to Stacy. I stood back up and brought her back into the room. Bella preformed the same ritual she had before, sniffing her owner all over, trying to understand why she didn't wake up. Bella laid her head on the edge of the casket near Stacy's cheek, whimpering quietly. Eventually, she pressed her nose to her cheek one more time, licked gently and turned to walk away. She knew now that Stacy was never coming home.

My brother took the dog from me and led her out of the building to take her home. I took my girls by the hand and brought them in to see their mom. The directors had set her casket back up, set fresh flowers in the room and prepared everything for the crowds that had come by to pay their respects. I closed the doors to the room to give my girls a few moments of privacy. Halle hugged her mom again and cried. I looked at Layla as she sobbed.

"Layla, honey, you can hug your mom as well if you want to."

"No, Daddy, I'm scared too touch her," she explained.

"That's okay, you don't have to. But if you change your mind, you just tell me and I will help you, okay?"

She nodded her head as she stood by her mother's side, wiping tears from her eyes. I gently brushed my fingers over Stacy's hair, every time I touched her the coldness tore at my soul a little more. The girls sat down in the chairs set in the room as I gently laid my head on Stacy's chest. The tears streamed from my eyes as I gasped between sobs.

"Why do you have to leave us like this?" I begged God to answer me.

Halle was by my side handing me a tissue, I stood up and dried my face. There were many people crammed into the building now. I knew our private time would be short, I just didn't want to be away from Stacy. My mom quietly entered the room and hugged us. I had known my mother to have her tears attached to a hair trigger, she cried at every moment. But she was very stoic now and had been through this entire ordeal, I hadn't expected it.

"Myron, you and the girls don't have to leave the room if you don't want to. We will bring in another chair and some water for you guys. But we should open the doors for everyone else soon."

I nodded my head and sat down with the girls to explain what was going to happen next and let them know we didn't have to leave the room. The doors slowly opened. I glanced up slightly to see the chapel packed with people. One after another they slowly made their way in to see Stacy one last time. Halle sat by my side, getting hugs from each person who came in. Layla sat on my lap and buried her face in my chest as she sobbed. I saw many faces, some I knew, some I did not. The ones I knew were friends, some I had not seen in many years and others had become family to us. Some faces I knew were relatives but I didn't know their names. Some spoke to me in a language I didn't understand. This is where the lines are blurred between what family means to others and what it means to me. My close friends who I call family are the people I lean on in times of need, the ones I can call for help knowing they would drop everything to lend a hand. The strangers who I didn't know and spoke a different language didn't even know my girls names. Those people might be blood relatives, but to me, they weren't family. We are not connected because of blood; it is a special bond that creates a family. Blood relatives so often feud over stupid things like religious beliefs or money. I absolutely refuse to allow myself or my girls to become a part of a family like that. Not when there is a world full of incredible people from many different walks of life who will accept you for who you are. Many of those great people were there that night.

The line seemed to be endless. One family after another would file in, say their condolences and file back out for the next one to come in. Once the line did finally end, I gave the girls some more time to sit alone with Stacy. The crowds of people had been a little overwhelming for them and they needed some space. They came out a few minutes later. Although they had been crying for hours it did seem like the time spent sitting with their mother was helping them in some ways. We walked into the waiting area where so many people were gathered. In the room were people I had been good friends with since elementary school, people I had worked long hours with in terrible conditions and some I had even fought with over things that seemed so irrelevant now. They were all here for the same reason. All differences aside, it was Stacy who brought these people together. The next day would be her celebration of life and, if this night had been any indication, it was going to be a packed house.

We left the funeral home that evening and for the first time in nearly a week I actually felt hungry. We stopped at a fast food joint and sat with my parents to stuff ourselves with some greasy takeout. It didn't take me long to feel full and a little sick. The past few days of not eating seemed to have shrunk my stomach slightly. But it was good to see the girls eat something for a change. We got back to the house and I did my best to get the girls to bed. They hadn't been sleeping much at all, but they needed all the rest they could get. Tomorrow would be a brutal day. I laid down and looked at my phone. I had turned the ringer off after Stacy's accident because I couldn't stand to hear it constantly going off with messages. I scrolled through dozens of messages from many people I hadn't talked to in years. The word had traveled far and wide about my beautiful angel tragically passing away. I replied to no one, there was nothing I could say. My phone buzzed with one more text. It was Sarah

"How are you feeling about tomorrow?" she asked.

"I don't want tomorrow to come," I replied.

"How come?"

"Because tomorrow makes this real. I will never see her again and I don't want to have to say goodbye."

"I know, sweetie, me and Jason are here for you always and we will be there for you tomorrow."

I set my phone down, my head filling with thoughts and questions again. I had taken sleep medication hoping it would help, but so far it hadn't taken affect. On the dresser I had a few papers filled with words I had written to say in front of everyone the next day. There is a side of me many people didn't know existed, which would become known when I read those words. I didn't care. It did not bother me to stand in front of hundreds of people and speak - not one bit. I just did not like standing down in the crowd surrounded by people. Tomorrow would be my last chance to touch Stacy's hand, feel the softness of her hair, and kiss her one last time on her forehead like I did every night when I had to leave for work while she slept.

I picked the biggest church around. It could seat twelve-hundred people. There were TV's to broadcast the service as well as a livestream service for those who couldn't make it to watch. The tribute video was done perfectly, the girls had nice dresses to wear, and the pallbearers were selected and ready. Everything was set, all I had to do tomorrow was go in and say goodbye. I closed my eyes, I covered my face with my hands and let the emotion take a hold of me.

I slept for about 2 hours before I woke up again. Time never stops no matter how hard you try and now this day had arrived against all my wishes. I poured some coffee and sat at the table going through the notes I had written. It was time for me to focus. If I had to go through this shit, it needed to be perfect for her. I never wanted to have to go through this, but if I can't make it go away, I was going to own it and I would wear it proudly. She had been my proudest achievement, my favourite person to brag about and I would continue to do that today. I showered and pulled my clothes off the hangers. The last time I had put them on was for a friend's wedding, the last place I had danced with Stacy. The girls finished eating what they could and put on their dresses. Layla looked adorable in the dress she had picked out and still had that innocence in her face. Halle walked out in her dress, wearing a pair of her mom's black high heels. I shook my head in disbelief. Where had my little, blonde, goofy girl gone? This petite young lady standing in front of me was supposed to be my little girl, but instead my daughter had grown and matured into somewhat of a young adult before her time. Her attitude had changed in the past few days, she no longer thought like an eleven year old should. Her thoughts had more depth and meaning to them now. I turned away, half smiling like a proud father would. If her mom could see her right now she would be standing in the kitchen, leaning on one leg with her arms folded. Shaking her head at the sight of her oldest child. She would've said, "Nope, turn around, get back in that room and come back out as my little Halle. I don't know who that person is right there!" Then she would have wrapped her arms around that girl and complained about how tall she was getting.

Our driving service had arrived, being piloted by a good friend of mine. It was time to go. I gathered everything I needed and guided the girls into the bus. They marveled at the custom interior, glowing lights, custom leather seats and a bar. We backed out of the driveway and headed to the church. Once we arrived, I got busy checking to make sure a few last minute details had been looked after. Kristin had come in early to do the girls hair. She had been Stacy's favourite lady to get her hair done by. The guys I had selected to be the pallbearers arrived and sat down with the family in a side hall away from the main crowd, who'd start to arrive soon.

The hearse arrived and the directors rolled Stacy's casket into the church and set it up in the main foyer. I took a deep breath. Now was my last chance to say goodbye. I looked at my beautiful daughters. They took my hands and we walked towards her. I stopped and knelt down beside them.

"Girls, this is our last chance to say goodbye to Mommy. After this we can only write to her and see her in our dreams, okay?" Layla's face lost all colour and tears instantly filled her eyes. She still didn't understand.

"Why can't we see her again, Daddy? I don't want mommy to go away. I want to keep coming in to sit with her, Daddy. PLEASE, I don't want to say goodbye!"

The dagger in my chest pushed deeper.

"I don't want to say goodbye either, honey, but we do have to let her go. But we will never stop writing to her, talking about her or dreaming about her. She will live forever in our hearts, and no matter what, she will always be in our minds. I promise, okay?"

She cried and nodded her head "Yes, Daddy." It took every ounce of strength I had to be strong for my girls at that moment. This final time to hug her, see her at peace and know that we will see her again someday.

We walked up to Stacy's side. Halle leaned over and hugged her again. I let her have her moment.

Layla tugged at my sleeve.

"Daddy, can I hug Mommy?" she asked.

I picked her up as Halle stepped back. I leaned Layla down. She reached her arm over her momma and laid her head on Stacy's chest. I gave her a few moments to hold her mom one last time.

Layla whispered, "Mommy smells like pretty flowers."

"Yes, honey, she does." I was doing everything I could to hold it together. She hadn't wanted to touch her mom out of fear until this moment. I was happy she'd been able to overcome her fear and gave her mom one last hug. I held Stacy's hand and ran my other hand over her arms, so swollen. I had seen her bare arms the day before when Halle had asked if she could have the shawl. The ladies at the funeral home had given me the opportunity to make that decision. Once I had seen her arms, I knew it was not possible to use it. Halle could have the shawl after today, but Stacy's body was far to beat up to remove it. I would spare everyone else from witnessing the extent of her injuries. How I longed to have been able to take all of that pain away from her, to trade places with her. It was never supposed to be this way. I was the one that should have been laying in that casket.

People were now streaming into the building, but I did not want to leave Stacy's side. Halle was in tears and I'm sure she felt the same. Layla seemed to be much more content after being able to hug her mom, bless her innocent heart. But I knew we needed to go. I knelt down and gave her one last kiss on the forehead, she was so cold. A tear rolled off my cheek and landed in her hair. I squeezed my eyes tight and tried to not cry.

I whispered my final words to her: "I love you baby, I'll see you soon."

I turned and walked away with my girls at my side. The time had come. We stood in the back corner, away from the crowds waiting for everyone to be seated. Eventually we were given the nod to proceed, the pallbearers came to the sides of her now closed casket and took hold of the handles. They lead the way in as we followed behind. The church was full. I did not see an empty seat available and there were still people coming in the door as the service started. I sat at the front and watched as my parents gave an amazing speech followed by her parents. I didn't know what their speeches would consist of or how long they would be, but both our parents had put together an amazing amount of memories and stories. As they wrapped up I knew it was my turn. I slowly walked up to the front with my papers in my hand. I wasn't uncomfortable standing in front of over 1200 people. I walked to the microphone and took a deep breath. I began to speak. I read every word I had written for her, I read the letter I had found that she had written to me so many years before and a letter the girls had put together for their mom. As I was reading my final letter I paused as my voice cracked with emotion. I was wiping some tears from my eyes when I felt a hand on my arm. I looked down to see Halle by my side. She had put her fear aside to come stand by her father who was struggling to get the words out. She stood by my side and held onto my arm until I was done saying what I had wanted to. I could have been up there for hours saying everything I could about my beautiful soul who had been taken from me. But I had done what I had set out to do. I stepped off the stage as her tribute video began to play.

There were a few more eulogies given by Sarah, my sister in-laws Charity and Twila, one of our race family moms, Carrieann and Stacy's cousin Connie. By the time it was over it had been nearly a three hour long service. If you had been there for me and didn't know Stacy very well, you sure did by the time it was over. As the service ended, we stood up and lead the way outside to the waiting hearse. The pallbearers brought the casket outside and we stood by as we watched them load it into the back of the car. I hugged my girls tight as the cold winter wind whipped around us, they closed the rear door and we turned to walk back into the building. I spent the next few hours hugging numerous friends and family and talking with so many well-wishers, some I had not seen in years. The sheer number of people that had arrived was far more than I had anticipated, but not a complete shock. The amount of lives Stacy touched throughout her short thirty-three years on this earth was unfathomable. The love she shared for so many people was the legacy she would leave behind. The love that she had shown towards others would come back to bless me in the months and years to come.

We left the church knowing she would have been proud of what we had done. If anyone was uncertain about how I felt about the love of my life I was sure I had removed all doubt. I walked away from that building never to see Stacy again.

Chapter 25

We arrived back at our home, the house was filled with homemade cookies, snacks, pizzas and beer. Many of my close friends followed us into the house to celebrate the life of an angel who had affected each and every one of us in a different way. My parents were staying for the night and were not accustomed to our loud talking, jokes flying back and forth and drinks being shared between friends. But this was my family, not by blood but by bond. These were the people I felt the most comfortable with. These were my people.

It was late into the night by the time the house grew quiet. I slipped off to bed, hoping to find the deep slumber that had evaded me for a week now. I laid in bed thinking again about why it had been her in the accident and not me. It was never supposed to be her that was gone. It had always been me who would be the one to be gone so tragically. I drifted off to sleep.

As I slept for the first time in a week, I began to dream. In my dream I was in her office at her work and I was a fly on the wall watching as she typed away at her desk. A man walked into her office and said, "Are you Stacy?" She looked up from her screen and nodded. "Your husband was in an accident and he was killed." It was the same words the officer had said to me when I had come upon the scene that fateful day. Stacy held her face in her hands and bawled as the tears flowed from her eyes. I felt the pain and anguish that was in her heart at that time, it was unbelievable. I had felt the sting of the dagger through my heart. I felt it as it twisted when my girls cried, but this was so much worse. The pain she was feeling was something I couldn't put into words. I sat there watching her, unable to say anything. All I could do was feel the pain as it rushed through her body after she heard the news that I had been killed. Then a voice came from beyond, "Is that what you would have wanted?"

I sat up in bed suddenly, sweating and breathing deeply. It was the first time I had seen her in my dreams. I had been praying to see her again, but this is not what I had been wanting to see. A rush of clarification came over me. This entire time I had been saying it should have been me, it was never supposed to be her. But now I had felt what she would have gone through, I never would have wished this pain on anyone and for as much as I loved that woman, the pain she would have felt, had the tables been turned, would have been far greater than what I had been feeling thus far. It was still dark outside but there was no way I would be able to go back to sleep, so I picked up my journal and began writing what I had seen in my dream. I was awe struck and unsure what to do with what I had just witnessed and felt. I needed to tell someone, but who? I had come to the realization that my mood or situation would dictate who the right person was to talk to at that time. I looked at the clock: 3:30 a.m. I wasn't about to call anyone then. It would have to wait.

I laid in the dark, staring at the ceiling and playing that dream through my mind over and over. If it had been me that was killed that day, what would she have gone through? How would she have dealt with everything? Would she be able to cope through this life without me? I thought she would have done just fine without me here. She had done it for weeks on end while I was gone to work, surely she would have been better at this than I would be. She knew how to take care of the house, the kids, all the birthday parties and special events. I couldn't figure out how to make a simple appointment for the girls. I didn't know what time the bus came to pick the girls up or what time school was out. I didn't know who to talk to about getting the girls back into class when the time was right. I had so much to learn. Would she not have been better at this than me?

Eventually night turned to day and I began to hear people stirring in the house. I walked out to the kitchen, the smell of beer bottles and stale whiskey glasses filled my nostrils. I hadn't drank much more than a couple, but with the amount of people who had been here, the number of half empty glasses sitting around had permeated the house with the stale stench of booze. I started cleaning things up with the help of my mom who was not used to the smell. I chuckled at my mother's curled up nose as she picked up empty bottles and put them into a bag. The family I loved may have been a bit rough around the edges and rowdy at times, but they were still the people I loved to be around and the ones I could call on at any time when I needed help. They might drink their fair share, they might cuss enough to make even a sailor blush, but they were my family, and damn anyone who would speak badly about them.

"Did you sleep?" my mom asked as we cleared the table off and started making breakfast.

"Yeah, a little anyways."

"Oh good. I think Bella is sleeping better now as well." The dog had calmed down after we had taken her into the funeral home and let her see Stacy.

"I saw her in my dreams last night," I said to my mom hesitantly.

"Oh, that's so good. I'm happy for you." She smiled.

I shook my head.

"It wasn't in a good way." I explained my dream to my mom. As I did, the dream began to make more sense to me. The fact was, yes, I wanted to trade places with her in the worse way. But had I been able to do that, Stacy would have suffered so much more pain than what I could have imagined. I could not wish this kind of pain on her, it would be unbearable to be gone and see her as she struggled to make sense of it all just as I was doing now. Although I felt as though the emotional pain I was in could not be matched, the pain she would have felt to be in my shoes would have been far greater. It did not make me feel any better at all, but it did change my way of thinking. I wouldn't wish this on her, not for a second. My mind set had changed now and would forever remain the same, I would bear the burden of this pain and wear it as a badge of honour to her memory no matter how great the suffering became. It was her love that would keep me going. I would need to carry on the love that she had for everyone just as she would have wanted.

"Well, that may not be what you had wanted to see, but maybe it's telling you something. Maybe you were meant to see it," my mother replied after taking a few moments to process what I had just told her. "I can't imagine what Stacy would have been going through had it been you instead of her." My mom was reading the thoughts that had rolled through my mind when I had woken from that terrible dream.

We made breakfast and served everything up for the girls. They had actually slept that night as well. They looked tired, but they were hungry and it warmed my heart to finally see them eat. I, on the other hand, was still didn't have much of an appetite. I tried to eat some, my body needed it as I was starting to feel weak. I had to go back into town that day to start on some of the paperwork. I was nowhere near being done with this whole situation and I would soon find out I had a very long road ahead of me.

I went into the funeral home with my parents and we sat in a room with a lady by the name of Tina. I was sure I had seen her before, but with the buzz of activity and my memory being on vacation at the time, I could not be sure. Then it dawned on me, she had driven my mom to my house on the day of the accident. She had also brought me to the school and brought us home after I had told my girls that their mother was no longer with us. She held out her hand to greet me. As we sat down in a private room to start going through the paperwork, she told me about her son who had died tragically in a vehicle accident. Except his vehicle had burned up and she was never able to hug him just one more time. No matter how bad it was for me, someone else out there has had it worse, this much I was sure of.

As we sat there going through one document after another, I began to feel very uncomfortable. I stopped replying to her questions with words, just nodding or shaking my head instead. My skin began to crawl. I was so uncomfortable I just wanted to crawl into a hole and stay there until this was all over. I thought it must have to do with the subject matter of the paperwork I was dealing with. The death of my wife, the life insurance, car insurance and funeral expenses. All of it seemed like a lot for me right then. I had never felt this feeling before and did not know what it was or how to describe it. I was short of breath, sweaty and just wanted to shrink into oblivion. I signed one paper after another, the entire time Tina had been very understanding and did not rush me. She let me know that the paperwork is the worst part and any dime given to me from this would be the hardest money I would ever earn. This was a great way to tell me the insurance money that will eventually come my way is very bitter sweet. It's not something you ever want to have to receive, and when it does come it will not make you feel any better at all.

Once we were finally done, we headed for home again. As we left the city my gross, uncomfortable feeling began to fade away. I was glad it was gone, but I felt so tired by the end of the day. It had been brutal for me and I did not know what caused it. The girls had been playing and were keeping themselves busy for most of the day. Grandparents and other friends stayed at the house while I was in town dealing with the things that a widowed spouse needs to.

That evening I sat at the table and began opening hundreds of cards and letters, reading through memories and looking at pictures that some had sent. Some were very beautiful; the few hand written letters were my favourites. I sat with my family and read one after the other, it was around 2am when I was nearly done. It felt good to do this and I was starting to feel tired, only a few cards left. I opened one, the name on it was one I did not know. A few words were written inside.

What happened that day saved my life, but took hers away. I am so sorry

I starred at the words and read them over and over. What the fuck is that supposed to mean? I flipped the card over and found a few more words written:

Semi swerved around black SUV and hit her.

There was an email address written at the bottom. My head swam with more questions, my heart raced as I tried to make sense of this letter. I still did not know any details of what had happened and this just raised so many more questions. What does this mean? How did she save someone's life? I quickly opened my phone and sent an email to this person. I needed to know what it meant. I went to my room and paced back and forth, my mind racing. I sat on the floor staring at the card, I buried my face in my hands and cried. How can this be happening to me? I stayed there all night wishing I had answers, wanting this pain to go away and praying I would sleep and hopefully dream about her in a better light. Sleep never came.

After a couple days, I had to go back into town to pick up a few small grocery items. I needed to get out of the house and get things organized for my girls who were already asking when they could go back to school. I got into my truck. My mom decided to come along since this would be my first trip to town while driving. I played music through the speakers as I normally would, but as the music played and each song came up on the screen I remembered where I had heard that one last or what Stacy had said about that particular song. She loved most of my music, but there was also my other music that she was not fond of at all. Metal, hard rock, hip-hop. I had nearly every genre that existed. She was straight country or classic rock, she did not like many songs outside of that.

I rolled my way closer to town. I needed to get a few groceries and it was a good excuse for me to get out of the house for a while. But as the vehicle carried us closer to town that sick and uncomfortable feeling began to rise up again. This time I took notice of what was going on. I still did not know what it was, but I hated it already. I felt like I wasn't in control of this situation and I hated that feeling. I was always able to control my temperament easily. Now to suddenly have something wash over me I couldn't stop was very unsettling. I made it to each stop I needed to make, everyone looked at me with concern. I didn't know these people. How did they know I had just lost my wife? Maybe they didn't. Maybe it was all just in my head. I wanted nothing more than to just fade into the background and become invisible. I didn't want anyone to know me anymore. I just wanted to disappear.

Once we were finished in town and were making our way home, that gross feeling began to lift off of me again. The further away from town we got, the better I felt. It was the same thing as before and I still didn't understand it. Maybe it was just the busy town filled with so many people. I wasn't sure, but I was glad to get home and relax. I was sure it would pass, tomorrow was another day. I knew I had to fill out some paperwork at the auto insurance place and go cancel Stacy's phone plan the following day. Two stops was all. I will do this on my own this time. I can handle it.

After another sleepless night and not being able to eat much again, I jumped into my truck and headed back to town. Once again as I drew closer to the city my heart rate increased. I arrived at the insurance office and walked in, a friend of ours worked there and quickly sat me down off to the side to wait my turn. My skin crawled as I sat there. I clenched my fists and squirmed in my chair. I was ushered to another desk where I signed one document after another. My voice began to waiver and become unrecognizable again. Dammit! What the fuck is going on with me? Why can't I shake this off? I headed to a cell phone store to cancel the phone plan. The last thing I wanted was for someone to call her number while I had the phone sitting beside me. I walked out of the building, my head was pinging and my skin crawled. I jumped into my truck and sat there for a few moments, needing to get myself together before I headed for home. My phone buzzed, an unfamiliar number came across the screen. Normally I would not answer it but I felt a tug, I needed to.

"Hello?" My voice came out raspy and weak.

"Hi, Myron, this is Christine. I'm the one who wrote that card for you. I'm sorry I told you like that."

The card I had read so late at night that had put my mind into a tailspin had been written by the lady on the other end of the line. She explained to me the details she knew about the accident. She had seen Stacy get hit. A semi-truck came up behind Christine's car in the north bound lane at a high rate of speed and did not stop. Christine had been stopped in a line of traffic as she waited for a light to turn green. She swerved to the right to avoid getting hit. The truck just scraped her rear bumper as the driver jerked it to the left...right into the front left corner of Stacy's car, as Stacy was heading south. There had been a sickening crunch followed by two more vehicles that slammed into Stacy's car that had been following her on the road. The first responders arrived in minutes but they could not get her out of the car. She never woke up from the hit. She passed away before they could get her out. As Christine told me the story, the scene unfolded in my mind. There would have been nothing Stacy could have done to avoid it, she was always a cautious driver and if there would have been any way to get away from being hit, she would have done it.

I got off the phone, wiped the tears from my eyes and took a deep breath. From what I understood she did not suffer or feel any pain. At least that is what I was going to keep telling myself. I made my way home, again the sick feeling slowly disappeared as I got further away from the city. I walked into the house and laid down on the couch, instantly falling asleep. I was exhausted.

Chapter 26

I woke up after a few hours, I hadn't slept like that in a long time. I did not dream of anything, I just slept. I was still confused as to what was going on with me every time I went to town. I had never experienced anything like that before. I called a friend of mine to talk to him about it. He had been a firefighter. He had also been through many terrible experiences in his life. Maybe he would know better.

"Dude, you have anxiety," Mike said.

"Anxiety? That's what that sick feeling is?" I asked.

"Yeah, man, kind of like you want to crawl out of your skin and just go hide in a corner right?"

"YES! Exactly!"

"Yeah, that's what it is. You can get medication for it if you need to. But just be aware of it, don't let it get too bad without seeing a doctor," he advised.

Medication? Doctor? No, no, that's not me. I'm tougher than that, I don't need any god damn meds to get through anything. I had never had anxiety about anything in my life. Riding bulls never made me feel like this and racing made me feel excited. This was completely different. Now I knew what it was, I just had to figure out a way to beat it. I was not about to back down from this internal fight and find medication for it. But was that even possible? I had heard stories of people who had it so bad they were unable to function without some kind of medication to calm them down. Fuck that! There has to be a way for me to kick this things ass.

I told my mom about it. I wanted to make sure a few other people knew what was happening to me. If I was losing it, they needed to know so that they could take over if I went off the deep end. I was planning to head to Stacy's work the next day to go through her desk and take her belongings home. I called Stacy's co-worker and good friend Jenni to let her know what I was going through with my anxiety. I told her I'd let her know if I arrived or if I turned around and headed back home. Jenni had lost her mom when she was the same age as Halle, so she understood what she was going through better than I did.

Next morning I sat in the kitchen, sipping coffee as my truck warmed up. This time I knew what was coming. I was preparing my mind for the anxiety attack that was sure to come. I kissed my girls and left the house. I hit play on my phone but the Bluetooth did not pick up the music. I was getting irritated, but didn't want to start fumbling around trying to fix it while I was driving. I was cresting the last hill before town as the anxiety crept back into my chest. I slammed the brakes and pulled off the highway. "FUCK YOU!" I screamed in anger for letting this feeling get the best of me.

I turned the truck around on a dirt road and sat. I could turn back home, or I could wait and continue on once I felt okay. I pressed a few buttons on the stereo trying to get my phone to connect to it again and after a few minutes I got it working. I pressed play and put the truck into gear. I idled up to the highway and waited for it to clear. One of Stacy's favourite songs came through the speakers: Redneck Girl by the Bellamy Brothers. I cranked the stereo to the max, tuned the wheels to the right and smashed the throttle to the floor. Black smoke poured from the straight pipes and sent the truck into a fish tail. Fuck this shit. *Anxiety can kiss my ass,* I thought to myself. I headed to town. My heart suddenly felt a little lighter as I tore down the highway. I had been driving like a nervous old lady for the last few days, it was not my style at all. The anxiety was still there, but it wasn't as intense now.

I made it to the shop and walked up to Jenni's office. I had not talked at length with her before, she was not someone I had ever really had a conversation with. But I sat down and chatted with her for a few minutes which turned into a couple hours before I stood up to leave. I went through Stacy's desk, finding little notes and reminders of what her next task was or who she needed to call to make an order of some sort. She had been the purchaser at a plumbing and heating wholesale shop. She had always loved the work load, although she would complain about it. I knew that she would've never changed it for the world. I continued to dig through Stacy's desk, finding pictures of the girls, a few pictures of us, and some messy hand drawn pictures the girls had made. I picked everything up and packed it out to the truck. I had always teased Stacy about some of her co-workers saying they were not 'my' people, they were not really country, they were not really into hot-rods or mud trucks. But as I left that day, my mind had changed. She loved them all like family. I felt compelled to be near those that she was close to now in spite of them not being 'my' kind of people. I got back in the truck and drove home. I could've taken the quicker route but that was the road that Stacy had died on. I wasn't ready to do that yet, so I took the long way through town.

I got home and hugged my girls, Layla was bouncing around like her usual goof ball self.

"Daddy, when can I go back to school?" Layla asked excitedly.

Her question caught me off guard, they had mentioned already that they wanted to go back to school. I just didn't expect them to want to go back so soon.

"You want to go back to school already? You don't have to go back so soon."

"I miss my friends so I want to go back," she pleaded.

Well, I guess I couldn't hold her back from wanting to see her friends. I called the school and let them know that the girls would be back on the following Monday. They let me know they had a counselor set up for the girls to see on Wednesday and I could sit in with them. I had never seen a counselor for anything, I wasn't even really sure what they did, but it probably wasn't a bad idea. I spent the weekend getting things ready for the girls to go back to school. I didn't feel ready for this. Stacy had always looked after this stuff, not me. What was I supposed to get them for lunches? Do they need anything specific I didn't know about? Halle helped me sort through everything and informed me of what they needed.

Monday morning I drove the girls to the school. The last time I had pulled up to this building I was going to walk in and destroy my girls' lives by telling them their mother had passed away. My stomach turned as I took my girls by the hand and walked in the front door. We stopped at the office to sign some papers and I walked them to their classes. Many of their friends were there to greet them. I hugged them and walked back out. That was a first for me--another first. How many of these would there be? It seemed like so many things were now a first time and none of them seemed easy. I went home and waited by the phone, expecting the school to call and tell me that the girls were crying and wanted to come home, but the call never came. I headed back when school was out to pick them up. Layla was happy to have seen her friends. Halle was okay, but much more muted about going back to school.

We continued this the next day. So far so good. Wednesday morning we walked in and headed to the office. Today we would meet with the counselor for the first time. We were ushered to a conference room where a young lady greeted us.

"Hi there, I'm Ashley." She reached out her hand. I shook it gently, suddenly very aware of how terrible I probably looked with my lack of sleep and not having shaved in a few weeks.

We sat down and listened as she explained what she does and how this all works. The girls sat and coloured some papers, not saying anything.

"Have you been told what we have been going through?" I asked. I wasn't sure if she had even known.

"Yes. I was told that you lost your wife in an accident."

Okay, good, I thought. I wasn't sure how much of this I was going to have to relive. We talked about how the girls were doing, how much sleep we were not getting and what we could possibly expect to have happen in the coming weeks. The girls sat very quietly, only speaking if spoken to. They kept their answers very short. Layla curled up to my arm in her shy way when asked anything.

I began to go through some of the story, telling Ashley some of the details as to what happened.

"I can't get the words the cop said to me out of my head," I said as I looked down at my trembling hands.

"What do you mean?" Ashley asked.

"When I came across the scene and found out she was killed."

Ashley covered her mouth with her hands. Her eyes glistened as they became damp.

"You found the accident scene and that's how you found out?"

I guess she didn't know all the details.

"Yes," I replied.

"Oh my God, I can't imagine how that must have felt."

How could anyone know? But now that I had thought about it for a while, I wouldn't have wanted anyone else to tell me. Having a loved one give me that bad news would be so engrained in my mind for the rest of my life. I wouldn't want that memory to be attached to someone I knew and loved. It was better to have a stranger tell me. No softness. Just rip the bandage off and tell me.

After an hour or so I took the girls to their class and went home. The counselor thing was not as bad as I had imagined it might be. I had envisioned a couch I had to lay on and explain why I felt a certain colour represented sadness or some stupid shit like that. I was curious what the girls had thought about it. I picked them up again, both seemed to have had an okay day.

"So what do you girls think of Ashley? Was it okay to go sit with the counselor?"

Layla was bouncing in the back of the truck. "I like her!" she said.

"You do? You didn't even say anything!"

"I know, I was shy, Dad," Layla explained.

"Okay, so do you want to go see her again next week?" I asked.

"Yeah!"

Alright then, I was happy to hear that. Halle had continued to write in her journal about her mom and would talk to me a lot about her. But Layla had stopped talking about, or even mentioning, her mom. I tried not to pry but I didn't want her to stop talking about Stacy. I would try to do small crafts or draw with the girls and get Layla to do anything that might involve her even just writing 'mom' on a picture, but she wouldn't do it. I finally had to ask her.

"Layla, honey, why don't you want to draw pictures about Mommy or talk about her anymore?"

Her eyes grew wide when I asked. The tears welled up in her eyes and she started to cry. "Because it makes me sad, Daddy. I don't want to be sad anymore."

My heart bled more as the dagger twisted in my chest. I knew how she felt. It wasn't always easy to talk about it, but hiding from it was not going to make things better either. I wrapped my arms around her and held her close.

"I know, sweetie. It's not always easy, but we can't just stop talking about her."

"Daddy, can I go watch a movie?" she asked.

I let her go. She was not ready to talk about this. I worried about her so much. The emptiness in my chest had not let up at all. I was still in constant pain, but I wanted to make sure my girls were looked after. I could push my agony aside and deal with it later, it was the girls who needed the most help. Layla had not cried over her mom in a week or more now. Once the celebration of life was done she had bottled up and stopped talking about it completely.

I picked up a new external hard drive and brought it home. I wanted to back up Stacy's phone and put every picture or video onto it for safe keeping. I sat at the kitchen table that evening scrolling through every picture and selecting every one that she was in. I watched every video, listening for her voice in the background and adding it to the file. Layla came over to see what I was working on. She sat down beside me as I watched one small video clip after another. Many of them showed Stacy on the floor when Layla was a baby just learning to crawl. Stacy spoke softly to that little curly haired girl as she crawled slowly towards her mom. I dragged the video into the file and started watching the next one, another clip of Stacy wrestling with Layla on the floor attempting to get pajamas on a wiggly little monster. Layla sat and said nothing, just watching the screen.

I kissed Layla on the forehead and said, "It's getting late, sweet pea. You should get to bed, okay?"

"Okay, Daddy"

Layla hopped off the chair and walked to my room to lay down. I continued to scroll through more files searching for more clips of Stacy. A few minutes had passed when I heard Layla suddenly start wailing. I jumped off the chair and ran to my room. Layla met me at the door, tears streaming down her face. I reached down to pick her up.

"Daddy, I miss my mommy. Why did she have to go? I want her to come home right now. I don't want her to be gone anymore!"

Those words came out and crushed my soul again. I squeezed her against my chest as my tears rolled down my face.

"I know, honey, I miss her to. I wish she could come back and hug all of us again."

Layla bawled, it was a cry filled with pain and torment. She had not cried like this since the day I told her we wouldn't be able to see her mommy anymore. A part of me was relieved she had finally let go and let herself cry, but I had not expected it to come out like this. Halle came out of her room and wrapped her arms around us. Tears rolled down her face as she ran her hand gently through Layla's hair. How could I ever make this life feel less tragic for them? My two beautiful daughters were so broken and felt so lost without their mother here with them. I was becoming drained of emotional energy and didn't know what to do to help them. I sat down with them at the table and looked at the laptop, then it dawned on me. Layla had sat and watched the videos of her mom playing with her on the floor as a toddler. She had heard her soft voice and seen her beautiful eyes again. It was what had finally broken through the walls she had put up.

"Do you want to see the videos of mommy again?" I whispered.

Layla nodded her head.

I clicked on a folder to open up the videos and we watched every one of them together. Layla giggled at herself as she watched the silliness that was once her normal. She watched intently when her mom was in view and listened for her voice. Stacy's voice was always sweet and soft. Even if she was angry, it still came out softer than anyone else's. It was the love in her that made it that way. It was something we all missed so terribly and we felt so empty without it in our home now. We took turns wiping tears from our eyes as we watched each video multiple times, remembering everything about her. After another hour or so, I picked Layla up and tucked her into bed. She fell asleep instantly. She was sleeping soundly for a half an hour when I heard her giggle in her sleep. The only time I had ever heard her giggle in that way was when Stacy would tickle her. I peeked into the room to see her fast asleep still. I smiled and walked back out. I was convinced that Stacy had come to visit her as she slept just to give her one more loving touch.

I went to my bed and laid there wondering if I would ever see her in my dreams again. I had not seen her again since the one dream I had of her at her work and felt her pain when she heard the news that I had been killed instead of her. Sleep evaded me. I picked up a notebook and started writing again, the ink flowed from the pen as much as the tears flowed from my eyes. The pain was relentless and unforgiving. If it wasn't for my two girls who I loved so much, I would've felt less determined to continue this fight on my own. I didn't want to live through this pain anymore, I didn't want to suffer anymore.

I wanted to die.

Chapter 27

I went to bed that night hoping to finally get some rest. I'd been able to get to sleep, but I would only sleep for a couple hours at most before I would wake up. I was completely drained in so many ways, yet I just could not seem to get the rest I needed. Some people were starting to suggest seeing a doctor to get medication but I wasn't up for that. Being the stubborn man that I am, I didn't want to admit I needed medical help to accomplish something as simple as sleeping. I popped a couple over the counter sleep aids and laid down. Eventually, I drifted off to sleep.

I began to dream that night. I could hear Stacy's voice on the other end of the phone as she drove to work. She sounded so beautiful.

"I love you, babe. I should probably let you go. I'm almost at work now," she said in her usual sweet tone.

Suddenly her tone changed.

"OH MY GOD, NO!"

There was a sickening, ear-piercing crunch that came through my phone.

"Stacy? What was that? Are you okay?" I pleaded.

I heard her cry out in pain. She was gasping for air.

"STACY, OH MY GOD! PLEASE TELL ME YOU'RE OKAY! WHERE ARE YOU?"

"It hurts so bad…"

I shot up in bed as if I had been stabbed, clutching my chest as my heart pounded. My eyes stung as they began to weep. My head swam with terrible thoughts of her final moments. I was told she was

201

unconscious and never woke up, but was that true? Were they just telling me that to spare me the nightmares? It wasn't working. The dream had been so vivid in my mind. I needed to get some help. I felt like I was losing my grip on life. I picked up my book and started writing again, but I could not bring myself to write down what I had just heard in my dream. Did I really just dream that? Dammit I don't need to have this happen to me now. I took a few deep breaths trying to gather myself up as my heart rate slowed back down. I looked down at my hands, they were trembling. I pressed them to my face, shook my head and cried. Why is this happening to me?

After a few hours I got up and made coffee. My mom had been staying with us to help me out with the girls. She walked into the kitchen and asked. "Did you sleep?"

I shook my head, I had slept for a short time but after hearing that horrific moment I wasn't sure sleeping was the best thing for me anymore.

"There is a fellow at the college who'd like to sit down with you and talk, just to help you through some of these hard times."

I nodded again, I knew I needed to talk to someone. But I didn't want to tell anyone about what I had dreamt about.

"Okay, that might be a good idea, I guess." I didn't want to sound too eager, but I was in a bad place and definitely needed some help. Mom set up a time for me to go meet this guy and I got the directions.

The next day while the girls were in school, I headed to the college this guy was supposed to be at. The parking lot was pretty empty. Most of the people had gone home for Christmas break by now. I walked up to the front desk to ask where this guy was, no one there. I waited for a while until someone finally came up the hall.

"Excuse me," I stopped her and pointed to the information on the note, "do you know where I can find this guy?"

She looked at the note and told me which way to go to find the right building.

"Uh-huh, okay then." What the fuck kind of directions were those? Whatever. I walked out and wandered around the campus looking for this mystery building. I eventually found what I thought was the right one and opened the door. It led to two more doors, neither of which had any signage on them to tell me which way to go. Must be the wrong one. I walked to the other end and opened those doors, it looked the same as the last. I walked to the side and tugged on that door, locked. Well, what the fuck? I looked back at the note, no phone number. My anger started to rise up in my chest. I needed help and finding this dickhead was like a Where's Waldo book. I turned around and stormed back to my truck, Piss on this guy. If he's that hard to find, he's not worth my time. I jumped into the truck and slammed the door. I looked at my phone. I had remembered my boss at work had given me a number for a help line we could use. I scrolled through my phone and dialed the number.

"Hello, help desk," a lady answered.

"Yeah, I'm looking for some help." I explained my situation to the lady and what I had been through.

"Okay, let me put you through to the right person."

Well, shit, I guess I wasted my breath on that one. I waited on the phone until another person answered.

"Hi there, how can I help you?"

I said my speech again.

"Okay, so you are looking for a counselor then. We can help you with that. Let me put you through to someone in your area."

For fuck sakes, really? My patience was really wearing thin.

Another voice came over the phone. "Hello Myron, I understand you have been through quite a bad time. I can set you up with a counselor right away."

Great, finally! I thought to myself.

"It'll be about 72 hours and we will get back to you with a time and place," she explained.

"Seventy-two hours? I need someone now!" I felt panic begin to come over me.

"It is a process that we need to do to set you up with the right person," she replied.

"So I can't talk to someone now?"

"No, I'm sorry. Are you in danger of harming yourself or anyone else?"

What the fuck was that supposed to mean? I wondered.

"No, I'm fine thanks," I lied. I was not fine. My anxiety felt like it was taking over me.

"Okay, we will get hold of you as soon as we have something lined up for you."

I hung up the phone. I didn't know what to do. My heart pounded, I felt like a wild animal cornered by a predator. I started my truck and headed back to the house. Just keep it together, you're okay, you're fine, just breathe. I pulled into the driveway and walked into the empty house. I paced every floor in every room. What the fuck is happening to me? The panic had completely consumed me now. I couldn't find help and I didn't want to call someone who knew me. I didn't want to cry anymore; I wanted this pain to stop. I ran back to my room and into the closet. I stared at her clothes still neatly hung on the rack. I pulled on her favourite sweater, one I had picked up for her in Colorado. I rubbed my face in it, but her scent was no longer there. I broke. I fell to the floor and cried so hard I couldn't breathe. The tears flowed from my face like a fountain. I screamed and punched the wall. My head and my fist throbbed with pain. I was lost and didn't know where to turn. I had done everything I could think of to remain calm. I had tried to be strong for my girls and tough for my family. But I had nothing left. I couldn't fight this anymore. I needed a solution, this pain needed to end. The house was so quiet and empty, except for Stacy's dog. She slowly stepped into the closet and nuzzled my neck whimpering. I pulled that fat headed pit bull cross closer to me. She crawled onto my lap and licked my tears as they streamed down my cheeks.

I had always thought that I was mentally tough, that nothing could break me down. No matter what was thrown at me in life, I could take it head on and own it. At that moment I had never felt so absolutely defeated. I didn't know how to pick myself back up from this terrible place I was in. I continued to cry as I slowly moved to the edge of the bed and sat down. I couldn't stop crying. I couldn't make the pain stop hurting. I never heard anyone come into the house, but I felt a hand softly touch my shoulder.

"Hey, sweetie."

It was Debbie and Jamie, I wasn't sure what had made them stop by the house, but their timing was impeccable. In all the years I had known them, they had never given me anything but love and respect. But I had never shown any deep emotion in front of them and now was not the time to try and hide it. This was real and as raw as it gets and I did not have the strength to hide it anymore. I told them what had happened when I tried to find help, the panic that had set in and the pain I was in. Jamie set his steel hands on my shoulders and spoke quietly to me.

"We are all in this fight together. I know you are feeling this pain worse than anyone else, but we are always here for you. We love you."

His words took me by surprise, I had known Jamie to be a hard-nosed farmer who never took shit from anyone. His way of showing affection was usually through humour, never through soft words but I knew he meant it. They both hugged me as I slowly stood up. They had come to my side when I was in the darkest place. I had felt I had lost control of everything and I wasn't sure I could take the pain any longer, but there they were holding me up and helping me take just one more step. I gathered myself back up and sat down in the kitchen. All the panic and tears had left me dehydrated and with a pounding headache. I took a few Advil and guzzled a couple glasses of water. We talked for a little while until I had calmed down enough to go get the girls from school again. I straightened myself out, toughened back up and left the house. My girls didn't need a train wreck of a father to lean on and I wasn't going to let myself fall to pieces like that again.

"Hi daddy!" Layla said with a grin when she saw me.

"Hi, sweet pea, how was your day?"

"Good! I got a new teddy bear!" She was clutching a new soft teddy under her arm.

"That's very nice, honey." I said. Her genuine smile warmed my heart.

Halle came out of the school and made her way towards us. She smiled at me but she was not looking as happy as her little sister. She wasn't ready to be that kind of happy yet and I knew it. I wrapped my arm around her shoulders as she came close to me.

"So, tomorrow we can go talk to the counselor again," I said as we walked to the truck.

"Ashley" Layla said with excitement in her voice.

"Yes, honey, is that ok?" I asked.

"Oh, yes, I like her. She's really nice," Layla replied.

I laughed at her. "You didn't say more than a couple words to her last time."

"I know daddy, but that's 'cause I'm a little shy." She giggled.

I smiled at her, it normally took Layla a fair amount of time to warm up to anyone. It felt good to see her so excited to talk to someone she had only met once. I was hoping it would help her to open up a little more and talk about her mom.

"Do you girls want to sit and talk with her on your own?"

Both girls shook their heads.

"Okay, that's fine. I will go with you again."

We headed for home where I busied myself with some things around the kitchen. I was feeling a little better now. My day had not gone well but I didn't need to dwell on it. I needed to get off my ass and keep pushing forward one way or another. I glanced over at the girls sitting on the couch beside the Christmas tree. It had no presents under it yet. I knew Stacy had finished all the shopping the day before her accident--another thing to make me wonder if she had known her final day was coming. I cleared the thought from my mind, I had enough torment for one day.

Next morning I drove the girls to the school and walked back into the conference room where Ashley was waiting for us. She greeted us with a big smile and the girls hopped up into the chairs beside me. Ashley had some small toys for the girls to play with and they quickly got busy building little people and houses as we started to chat about the last week's events. I explained what had happened to me the day before and told her about the nightmares I had been having, although not in detail. We talked about how the girls were doing and what we had planned for the coming weekend. The girls began to talk a little more, Halle being the most talkative as usual. I found Ashley to be easy to talk to. Maybe it was because she did not who I had been before all this happened. I wasn't sure, but I felt comfortable talking about what was going on in my head. We were there longer than I had thought, but Layla was happily playing and every now and then she would speak up about one thing or another and I didn't want to cut that short. Eventually I needed to get going, Ashley offered to let the girls stay longer if they wanted to. They both smiled and waved goodbye to me. *Well, alright then*, I thought, *this is a good thing!*

I walked out of there feeling confident that my girls were in good hands. Both of those little girls of mine had always been great judges of character. If they were ever uncomfortable around someone, I would take notice and distance them from that person. But Ashley seemed to have really hit it off with them.

I received a call back from the help line I had called a few days earlier, they had set up an appointment for me in town for the next day. I planned it out for the afternoon and made sure my mom was around for the girls when I went in. I wasn't sure what to expect at this place. I guessed if I could find the person that would be a good start. I walked into the building. No one was at the front desk. Great, not this again. I slowly walked down a hall to an open door and I peaked in.

A man was sitting in an office. "Oh, hello there, are you Myron?"

"Yep."

"Come on in and make yourself comfortable."

I sat in a plush office across from a fellow in a suit who appeared to have taken more time in doing his hair then I did setting the valve lash on my race engine. I sat there for an hour explaining what I had gone through in the past few weeks. He analyzed every word I said and took notes, not giving me much more than the odd mmhmm. I guess this is what this is supposed to be like: uncomfortable, perfect. After the session he booked me in for another appointment a couple of days later.

I returned to the same building for the next appointment right on time. I sat down in the waiting room. This time there was a lady working at the front desk. She glanced up at me and continued typing. I sat and waited, I glanced at the time, five minutes after when my appointment was supposed to start. Maybe his last session was running longer than expected. The lady at the desk got up and walked down the hall, spoke with someone and came back. I waited some more. Where the hell was this guy? I double checked my phone to make sure I wasn't there on the wrong day. Nope, I was here at the right time and the right day. The lady made a couple phone calls and then came out to me.

"Myron, I don't know where he is. He is not answering his phone, but he should have been here already. I don't know what to tell you."

"Great! Well I guess that's just par for the course that I have been on," I said in frustration.

She was very apologetic and offered to set me up with another counselor for the next week. Sure, whatever. Why not try another one of these quacks who don't seem to give a shit about what I was going through. I made the appointment and headed for home.

The next time I went in, the person I was seeing was there. That was a good start. She brought me into the room and I had to walk her through the same story all over again. I couldn't help but feel like I was constantly having to start over, but never make any sort of progress. She seemed nice enough and had more input. Towards the end of our meeting she said she didn't know exactly what I was feeling, but understood the pain, because she had been through a divorce. Okay, I'm done now. I'm just gonna go home and sort this shit out on my own. I was done with counselors. I wasn't sure what they were supposed to do, but this sure as hell was not helping me. No one could ever understand the pain I was going through. Divorce was not the same kind of pain.

I headed home and suffered through another few days of sleepless night and consoling my grieving children. I continued to write, it seemed to be the one thing that sometimes helped me. The following Wednesday the girls were excited to go see Ashley at the school again. I was happy for them to have found someone that they were comfortable with. I enjoyed talking with her as well. She seemed more down to earth than the other train wrecks I had seen. We walked in and she greeted us with her usual smile. The girls sat down and went for the same toys again. They both talked more this time, explaining some of the feelings they had been dealing with and some of their favourite memories of Stacy. We sat and chatted for a couple hours that again only felt like minutes. Soon the time had come for me to get going. Ashley then explained to me that she would be moving on after this day, she would no longer be here to sit and talk with my girls. My heart sank to my stomach. I had been through enough counselors already and I did not want my girls to have to go through the same thing as me.

I nodded. I understood life changed for everyone and I couldn't argue the fact. I did not know what her life was like or what had happened to make her change jobs now. I stood up to leave and Ashley hugged me before I left. She had been the one person I really enjoyed talking to about the hell I was in. She may not know how it felt, but she had made a lasting impression on me and my two girls. I felt terrible for them, but we had to keep pushing forward. I left that day feeling a little helpless and lost. Every time I seemed to reach out for help it would be pulled away from me. I went home and thought about what I could do to help the girls. I needed to find help for myself as well but I was done looking for someone to do that, now I needed something different.

I walked into the house. The girls would be on Christmas break in a couple days. It sure didn't feel like Christmas, though. The house was covered in pictures and memories of a person who had once brought the Christmas spirit into this home. I dreaded the day now. I hoped it would just pass by with nothing more than another check mark on the calendar. But that's not what the girls would have wanted. It might be a brutally tough time for me, but I needed to make it special for them, one way or another.

Chapter 28

With the girls out of school for the next couple weeks for Christmas break, I tried to keep them busy with things around the house. It was terribly cold outside, so they were not very interested in going out. I didn't blame them, I always hated the winter months as well. I sorted through the piles of paperwork that had to be filled out, signed and mailed back to the insurance companies. It seemed so overwhelming to me. All these official documents were Stacy's department. I never had to deal with this garbage before, but I didn't have a choice now. Tina at the funeral home had been putting in a lot of time to help me through most of it and I appreciated it very much. But it was still such a daunting task to get through it. Every paper requested a death certificate, a signature, policy number, dates and times.

I pulled up another document, it was requesting a doctor's notice of death. I stopped and stared at it. Anger flew through me as I read it over and over. THERE WAS NO FUCKING DOCTOR, SHE DIED BEFORE THEY COULD GET HER OUT OF THE FUCKING CAR YOU DISRESPECTFUL FUCKS! I slammed the paper down on the table and walked away. I couldn't deal with that right now. I paced around the house again trying to maintain my composure. Why was I angry at the paperwork? Shouldn't I be angry at the driver of the truck who hit her? I thought about that in length some days. I still didn't know exactly why the accident had unfolded the way it did. Maybe his brakes had failed; it could happen. I could not feel mad about what I did not know yet. It had been a month since that day and I still had not received any more information from the police. A part of me hoped it had been a mechanical failure, or something I could not blame an individual for. Just an accident that claimed a life. It happens every day all over the world. This time it just happened to be my wife who lost her life, the one person in this world that made me feel whole.

Sarah came to the house that evening to help me pull all the presents out and start wrapping them. I laid everything out on my bed. I knew who some of them were for, but there were some that I had no idea. Well shit. Then I remembered seeing a list somewhere. Stacy's purse. The police had brought it to the funeral home and I had received it shortly after. I went into the closet and opened it up. I found an envelope inside, filled with receipts for each present. Behind them was a hand written list perfectly itemized, just like she would do. Dammit woman, how did you know I would need this? I pulled it out and set it on the bed. Sarah wrapped each gift while I wrote names on cards and stuck them to the boxes. Stacy had gone all out on the kids this year. I would always tell her to stay within a budget. My budget was always different from hers, she always went over and above what anyone would have expected. Just another way that she would show others she loved them.

Once everything was wrapped or put into gift bags, I put them under the tree. I kept two huge burlap sacks hidden in my closet that contained a ton of things for the girls. I would wait until Christmas Eve to put those out. I sat and talked with Sarah until it was quite late. I hadn't talked to many people over the last few days. She had been such a big help and strong shoulder for me to lean on through all this. I was worried about how Christmas would go. I was not looking forward to it at all. Everyone had plans to be with family and loved ones. I would have loved to do the same, but my family was missing the biggest part of all. Stacy was not here to share the excitement with the girls and I wouldn't get that early morning kiss as she crawled on top of me in bed and tried to wake me up with teasing tickles. I wouldn't get to share our usual huge breakfast and mimosa's after the gifts were opened. She wouldn't pull me back to our room while the girls were distracted by the new toys for some much needed alone time together before we would be surrounded by more family. This was going to hurt and there was no way to avoid it.

I did my best to plan the day out. This was the first year Stacy had wanted to just be home and not go anywhere. Just have the day to ourselves. I asked the girls if they still wanted to just stay home or if they would like to go to the farm on Christmas. They both wanted to stay home like Stacy had wanted to do. I wasn't going to try and change their minds. Christmas Eve would be spent at the farm anyway.

Our community had pulled together and provided us with dinner for the past couple weeks. I was grateful, even though I didn't have an appetite. I was hoping I'd be able to eat something by Christmas day. Tomorrow was the twenty-third and I planned on taking the girls to Stacy's favorite place. I needed to go to the cattle lease and visit the spot where we'd been married.

Sleep evaded me again, as usual, but I made myself get out of bed and roust the girls up. We gathered some winter gear and dug out their sleds. With all the snow we had been getting, the hill should be in good shape for them to slide down today. We drove out to the end of the road where it became more of a trail leading into the lease. I was not sure how my mind would react to being back in her favourite place, but I felt a tug at my heart to be there today. We pulled up to where the fire pit was set in a stand of trees. The girls couldn't bail out of the truck fast enough and they ran up the hill. More family showed up to join us. Jamie worked up a decent fire for everyone to stay warm and cook the usual hot dogs over. My stomach was still in some pretty serious pain and I was not hungry. As everyone sat and chatted and all the kids took turns sliding and wiping out on the hill, I slowly stepped away. I needed to go somewhere. I walked off towards the edge of the field where the land swept downwards towards the river. I stopped and looked over the valley. It was still the most beautiful place around. I took a few more steps and looked around. I was standing exactly where I had stood years ago as I slipped a wedding ring onto Stacy's finger. A sense of peace came over me in that moment as I relived our beautiful day in my mind. It had been perfect.

The wind whipped around me, I was not dressed very well for the weather but the cold didn't bother me right then. I stayed there soaking up the view, lost in thoughts of happier times. I took a few steps back and looked around again. I had an idea. Stacy had loved this particular spot so much. Every time we came through here she would stop and just take it all in. She had been cremated after the celebration of life. This is where she would want to be. But I needed some kind of marker, something to show anyone else who might pass through here that this spot was a special place to someone who meant the world to me. I didn't want a headstone, that wasn't right. It needed to be something she would have wanted in this place. As I stood there thinking, the cold began to penetrate my right knee making it ache. I needed to…sit. That's it! I needed a memorial bench, something beautiful but not wood. No this needed to be something that could withstand the weather, I needed a marble bench. That was perfect. I smiled, still feeling the peacefulness of this place. It felt like she was here, this was her place.

I turned and slowly made my way back to the fire. The kids were gorging themselves on hot dogs and sweets. My stomach turned, the pain in my gut wouldn't ease up. But I had a plan to put into motion when I got home now. I sat quietly by the fire as everyone else chatted. My own demeanor had changed, though. I did not have energy for small talk anymore. I would easily talk in depth with certain people but only when it was one-on-one. I did not feel like chatting when there was more than a few people around. I watched as Halle slowly climbed to the top of the hill to the highest point around for miles. Her tiny figure was barely a spec on the crest of the hill. She wandered around up there and I knew she was taking time for herself. She deserved to have time to reflect. I had told her many times how much this place meant to her mother. She sat down and stayed there for a long time. But before she was done, she was surrounded by her younger cousins. They all loved to hang off Halle. She didn't mind usually, but I hoped it hadn't ruined her time up there. She slid back down with the rest of them and came back to the fire. By then it was getting late and we needed to get home. I was still in pain and needed to try and get some rest.

We packed up and started heading out. I paused one more time to look out over the valley, it was the perfect place. I headed out on the trail towards the road, Halle looked over at me as we idled through the trees.

"Dad, I felt like mom was there with us."

I smiled back at her. I knew exactly how she had felt because I had felt the same thing.

"I know, honey, I felt it too. It felt very peaceful there today."

She smiled at me and turned back towards the window. Despite the pain I was in, it had been an okay day. I had been worried about what sort of torment this day could bring, but it was not a terrible moment at all. It had been wonderful. If it hadn't been for the cold wind and the pain I was in, I would've wanted to stay there all night.

When we got back home I opened the laptop and started searching for what I wanted. I flipped from one website to the next until I found exactly what I had in mind. I quickly sent an email to the company to inquire about the bench I wanted. I knew it was the right one as soon as my eyes came across it. Satisfied with the day, I sent the girls to bed. They had not been sleeping in their own rooms yet. Instead they had been sleeping on the couch, I felt more comfortable with them being close to where I was rather than all the way downstairs. I knew they would have to get back to that normal routine soon, but not tonight. I stood up to head to my room. I hadn't eaten all day. The pain in my stomach was still there and I couldn't bring myself to try. I laid down to suffer through another sleepless night.

In the morning I got the girls bathed and dressed. We would be celebrating Christmas Eve at the farm. I wasn't sure if I was ready to celebrate anything, but I would make an appearance anyway. I hadn't been out to the farm since the day I shot the elk, the one I had used to make Stacy a special dinner to celebrate the anniversary of the day we met. The last dinner we would share together. So many memories tied themselves together like a string. A chill went up my spine. I hoped I would be okay. I felt a light twinge of anxiety through my chest. I had never gone out there for Christmas without Stacy by my side. Another first to conquer.

I packed up the girls and headed out. We arrived at the farm and made our way into the house. Debbie walked towards me to give me a hug, I looked down at all the gifts.

"Fuck." I shook my head.

"What's wrong?" Debbie said as she hugged me.

"I'm sorry. I forgot all the gifts at home." *I'm such an idiot*, I thought. *Who forgets the gifts at home?* Stacy always made sure to grab all those things. She double checked that each gift for each child had been accounted for before we would leave the house. Another twist of that dagger in my chest. Every small reminder that she wasn't here to do this anymore just hurt me over and over.

Debbie held me in that hug and whispered, "Its fine. Don't worry about it." She knew I felt bad about it, and she knew it was Stacy who would have always looked after that detail. She wiped a tear away as she turned toward the kitchen. I was mad at myself, but I walked in and sat on the couch. I was still in a lot of pain but I tried to make the best of it. Jamie sat down near me and chatted about this and that. I told him about the bench I wanted to get to set in the lease. He liked the idea and thought it was perfect as well. I didn't have a lot to say again, but I tried to be conversational. Everyone else ate a good supper, but I couldn't eat again. We spent the evening together until I began to feel weak and tired. I needed to get home and try to get some rest. I packed the girls up, we hugged the family and went back to a house that still felt empty and cold.

I talked the girls into sleeping in their own rooms. They were a little uncertain, but Halle helped me convince Layla that it was a good idea. How was Santa supposed to show up if they were sleeping on the couch? They decided to snuggle up together in Halle's room. That worked. I went back upstairs and waited until they were asleep. Then I carefully set out the huge burlap sacks Stacy had picked up and filled with so many thoughtful gifts for our girls. I set everything up the way she would have done, then stood back to look everything over. The dread of the coming day hung over me like a dark cloud. I had to do what I could to make it special for them. I went to my bed and stared at the ceiling until I finally drifted off to sleep.

A few hours later I was woken up by two little girls who were tugging at my hands to get me out of bed, Layla had her usual ear to ear grin.

"Come on daddy! It's Christmas morning!"

Halle giggled at her half-heartedly. She was happy to see the gifts all set out but I could tell she was feeling the emptiness like I was. I got to my feet, the pain still in my stomach but managed to get to the living room and sit back down.

"Okay girls, before you open anything I want you to know something."

They both looked up at me.

"Everything that is here for you, your momma did all of this for you. She had everything ready for you before her accident. She loved Christmas time and was always as excited to see you girls open everything. This is her gift to you."

Halle stood up and hugged me, I covered my face with my hands. *Don't start now, not yet, just keep it together for a little while.* I thought to myself.

"Okay girls, go ahead"

They tore into the bags, every item that came out was thoroughly examined before they would reach in for the next one. Every gift Stacy had found was so thoughtful, each one had some special meaning. I watched as they played with each toy, tried on every article of clothing and flipped through each book they had received. There was little joy in my heart this time, I didn't have a lot to feel joyful about. But knowing Stacy had put her usual amount of incredible love into this season, I tried my best to be happy for the girls. I gave them all the time they needed to open everything. They hugged me and gave me kisses as I stood up to start on breakfast for them. The girls got up and headed downstairs coming back up moments later with a box.

"Dad someone brought this here for you."

I looked at the box. No card or name on it.

"Who was it?" I asked.

"We don't know. They said to give this to you today."

I slowly opened the box, inside was a wooden sign. It was one Stacy had wanted to get for our room. In bold white letters it said: We go together like moonshine in a mason jar. I could not hold it back anymore, I wept uncontrollably. The pain of that loneliness was terrible. She should have been there with me, helping me get breakfast together. She should have had her arms wrapped around me and been flirting with me like she always did. My heart ached with the pain, the sign was beautiful and very thoughtful. I loved it, I was happy someone had thought about this. The girls hugged me as I wiped the tears away.

"Oh, and these too, Dad."

Halle handed me a small bag. I opened it up and inside was a pair of socks. On the bottom were some words: If you can read this, bring me a beer. I laughed. Well, that was worth a try. I slipped them on my feet. I got some food for the girls, then sat on the couch and watched as they went through all their gifts again. I picked up a blank piece of paper and started drawing. I had been thinking about Stacy's beautiful eyes for a long time but I couldn't find a picture that was clear enough for me to really see them. I did my best to bring that vision to life on that paper. When I was nearly done I drew a tear coming from the corner of the eye. I set the pencil down and let my own tears roll down my face. This day had brought on the loneliest feeling I had ever felt and I just couldn't hold it back anymore. I couldn't help it, I cried for hours that day.

Chapter 29

I'm not sure how, but we had made it through our first Christmas without Stacy. Another first to check off the list. It had been terrible. I tried to make it fun for the girls, but I just couldn't get past the loneliness. I didn't know how to get away from it, the sadness that had become of my life was depressingly constant. I talked to friends and family regularly, but I didn't always have much to say. What could I say? My life had been ripped to shreds, my daughter's hearts had been shattered and I did not know how to move on from this point. I sat down at the table one day and opened the laptop to check my email. When Ashley had told me she was moving on I had sent a message to the school to see if she was still going to be in the area and if she might still be able to talk to the girls from time to time. Since I had not received a reply, I had assumed she would be unable to do it.

Once my email was open, I scrolled through deleting them as I went. Nothing of any importance, just social media garbage, all of which I had completely cut myself off from. It was all just full of everyone else's lives moving on as if nothing had happened. Meanwhile mine had stopped completely. I opened my junk mail folder to clear it out, scrolling through quickly just to check that there wasn't something in there I might need. I scanned through and stopped on one that looked different. It was a reply from the school and I opened it up. They had replied to me on the same day I had sent my original message. I had an email address for Ashley and was told to send a message anytime. I sent one immediately. If it would help the girls at all I was going to try. My spirits were lifted ever so slightly.

The next day the girls were itching to go hang out at a friend's house, something they hadn't had a chance to do lately. Sarah called and asked if we could meet for coffee. Seemed like a great plan, the girls would get some time away from the house to play with friends while I made a trip to town that did not involve death certificates or paperwork. I stopped to get the mail before I left, in the box was a memorial bracelet I had ordered. It was a metal band, black with laser etched words on it.

Love of My Life
Stacy Ann Krahn
July 23 1984 - Nov. 22 2017
I love you, I love you more, I love you most

I quickly took it out of the package and set it on my wrist. I admired it for a moment. I had also requested they etch a picture of Stacy on the band. It had turned out perfect. My eyes glanced to my ring finger where I had her name tattooed. I thought about the day I had done it. The shocked look on her face when I showed it to her was priceless. The memory made me smile. I had captured that moment on video and had come across it while I searched for clips of her.

I headed to town excited to show Sarah the bracelet. I spent a few hours chatting with her over coffee, it was the first time I felt somewhat relaxed in public. The girls were in good hands. I was not worried about them, I was in good company and I felt no pressure to be anywhere at any certain time. It was a relief to have after the Christmas I had gone through. I stopped to pick up a few groceries before heading back to pick the girls up. They were bouncing off the walls when I walked into the house, smiling and giggling. It had been a good day for them as well. They were not ready to go home but it was getting late.

We pulled into our driveway, Halle rushed out of the truck and inside. I grabbed an arm load of groceries and worked my way into the house.

Halle yelled from my bedroom. "Dad! There's something wrong with the water!"

I didn't know what that meant, but it couldn't be a good thing. I dropped what I had in my hands and ran to see what the issue was. My feet were soaked by the time I walked into my room. Water was spraying everywhere. A water line had broken off in my bathroom while we were out for the day. I quickly shut the valve and stopped the water.

"Go get towels, quickly," I instructed.

The girls ran around gathering what towels they could find. I threw them on the floor of my room and started mopping up the mess. I worked my way towards a corner where the heat register was and saw the water rushing down into the duct.

"Shit. Girls, stay here, I need to go check the basement."

I ran down, the breaker had flipped and it was dark. Using my phone as a flashlight, I made my way towards the kid's rooms, the water was deeper. It sounded like a tropical rain storm in the basement. I shone the light into the girl's bedrooms.

"Oh my God, this can't be happening to us."

The rooms were completely destroyed. The ceiling had caved in, the walls were swollen with water and all of their possessions were soaked. I heard a gasp behind me. I turned around to see the girls standing there, mouths wide open as they looked at the destruction. Layla held her face and started to cry.

Halle grabbed her sister by the shoulders. "Layla I know this sucks, but it's not the time to cry. Get anything of moms out of your room and move it to a dry place," she instructed.

Layla stopped crying, pulled off her socks and rolled up her pant legs. She ran into her room, ankle deep in freezing cold water and got to work.

I smiled at Halle and patted her head. "Good job, Stacy Jr."

Halle looked up at me and grinned. She said the exact words her mom would have said if she were here. Then she followed suit by rolling up her pant legs and running into her room to start pulling out what she could. I made a few frantic phone calls and soon had a few people running in to help us get out what we could. I was upset, but I didn't have time to think about the situation. A restoration company came on to the scene and began sucking water up. I ran back to my room and started taking things out of there. My own stuff was of no concern. It was anything that had belonged to Stacy I was worried about. I moved boxes and possessions I had set on the floor. I still had many items from the day of her celebration of life, pictures and memories everywhere. I had planned to put pictures all over our house of her. I found them and got them to a dry place, frantically digging through the closet to make sure her things were safe before returning to the basement. I started to assess the damage. I entered the furnace room and looked around. The furnace was out and water was streaming out from inside. Great! It was freezing cold outside and now the furnace was dead and not likely to work after being filled with water. We made some more late night emergency calls and soon had a guy coming to see if he could get it working for now.

I was sure I knew who was coming to our aid. Gord had known Stacy for many years and would visit with her every time he ran into her. My mom answered the door when he arrived.

"Hi," my mom said, "do you know whose house this is?"

Gord looked a little puzzled.

"This is Myron and Stacy's home," she told him. As far as Gord had known, this was just another call out. He hadn't known who the home owner was when he received the call.

Gord walked into the house and found me. He wrapped his arms around me in a big bear hug. "Hey mister, how are you doing?" he asked.

"Well, to be totally honest, not worth a fuck," I replied.

He nodded in understanding and headed to the basement to see if there was anything he could do to help us out.

Kelly arrived to help out. I'd known him since I was Halle's age. He quickly loaded my guns and ammo to get it out of harm's way. The moisture wouldn't be good for the guns and it wasn't like I needed them right now anyway. We worked feverishly until there was nothing left to do but head to a hotel. I packed the girls into the truck. There was nothing else to do, the house was destroyed.

Sarah met me at the hotel she booked us into and had everything set up for us. I wasn't sure what I would have done without her around. I wasn't sure how Jason was coping through all this, every time Sarah jumped up and ran to our aid, he was left with their rambunctious twin toddlers. Sarah helped me pack our bags up to the room. I set everything down and Sarah handed me a bottle, "Jason said you needed this more than he does."

It was my favourite bottle of whiskey. I smiled and set it down on the counter. I wasn't known for being a big drinker, but I was gonna have one tonight. I settled the girls into their bed and got them to sleep. I sat down on mine and picked up a book to write in, I only came up with three words:

What the fuck

I sipped my whiskey and thought about the day's events. It had started off so well, but ended up terrible. What a mess. I hoped the damage wasn't as bad as I feared, but who was I kidding? Things apparently didn't work like that for me.

I laid my head down knowing I wouldn't sleep.

Next morning I got the girls up and found some breakfast then headed back to the house. The restoration crew was there trying to pull water from walls, tearing wet walls down and pulling up wet floors. The house was a disaster, the furnace had been patched up last night but it was dead again. Gord was running around town trying to find enough parts to make it last until he could get a new furnace in. The house felt cold, and not just because the furnace had quit. Last night I had been forced to pack up a bunch of Stacy's things I wasn't ready to have moved, things I did not want to have moved because they meant something to me. My girl's rooms that they had just started sleeping in again were now completely ruined. Nothing was left. All the work Stacy had put into the basement to make it nice for the girls was now in tatters. All of the girl's clothes were wet and had to be taken out to be cleaned. All the gifts their momma had got them for Christmas were shoved into a dry corner of the house. There wasn't much I could do about it right now, so I moved a few more things around and then headed back to the hotel. The girls did not want to see the house any more than they had to. There was a pool at the hotel and they wanted to go play.

The crew finished what they could. They left many fans, dehumidifiers and heaters running all over the house. It would be a while before it would dry out now. I headed back to the house on my own this time. Mom had the girls for a little while. I walked in and was hit by the humidity of the house and the loud howl of all the machinery running. I scanned through each room, now fully gutted of any damaged walls, floors and ceilings. The insurance adjuster had been there already and said 2/3 of the house had been destroyed. Every bedroom had been damaged, two bathrooms were now ruined and not useable. Every floor in the house was going to have to be ripped up and replaced. I walked from one room to another, looking at the damage to our home. I tried to just be angry about the whole situation, but it wasn't working. The panic in my chest had already started to creep up. This had compounded an already terrible situation for us. We had just began to sort things out somewhat and move forward. And now this.

My knees weakened, I folded my arms trying to get a hold of my emotions. I fought it as best I could, but there was no stopping it. I hit the floor and burst into tears. I was so overwhelmed with everything that had been thrown in my face over the past few weeks, now this. I was alone, I screamed,

"WHY THE FUCK IS THIS HAPPENING TO ME?"

I sat on the floor and wept. So many people had told me I was the strongest person they had ever met, that they would have never been able to make it through all this and still be a functional human being. I disagreed completely, I was a mess. If they could see me when I was at my worst they would not say the same. If they could look inside my mind, even for a moment, they would see the truth. I did not feel strong at all. I was lost in this shit storm that had become of my life.

I waited there until I was able to get myself back together, took one more glance around our ruined home and walked out.

I headed straight for the hot tub by the pool where the girls were happily splashing and playing together. I eased down into the steamy hot pool with a cold whiskey in my hand. I glanced around at the other patrons enjoying the heat. I was the only one with a drink in my hand. Too bad for them, I guess. I sat and thought about how much work it was going to be and the amount of time it was going to take to fix everything. I remembered Stacy arguing with me about wanting to rip out the en suite bathroom and remodel it. I had said no; it was way too expensive and so much work. I had nearly brought my glass to my lips when I stopped. That's where the line had ruptured. It had all started in that bathroom. I shook my head and smiled. Even though she was no longer here, she was still winning every argument. Damn woman, she always got her way. God how I missed her.

Next morning I called Jenni at the shop. I needed to sit down and talk about ordering some things. Not just any old things; I had a list. The list was everything that Stacy had wanted to do in that bathroom. Obviously Stacy still wanted her dream bathroom and I wasn't about to mess it up for her. In her typical fashion, nothing was easy. All the items she had wanted were custom order, top of the line and expensive as hell. I didn't hesitate though. Do it and get it over with. If the house had to be redone, it was going to get redone the way she wanted and that meant everything. Nothing was going to be half-assed, that wasn't my style or hers. I swore up and down Stacy had come back to the house when we had left that day and kicked that damn line off just to set a fire under my ass to do all the house renovations she had wanted to do. She knew there was little to no chance I would have done it otherwise. I just wished she was here to see it whenever it was done. I wished she was here to help me make all the decisions.

I just wished she was here.

Chapter 30

We stayed at the hotel for about ten days before we were able to get back into what was left of our home. It was still a mess, but we were tired of being in the hotel. We sorted out some make-shift rooms for the kids, not much more than a mattress on a plywood floor but it would have to do for now. The girls Christmas break hadn't been exactly what I had planned for, more stress was not something any of us needed. The girls were going back to school in a couple days and I needed to find some kind of stress relief for all of us but wasn't sure what to do. I went through my phone to see if I had anything to remind me. I found the last email from Ashley, I had not thought about it much with everything that had happened, but maybe I should see if she had time to talk to the girls.

I got hold of her and she suggested FaceTime. I had not used it much at all and was not sure how Layla would do, she was not much of a phone talker. But it was worth a shot. I set Halle up first and made the call. As I expected she babbled on for an hour, but it was good for her. I had been running out of things to say to help her with everything we had been through. Ashley seemed to have a way of getting her to open up about all the little things and encouraging her to stay positive. Once Halle was done, Layla sat down and looked at the phone screen to see Ashley's face. She smiled and bounced on the bed which I'm sure must have looked like a big ball of hair on the screen. I closed the door and let her have her own space. I busied myself in the kitchen, cleaning up the mess from the flood. I had a lot of help from family and friends that evening so we made short work of it. I wandered around and sorted through laundry, school supplies and more paperwork from the accident.

I glanced around a while later, Layla was still not out of the room. I peaked in the door. Yup, still chatting away after nearly an hour. That was awesome to see. I didn't expect her to actually stay on the phone for long, but this was a good thing. They needed someone to talk to who wasn't family for a change. I had found it was sometimes easier to talk to someone who hadn't known me before Stacy's accident. I felt I had changed a fair bit in my own personality and anyone who had known me for years was likely waiting for that person to come back. I wasn't sure that person even existed anymore.

Once Layla was finally done I talked with Ashley for a few minutes to see how it had gone. She let me know the girls were incredibly strong and doing very well for what they had been through.

"You are doing an awesome job with those girls. They're lucky to have you as a father."

I wasn't sure I felt the same. I was trying, but I didn't feel like I was going above and beyond what anyone else would have done in my situation. We chatted for a little while longer. I let her know about the house, the stress and the lack of sleep that continued for me. She told me that even though they seem to be making good progress sometimes people end up taking a giant step backwards around the two month period from the passing of a loved one. I made a mental note of that. We were getting close to that time now. We set up another phone date for the girls and I said goodbye, it had been good to talk to her again.

The next couple days were pretty quiet, almost too quiet. With all the activity of past few weeks I had been looking forward to some down time, but now I was not liking it. Normally I would be in the garage turning wrenches and listening to music, but I hadn't set foot in their since the accident. I didn't want to. It had been my life for the last several years, but now I didn't give a damn about anything in there. I was convinced I was never going to race again. I'd sell the engine, part out what was left of the race truck and walk away from it all. Halle, however, said I couldn't sell it.

"Would mom want you to sell the race truck and stop racing?" she asked.

I contemplated her question for a moment before replying. "Well, no probably not, but…"

"Then don't sell it. Mom wouldn't want you to stop racing."

What the hell? I was getting advice from my 11 year old now? Fine, it can get shoved into the corner of the shop and stay there.

Halle asked, "Dad, when are we going to start working on Mom's truck again?" She had been looking at the '75 F-100 truck sitting in the garage beside the race truck. It was now getting covered in dust. I hadn't thought much about the truck either, though I didn't want to get rid of that one. That truck was meant to be built for Stacy to drive. I just wasn't sure when I was going to have the energy to start on it again.

"I'm not sure if I can start working in the garage again yet, Halle"

"You don't have to, Dad. You just tell me what to do and I'll do it. You just have to sit there and tell me," Halle eagerly replied.

"You want to get working on it that bad?"

"Yes, I want to be able to ride in it again this summer."

Ugh. Well, I couldn't fault her for that. I wanted to drive it again as well, but there was a lot of work to do. I thought about it throughout the night since I wasn't sleeping anyhow. When I got up and walked out to the garage, it was a mess. Between the things that had been stored in there shortly after the accident to the stuff that had been shoved in there after the flood, there really wasn't room to work now. I started cleaning things up and organizing some sort of work area. I set the race truck on some rollers and shoved it against the back wall. It wasn't going to get any attention anyhow. I rolled an engine into a cleared area in the garage. The engine had originally been in what had become the race truck. Stacy wanted it put into her F-100. It was in need of a rebuild and some more go-fast parts, but it needed to be torn down first.

Once the girls were up I let them know they could tear down the engine for Momma's truck if they wanted to. Halle's eyes lit up. Layla was just happy to come out and help. We went out to the garage together. I broke the bolts loose and they started ripping parts off. One piece at a time, the old parts were hitting the floor. I flipped the block over to start getting the main caps out. The girls were covered in engine oil, but happy to be working on their mom's engine. Halle used my dead blow hammer to knock the main caps out, but the last one was being stubborn. She bashed it left and right and chunks of the hammer were flying everywhere. She missed a few times and smashed her knuckles into the steel cap, but kept working at it until it finally came loose. She pulled the cap out and set it with the rest as I lifted out the crankshaft. It had taken them two hours with some hand tools to completely strip the engine down to the block. I looked at the girls. Layla was wiping her oily hands with a dirty rag and Halle's hands were covered in oil and bleeding. I couldn't have felt more proud of them at that moment.

I finished cleaning up the tools and old parts. I would be sending the block to my engine guy to get it prepped and machined for the new parts I planned to put in. I had been dreading any time spent in the garage, but this had turned out to be a good day. Usually Stacy would have come in to check on my progress. She would sit down and chat with me as I worked away. Sometimes she would come out with a cold beer and some food because I would forget to eat once I got busy. She was always looking after me and the girls. Now I had to figure out how to look after myself and the girls. The insomnia thing was getting old. *Maybe I should see a doctor*, I thought. Over a month of not getting much sleep can turn into some serious health issues and that's not something I had any strength for. I didn't want to admit it, but I needed help.

I finally made an appointment to see the doctor in mid-January. He prescribed some meds to help me sleep, but warned that they could be addictive. Great! I wasn't really wanting to take anything before, and now if I took them too much I'd get addicted? Awesome. Guess I'll just have to take my chances. I went home and looked at the bottle of pills. I've never had to take meds for sleeping before, only pain meds for broken bones. First time for everything, I guess.

The girls had another chance to talk to Ashley on the phone. They always looked forward to the call like kids waiting for their birthday party to start. Once they were done, I spoke with her a little about the pills I had to take. Besides being a counselor, she was also a nurse. She explained what these pills were and that they could be addictive, but only if you had that type of personality, which she did not believe I had. I agreed. I was too damn stubborn to get addicted to that crap, or anything for that matter. Being a control freak does have some benefits, I guess.

"So, I think you should still be seeing a professional counselor. I want to continue these conversations with you and the girls, but I am not taking notes or anything a counselor normally would. This is strictly on a friend's basis now," Ashley informed me.

"Okay, fair enough." I was assuming I would have to find some more help for the girls. Yet, I was pretty much done looking for myself at this point. Counselors did not seem to work for me very well anyway. We chatted for a while longer, which turned out to be over an hour by the time we said goodbye. I took one of the pills and headed for bed. For the first time in nearly two months, I slept a solid eight hours.

Over the next couple weeks I started going back to work. I had been offered a different position that would no longer have me in the field. It wasn't something I expected, but was honoured that they had thought about my circumstance and decided to pull me out of the field. The girls seemed to be doing okay in school for the most part and were starting to get into some sort of routine again. Halle had some issues with friends at school but we worked through them. I know it's hard for kids to understand what she is going through but man, kids can be little assholes at times. Her friends didn't understand how she could be fine one day and upset the next. Many try to say they know how she feels because they felt the same when their cat, grandparent, neighbour or some distant friend died. They have no idea the depth of pain the girls had to deal with. It was infuriating for me to see Halle have to go through that. I wanted to knock each kid on the head and scream in their faces for making her feel upset. It wasn't fair for her to have that to deal with on top of everything else. What made it worse was not knowing what to say or do to make it better for her. I used the resources I had and got her on the phone with all the main contacts I felt could help her. She eventually got through it thanks to many incredible people who spent hours chatting with her and helping her through some rough days.

As the 22nd of January drew near I felt like we were starting to move ahead in some ways. The house was still a disaster but we were slowing getting some sort of life started. I knew the date was coming but didn't draw attention to it. I wasn't going to try and make the 22nd of every month a bad day. But just as Ashley had warned, everything seemed to fall to pieces. The school called and said Halle had broken down in class and needed to be picked up. She had been doing pretty well and was acting as if everything was fine, but it was all very far from fine for her. She missed her mom terribly. They may have butted heads regularly, but that never lessened the love they had for each other. Layla seemed to be a little more oblivious to the fact it was the two month anniversary of Stacy's death and I was okay with that. She didn't need the reminder. I sat up with the girls again, not sleeping just chatting and trying to help them through this set back. I didn't want to admit it but I was starting to feel very cornered. I love these girls with all my heart, but my own heart was aching and I didn't feel like I had anywhere to go to release the tension and strain. I didn't want to leave but I was going to have to do something to try and recharge myself.

I called Ashley one evening to tell her that she had been correct about the two month set back she had warned me about. I explained what the girls had been going through and what I was doing to try and help them. Then as if she was reading my mind she asked.

"So what are you doing for yourself?"

I didn't really know what to say. In my mind it had nothing to do with me. My entire focus was on the girls and doing whatever I could to help them. But I admitted I was feeling worn out mentally. I just didn't have anything to really boost my mood enough for the girls to keep drawing from when they were down.

"Not really anything. I don't know what to do. I'm starting to feel like I need to get away for a weekend, maybe head south to the city or something just for a night. Try to get my mind away from all the stress."

I wasn't sure how she was able to do it so well, but she had been quite intuitive as to what I was thinking without having to say it. She was no longer a counselor for us. She had turned into a friend and one of the favourites for us to talk to.

I began searching for different events that would be happening in the city in the next couple months. There was a Brantley Gilbert concert coming up. I was a big fan of his music but the crowds worried me. I seemed to have gotten control of my anxiety issues but I still seemed to struggle with huge crowds of people. Maybe that was not the best idea just yet. I searched some more until I came across a Professional Bull Riders event coming in late March. It had been years now since I had been to any sort of bull riding event. I had pretty much just avoided them because it was hard for me to go and not be riding. I felt like I was way past that now, though. Maybe that would be fun to go to. I thought about it for a few days and decided that's what I wanted to do.

I ordered my tickets and started planning the trip. It was still two months away but given my circumstance, a little extra planning was probably a good thing. I was excited about it. I had something to look forward to now! But until then I had to continue the arduous task of our new everyday life. I was starting to see a pattern with Halle, she would start each week very down and depressed and as the week went on she became better. Sunday evening I could see her go back down. I talked with her about it, so she was aware of this cycle. She was pretty easy to read most days. I could tell in the first thirty minutes of her getting out of bed what kind of mood she was in. I'll admit, it was wearing on me. I completely understood when it was just due to her missing her mom and if that's what was causing the depression I would stay with her and help her through it in any way I could.

On one particular morning she was showing the usual signs that she was having a rough morning. I was busy trying to get them ready for school and she ran off to hide in her make shift bedroom on the floor. I walked in and sat down beside her. We chatted a little but she wasn't really letting me in on what was going on. She said it wasn't only missing her mom that was hurting her today. I kept digging until I started feeling frustrated. I got up and let her sit on her own for a while. Eventually she came out of her room and started talking, but she was bringing up things about her friends we had already dealt with weeks ago. My patience had worn thin and my ability to be soft about her situation was now gone. I snapped.

"Halle, we talked about this weeks ago and we worked through it. Is this happening again?"

"No," she replied, a little irritated that I wasn't sounding very supportive now.

"So every time you feel like having a sad day we are just gonna drag up some shit from weeks ago so we can relive that garbage?" I asked raising my voice. I was angry at her for bringing up more stuff for me to deal with. Old stuff I didn't have the energy for. I was mentally and emotionally exhausted. I didn't have the capacity to be soft hearted anymore. I had no one to calm me down from my overwhelmed mental state.

"Dad," she cried, "You're being really mean and not helping me!"

"Well I don't know what you want from me" I snapped, "I can't just let you have sad days just because you want to drag up shit from weeks ago. I don't know what you want me to do to make it better. I don't know how to make it better. I don't know how to do this on my own. I don't know what the fuck I'm doing! I have never had to do this without your mom here to help me."

My voice cracked. The dagger twisted hard in my chest and I covered my face with my hands as I started to cry. I didn't mean to be so hard on her or to yell and swear at her. She didn't need that. I was just out of gas and had no more energy to help her with her emotions when my own were still so raw. Halle's eyes grew wide, she hadn't seen me so upset in over a month. I had done a good job of hiding it from the girls when I could. At that moment my heart had been ripped open and Halle could see directly inside of it. She had witnessed the pain I was in. It came as a shock to her to know how lost and alone I felt. I had been trying so hard to be strong for them, but everyone has a breaking point. She had just found mine.

Halle walked over to me and wrapped her arms around me as I sobbed. Layla quickly ran over and did the same.

"I'm sorry," I whispered, "I didn't mean to yell at you like that. I just don't always know what to say and it frustrates me that I don't always have the answers for you."

"I know, Daddy. I'm sorry too. I love you, Dad," she said.

I took a deep breath and tried to stop crying. "I love you more."

Halle looked up at me and smiled. "I love you most!"

Layla looked up as if something had just clicked in her head, then her eyes brightened.

"Daddy! That's what Mommy said to me that morning!"

"See? I told you she never left the house without telling you that she loved you!"

Layla had been tormented with the thought of not telling her mom she loved her. In that moment with our emotions raw and ragged it suddenly came back to her. Our hearts were lifted slightly. It had been a brutal morning, but I learned in the last couple months we would get through this together, one day at a time. I hugged my girls close to me and took a deep breath. We would get through this, together.

Chapter 31

As we continued our daily struggles of dealing with the grief, we learned how to help each other out a little more. I wouldn't say we were off and running, but we were crawling through this pile of shit that had become our new lives. It wasn't a sprint, but we were moving forward. We were starting to have the odd day where we could laugh and feel a little happy without the sting of guilt that would sometimes hit afterwards. I was getting back into a somewhat regular schedule at work and slowly getting myself integrated back into the daily grind of oil field work, but now it was more of a desk job. I was happy to have the opportunity to get out of the field. It wasn't what I had planned, but life changes things on you when you least expect it.

I was trying to sort out the weekly chores Stacy had usually done without me knowing. Things most dads would take for granted, especially when working away from home. The girls needed socks, new pants, and snacks for school lunches, there were dentist appointments and birthday parties to go to. Stacy had always made it look so easy, but it was exhausting to me. She could balance a fulltime job, make dinner, keep the house clean and still be on top of all these little details. I had always known she was something special. There was never a doubt in my mind that she was Super Mom. I sure wished I would have had time to ask her how to do all this on my own as well as she had done for so many years. I messed up a few times. I hated failing at anything and it drove me crazy if I forgot something the girls needed. I know I was being a little hard on myself at times, but I wanted to try to live up to the standards Stacy had set before me. I wasn't sure if I could ever meet that standard, but I was going to try.

On one of our trips to the dreaded mall, we ran into my old travel partner from my rodeo days. Ryan was having just as much fun at the mall with his kids as I was. We talked a little about our old riding days. He told me his kids were in the new junior rodeo circuit and how they were doing in it.

After we left, Halle started asking questions, "What's junior rodeo, Dad?"

"It's setup for younger kids, mini broncs, steers or mini bulls, barrel racing and things like that."

"Huh, so I would be allowed to ride?" she asked.

I wasn't sure where she was going with this, but I had a bit of an idea.

"Well, yeah, if you wanted to you could, but in what event?"

"Could I ride the mini bulls?"

"Whoa now, you're not just gonna run in and ride. That's what I did and I won't let you do the same. We can go to the next event and I'll take you back behind the chutes and show you how it all works. You can watch the other kids ride. If you still want to try after that, we can start training. Deal?"

"Deal! I'm excited." She grinned.

I wasn't all that excited. I had been away from this sport for so long, but if she really wanted to do it, she was going to have me as a coach. She might not like that because I wouldn't let her half-ass it. That's how people get hurt. She talked about it for a few days, asking me questions about how it all works and watching videos she would find of other kids riding. If she did get on, she would be a third generation and the first girl in the family to be a bull rider. She really liked the sounds of that. I wasn't going to encourage it, but if she wanted it bad enough I wouldn't hold her back. She needed to understand what she was getting into before she got on.

A couple weeks passed before I packed the kids up and headed to the arena. I walked in and was instantly hit with all those familiar smells an indoor rodeo arena has, horse sweat, dirt and manure. It's not pleasant but it sure brought back a flood of memories. We found some seats to watch the timed events that were going on. The kids seemed to enjoy it. It took a couple hours before the rough stock started and I grabbed the kids and walked back to the chutes where I found Ryan, his wife Nicky and their kids. Kennedy was riding her horse in most of the timed events while Pacen was getting ready to get on his mini bronc. I took Halle behind the chutes to show her how to rig up a bull rope. I showed her the spurs and explained what the kids were doing in the chutes as they got set to ride. She watched with interest until one kid landed on his head.

"Whoa, that looked like it hurt, Dad," she grimaced.

"He'll be fine. If he ain't, he won't be riding long." You couldn't be a wimp and think you were going to rodeo for any length of time. There really isn't any way around it. You can either take the pain and keep riding, or pick a different sport.

We stayed around to watch Ryan's kids do their rides, both doing really well. Being back there was a good feeling, but I wasn't sure I wanted to get back into this sport with Halle. I was an over protective father and I wasn't sure I would be able to see her get beat up, which was bound to happen if she rode. As the show ended I packed the kids up and started walking out. Halle hadn't said any more about riding.

"Halle, I'm never going to tell you to get on. This is up to you, but if you want to do this, you have to want it bad. You have to want this more than anything else, because if you don't you're going to get hurt. You have to come to me and tell me that you want this because I'm never going to ask you to do it. Understood?"

She nodded her head at me and got up in the truck and didn't say a word the whole ride home. There was a small part of me that wanted her to be able to experience what I had at her age. But I was not willing to push her to do it; she had to have the drive to do it herself. I had seen other kids when I was riding with their dads yelling at them to try harder, screaming at them if they got tossed off. I wasn't about to do that to her. I never brought the subject up again and neither did she.

We were still in a torn up house, the girls were constantly getting slivers in their feet from the plywood floors and I was getting tired of waiting to use the bathroom every morning. Slowly things started to get worked on, but it all seemed to be taking a ridiculous amount of time. I wanted everything done like yesterday and I wanted it done properly and at a good price. Most of the renovations were covered by insurance, but the things Stacy had wanted to upgrade weren't. She had good taste. That was never a question. (She did marry me after all.) I ordered all Kohler products just as she had wanted. It had come to a small fortune, but I didn't blink at the cost. Just do it and get it over with. I had gone in to her shop and paid for it all. Of course, it was all special orders because she was not the type to get whatever was sitting on the shelf. A couple days later, Jenni called me and said I needed to come back to the shop.

"Why? Did I forget something?" I asked.

"Well, no. I put the order in and you know how Stacy always dealt with the Kohler people on a daily basis, they called back when they found out who the order was for and told us to refund your money. They're covering it."

"Huh?" I didn't know what else to say. I did not expect this at all. I had no plans of getting a hand out of any kind. I had never had one in my life yet. Why now? Stacy was the purchaser at the shop so she talked with all the main representatives weekly if not more. The Kohler rep sat with her many times, going over what they were going to bring in for new product and planning what future new releases to bring in as well. It was just another example of how much people respected who she was. The incredible person she was to everyone was still affecting my life now. I could only try to be more like her.

The kids and I continued to talk to Ashley whenever we could. Her busy schedule was not always easy to match up with our own, but I had taken her advice and found another counselor for the girls in town. They seemed to be okay with this one, but they still preferred Ashley. I still suffered with insomnia and had to take medication or I wouldn't sleep for days on end. I had been working out every day for the last couple months. It seemed to help curb my stress levels a little and it did help me to get a better sleep at night. The side effects were not all that bad either. I was never a big person, but I lost about 25 lbs. I was sure that some of the weight was shed due to stress, but I was trying to eat better too, or at least eat something. I didn't have to be clean shaven for work anymore so I stopped shaving. I also got laser eye surgery done. After all that I found I could walk through a busy place and not get recognized so easily. This made me feel a little more comfortable. It wasn't likely to last long, but for now I was happy. I was not the same person I had been a few months ago, why should I bother looking the same?

My trip to the Calgary to go watch the Professional Bull Riders event was coming up pretty quick. With me and the kids under each other's feet constantly, I was thinking it might be a good idea for the kids to split up for a couple nights as well. They had been fighting like sisters do, so Halle would go to the farm and help Debbie and Jamie with the cows since they were heavy into calving season. Layla was less interested in the calves, so she was happy to go to my folk's acreage and hang out with the cats in the barn. I had a flight out early Saturday morning so the girls headed out on Friday for their weekend away from it all. I was pretty excited to go, but also a little nervous. This was my first trip away from the kids since the accident. Another first to get through. I wasn't worried about the kids too much, I was hoping they would be able to cope with being away from me for a couple nights. I was more worried I would have one of those stupid anxiety attacks. There would be a lot of firsts this weekend for me. I didn't sleep much that night at home alone in spite of taking my sleep meds.

I got up early and headed to Sarah and Jason's house where I dropped the dog off and Sarah drove me to the airport. First flight out - check. I landed in the city and walked towards the exit. I found a ride to a good book store, got a much needed coffee and searched the store for something for the girls. So far so good. I actually felt relaxed and comfortable. I was a little surprised I wasn't feeling the pins and needles of anxiety at all. After some time looking through books and finishing my coffee I had some time to kill. The rodeo didn't start for a few more hours. I knew there was a decent indoor shooting range in Calgary that I had been to before.

I walked into the establishment and heard the familiar pops coming from the range as shooters sent rounds towards the targets. I walked through checking out all the firearms on the walls. I had always been into hunting and sport shooting. Guns were fascinating to me and a lot of fun, as long as you were in a good place and doing it safely. I had spent many hours with my girls teaching them how to safely handle rifles and really enjoyed watching them learn how to reach out to those far away targets. The range was pretty full and I waited for an hour for a lane to open up. I glanced over the handguns available for rent and selected one that fit my hand properly. Walking into the range, smelling the spent gun powder brought a smile to my face. Surrounded by strangers with guns in their hands was oddly comforting for me. I set up my targets and spent an hour squeezing off round after round, each crack of the pistol seeming to relieve just a little bit more of my built up stress. It had been a long time since I had been able to relax with a gun in my hands.

With my ammo spent and the show starting soon, I decided to head towards the venue. I walked in to the building, that all so familiar scent filling the air. It had been years, but I still loved that smell. Anyone else that had not grown up around it would've hated it, I'm sure. I grabbed a $10 beer and found my seat. I had been able to pick where I was going to sit when I ordered the ticket and had chosen the perfect spot. These events were always a bit of a show, pyrotechnics blasting off, fire, smoke and lights blazed over the arena as they introduced the riders. I had been involved in an entry like that before. It was a bit of a pain as far as I was concerned when I was riding. I was already getting my mind set and didn't want to have to go out and be introduced with all the fan fair.

The bullfighters came out with the riders and were introduced. Those were always the guys that we had a ton of respect for if they were good. They could save your ass from a terrible wreck, as long as they knew how to do their job. They could also end your career as a rider if they sucked at it. Soon the show was underway. One rider after the other came out to attempt to score big and many hit the dirt before the buzzer sounded. I sat and watched, feeling a little anxious but enjoying every minute. All too soon it was over, but it had been a blast. I had really enjoyed the show and all the memories it had brought back. I got to a hotel and headed to bed. I laid there unable to sleep the entire night, wondering how the girls were doing. I worried they might have a rough night and I was not there to help them. I looked at my phone, 4:00am. Eventually I drifted off to sleep.

I began to dream again, I could hear Stacy's voice over the phone.

"Well, I should probably let you go babe, I'm almost to work now…"

I knew what was coming, I forced myself to wake up. I didn't want to see that dream again. It had been reoccurring for a few months and never ended better than the last time. I laid there staring at nothing in the dark. An hour or so passed before I decided to get up and find some coffee. I walked for a couple hours, eventually finding a little coffee shop and getting some kind of green tea latte? Or something like that. I will admit, whatever it was, it wasn't half bad. I laughed at myself for having such a city-boy cup of whatever the hell this was.

I walked for a couple more hours along a river bank through the city. The early spring air being warmed by the sun felt good on my face. As I walked I thought about everything we had gone through in the last four months. We had all been fighting so hard to push forward and stay positive. My girls had gone far beyond what I could have ever asked of them. They matured so much, helped me out when they could and were there for each other when one was not doing well. I suddenly felt homesick. I hadn't been gone for long but I was ready to get home.

Chapter 32

I got off the plane, walked to Sarah's car and hopped in, instantly greeted by her crazy twins in the back, "Hi, Unco Mywin." Their energy never seemed to dissipate. Thank god they had parents who seemed to be able to keep up with them most of the time! I wanted to stay and chat with them, but I needed to get home. It was going to be a late night and an early morning as it was. I headed back to my house where my mom was already hanging out with the girls and getting them ready for bed. I felt like I had found a refreshed energy and was ready to face this next week without anything holding me back. The weekend full of new faces and events had given me what felt like a week of rest. I was happy to see my girls smiling faces. They had missed each other since they had been split up for the weekend and both begged me to keep them together next time. I laughed, thinking if I gave them a couple weeks together again, they might change their mind.

Next morning started as it would for any single parent on a Monday, rushing to get the kids ready for school and get myself off to work. But I was in a good mood and ready to get after this new normal life. I spent the day working away on a new project. I worked straight through lunch until I was nearly ready to head back home and make dinner for the girls. Just as I was packing up my laptop my cell phone rang with a strange number. Normally I wouldn't answer it, but given the situation we had been in I thought it best to answer. It was the police department calling to give me an update on the investigation into the accident that had taken Stacy's life and turned mine upside down. The officer explained the basics I already knew, which wasn't much. I still had not heard much detail other than what first-hand accounts had told me. It had been just over four months now and I had settled into the thought that some things are better left unsaid.

"We are just waiting for the driver's toxicology reports to come back now."

"What toxicology report?" I asked somewhat perplexed.

"The driver's blood was taken a few hours after the accident and we had found him to be at the maximum legal blood alcohol level, so we are now working on an analysis to see where his level was at the time of the accident."

"Are you telling me that this mother fucker was drunk?" I lashed out in anger.

"Well, as of right now, I can't confirm that until this analysis is complete and we can say for sure."

"So his blood was taken hours after the accident and he was shown to be at the maximum legal limit then, so given the time it took for that to happen, he was likely over the limit at the time of the accident, making this a completely preventable accident and maybe if he was fucking sober, my wife might still be alive?"

"I'm sorry sir, I cannot speculate one way or the other. I just wanted to give you an update of where we were in the investigation. I know it's taking a long time. We just want to make sure we have everything one hundred percent correct before we move forward with possible charges."

"Yeah, ok, thanks"

I hung up the phone completely stunned. I quickly grabbed my things and got the hell out of the shop. I needed to process this quickly before I lost my mind. All this time I hadn't been able to feel angry. I had hoped it was all simply an accident, no one's fault, just something that happens every day all around the world, but this time it happened here and it was Stacy who lost her life. I didn't want to feel angry and blame someone. I didn't want to know this had been a preventable accident and that she could have still been here with me carrying on our true love story. My mind was racing a million miles per hour, which slowly started turning into rage. I had been angry before, plenty of times. I have punched my fist through walls in anger. I had punched someone's face when they pissed me off, but I had never in my life experienced what I was feeling now. I was completely apoplectic. I had lost the ability to communicate and could not sort out a way to deal with this furious state I was in.

I got to the house and walked in to see the girls smiling and having fun. Halle had brought one of her friend's home from school to work on some sort of project. I dropped my bags off and went back to the garage. I couldn't tell them this new information, I was sure it wouldn't help them right now. I needed to calm down, I needed to breathe. My heart pounded in my chest like a drum and I paced back and forth, pulling at the hair on my head trying to keep it together. I wanted to scream but I didn't want to alarm the kids. I sat down on a stool, trying to think of what to do. I needed to talk to someone, but who do I tell? I texted Ashley to see if she was busy. I didn't want to bother her with this shitty mood that had suddenly been slammed down on my already burdened shoulders. I hoped she wouldn't answer, but she messaged back right away. I picked up some tools and tried to start working on Stacy's truck. I had to keep my hands and mind busy, do something to keep my mind from exploding. Minutes later my phone rang.

"Hey, what's up?" It was Ashley.

"I'm sorry, I didn't expect you to call." My voice was noticeably shaky.

"What's wrong?"

"Um…" I took a breath, trying to get myself gathered up. "The police called with an update on the investigation…the driver was impaired. This whole thing could have been prevented. She could still be alive, but he was fucking drunk" I broke down, but I did my best to suck it up. I didn't want her to hear me cry.

"Are you fucking kidding me? Oh my God, I'm so sorry…I don't know what to say."

"What can you say? What can anyone say right now?"

She stayed on the phone with me for a half hour, trying to calm me down. There wasn't much anyone could have done at that moment to pull me from the rage I was feeling. It would be one of the last times I would ever have a chance to talk with her. Life changes for everyone and her work was taking her to new places. I appreciated all the time she took to help my girls and me through some hard times. I would've never started writing my memories down if she hadn't inspired me to do so. I got off the phone with her and called Debbie. I didn't want to tell her, but she deserved to know this son of a bitch who killed my wife deserved to rot in a fucking jail for the rest of his useless life.

I dialed her number and broke the news to her. She started to cry. Last time I had called her and broke bad news to her was when I had to tell her that her baby girl was gone. My heart was crushed all over again listening to her tears over the phone again. She was angry like I was. She gave me a number to a lawyer who was a friend of a friend.

"I think we need to fight this," she said. I was with her, but that's not the way I wanted to fight right now. I wanted to bash this piece-of-shit's face into a concrete curb and make him suffer. I wanted his useless life to end in as much pain and suffering as possible. But I stopped myself. That's not how I wanted my girls to see their father, a man possessed with rage, a man who at this moment would be capable of taking someone else's life and snuffing it out - even if he deserved it. Stacy deserved to live the rest of her beautiful life with every one of her dreams coming true. My girls deserved to grow up with a mother who loved them more than anything in this world. I deserved to live the rest of my life with my happily-ever-after love story. None of us deserved to go through the incredible pain that we were feeling. The dagger in my chest had been pulled out and stabbed back in hundreds of times that day. I felt the bleeding of every emotion I had ever known pouring from every vein in my body. I could never put into words how much pain and rage I was in, and yet I pushed it down. I sat on the concrete floor of the garage and bawled for an hour before I was able to stand back up, get my shit together and go back in the house to make dinner for the girls.

Halle, in her uncanny way, knew that something was up. She asked me several times what was wrong, but I couldn't bring myself to tell her. I wasn't sure how she would take it. I wasn't sure she would understand. Although she was wise and mature beyond her years, I didn't want to repeat those words to her. I would tell her one day, just not today. I struggled through the evening. I tried getting hold of a few other friends, but I hate asking for help. I refused to tell anyone else this information over the phone. I didn't want anyone to rush to my side out of pity. I wanted to call Sarah but her and Jason had just left for a long overdue vacation and I was not going to ruin that for them. I went back to the garage and sat alone while my girls put themselves to bed that night. I had never let them do that before and it added to the terrible feeling I already had. I thought about opening a fresh bottle of whiskey and doing my best to find the bottom of the bottle, but that was not the answer either. I was tougher than to be a weak-ass pussy who had to drown his sorrows in alcohol.

Instead, I worked for hours on Stacy's truck. I discovered my welding skills, which were usually pretty decent, went right out the window when I was angry. But I kept at it until I had calmed down enough to take some more sleep meds and head for bed. It would be a short sleep, but life didn't stop just because I was angry. I had to get up and get my girls back to school and keep them pushing forward on this dirty, dusty uphill trail that had become of our lives. In spite of the sleep meds, I didn't sleep that night. I got up before my usual alarm and made a decent breakfast for the girls. It always made me feel better when I saw them wake up happy to see fresh bacon and eggs ready for them to devour before they headed off to school for the day. Sometimes when you can't do anything to make yourself happy, making someone else happy will lift your spirits enough to carry on.

I didn't go back to work that day. I decided to run for a few miles, which was much harder than I had anticipated. I lifted weights for another hour, still working out the anger I was dealing with. I worked out until I threw up and then worked out some more. Once I had physically exhausted myself, I headed back to the garage to turn more wrenches. I thought about the day Halle had asked me to help them work on the motor for the truck. I stopped what I was doing and looked around the garage. Covered in tools, old parts that had gotten pulled off and new parts awaiting to be installed. If she hadn't pushed me to get back out here and start working again, I'm not sure what I would've done to help myself deal with all this insane rage. I smiled and shook my head; Halle was so much like her mom sometimes. I had told Stacy many times, when the two of them would butt heads that it was like watching her argue with a younger version of herself. It used to piss her off so much when I would say that, but it was the damn truth. I never thought that one day I would be so happy that Halle had turned out so much like her.

I spoke with the lawyer for an hour and he talked me through what the basic rules were and what my rights were in this situation. He asked what the driver's insurance company had told me. I told him they hadn't contacted me yet and he was shocked to hear that. I sent him the police report I had, which really didn't tell me much more than the names of every person involved, what they were driving and the insurance company names. He said he would be making a few calls to get the process started. I had to make plans to head south to the city again in the near future to meet with him face to face and go over what I needed to do from this point going forward. I had never wanted to go down this road at all. I wanted this terrible time of my life to come to an end so my girls and I could move on with our lives without this cloud of dread constantly hanging over our heads. I wanted the sun to shine on us again. I wanted us all to feel happy again, if it was ever possible. But here I was, having to relive that day all over again. I wasn't out of this depressing darkness yet. But I wasn't going to quit fighting until I could look back and tell my girls we were in the clear so we could look forward and begin our new lives as our emotional scars healed over.

The next day Halle came home from school and pushed a form in front of my face.

"Daddy, you need to sign this," she demanded.

"What the hell is this now?" I tried not to be impatient but I was in no mood to be told what to do by an eleven year old.

"It's for football. I want to play."

"Huh? Football?" She had never even sat to watch one Super Bowl with me, aside from the lame half time shows they had had on in the last couple years.

"Yeah, I think I'd be good at it. I'm the fastest runner in my grade, I can throw better than anyone else and I'm tough enough to take a hit."

I sat and looked at the form, then back at Halle. I couldn't deny what she was telling me. She did have an arm on her. She was only five years old when the daycare had to take the balls away because she kept whacking other kids in the head with them when they would play. She would say, it's not my fault they can't catch. I'm throwing it right at them. She was definitely fast; I couldn't even keep up to her long-legged strides anymore. And she was one of the toughest kids I knew. She laughed at pain and kept on moving when she got hit.

"I'll sign this, but you are not allowed to quit halfway through the season. You'll likely be the only girl on the team, but I expect you to keep up and pass those other kids. I will not accept any half-assed effort. It better be all or nothing, no complaining."

"Deal. Sign here." She pointed to the signature line at the bottom of the page.

I signed the papers and paid the fee online. Her first practice was the next week. Then Layla came up with her big brown doe eyes.

"Daddy, can I play soccer this year?"

"What the hell has gotten into you two kids?"

In unison they answered, "We wanna play sports!"

I wasn't going to hold either of them back from something they wanted to do. I signed Layla up for soccer and we headed to town to find some cleats. If life had any empty spots in the near future, they had just been filled. Game days were now going to be three days each week. I wasn't sure how any single parent was supposed to juggle this lifestyle, but I wasn't about to let them down. Maybe this is the distraction I needed to get away from the rage I had been feeling. If I could focus on those two beautiful girls that were still so full of life after all we had been through, maybe the rage wouldn't consume me. I'd be there to support them in every way possible. There had to be something positive in our lives and maybe this was the start of it all. I couldn't stay down for long, it's not a place anyone should stay for any length of time. You have to get up and get living while there is still life to live.

Chapter 33

Before long we were taking Halle to her football tryouts. I was hoping this would be a good change of pace from the havoc that had ensued at the house. With contractors constantly coming and going, the house was always in a terrible state and not comfortable to be in for any length of time. We headed to the indoor football field at the rec centre and met up with a packed crowd of parents and kids all trying to figure out where to go. I brought Halle onto the field where coaches and kids had gathered.

"Good luck, sweet pea. Listen to the coaches and do your best," I instructed.

Halle nodded at me. She was pretty nervous looking around and noticing that she was the only girl. I headed up to the bleachers to sit and watch how this was going to turn out. The coaches split everyone up into groups and gave each kid a chance to work on different skills. Halle, being slight in size, was not expected to be much of a blocker, but she could hit, catch and run her ass off. She did quite well for having never played the game before. Towards the end of the tryouts they lined up the kids to do a timed run. I sat listening to the times that were called out as each kid got their turn to run.

4.1...4.3...4.8...4.0 One after the other, then came Halle. Holy...3.7!

I smiled, but said nothing. I heard a few parents asking who she was and who her parents were. I secretly hoped that no one would recognize me. Halle walked off the field with a smile that could not have been wiped off with a grinder. I hadn't seen a smile on her face like that in months. It was beautiful.

"Dad, that was SO much fun! I can't wait until we get to actually play a game!"

"Yup, you did really good, kiddo. You do know eventually they're going to get into full contact right? You are going to get hit at some point and it's not going to feel awesome."

"Yeah I know. I'm good with that. I'm going to be able to hit other kids too though."

I laughed. Little Miss Bright Side was feeling good and it made my heart feel a little lighter. Layla found it boring, which she reminded me of every couple minutes during the tryouts. She was a little bummed out that soccer had not started yet. There was still snow on the ground from the brutal winter we had gone through, which was likely going to mean a late start for her.

If I had thought my life had become busy already, it was only beginning. I had been using any spare time I had to get Stacy's 1975 F-100 ready for summer. I wanted so badly to get it back out on the road and take my girls for a ride in a truck their mama had fallen in love with as soon as she had seen it. Parts rolled in and I would get busy putting them on as quickly as I could. It was slowly beginning to take shape. Late nights of grinding, welding, skinning my knuckles and getting stuck under the truck that was much lower to the ground than I was used to. It had become something that helped my mind take a deep breath. After the accident I hadn't wanted to step foot in my garage, but now it came as a peaceful place for my mind to turn off from the pain and concentrate on what was in front of me. The girls would come out and get excited to see things starting to come together, constantly asking when we could take it back out again.

Football practice continued. I could hardly stand the cuteness of my not-so-little-anymore blonde girl in her gear. She looked so adorable. I made the mistake of telling her that once and she promptly corrected me.

"Dad, it's not cute, football players are not cute!"

Right! I'll try to remember that but I'm likely to forget, more than a few times. After a few practices, the players all sorted into the positions they would play as they got ready for the first game of the season. We packed up early one Saturday morning and headed into the city. I hadn't been to this field before, but it looked like a pro football field compared to the cow pasture we had in our small town. We were playing a team who had traveled from High Prairie to play. They had an obvious size advantage compared to our team, but that's not really the winning factor in any game.

Halle was quiet as usual, not saying much and feeling a little nervous. She held onto me and shivered in the cool morning air.

"Dad, I'm cold."

"I know. You'll be good once you get out on the field. Just pay attention to what your coach tells you and do your best."

She ran off to start warm up with her team. Layla sat in a chair completely covered in a blanket reading a book. She was not interested in football.

As the game was about to start my stomach tightened. I don't know why I felt nervous. I knew Halle could handle herself just fine. I just wanted more than anything for her to get something out of this, something that could help lift her spirits. Halle walked out on the field, cute as ever, stepped into her position for the kickoff. Whistles blew, kids ran around looking a little lost at times, coaches hollered orders. Halle was playing corner back, she blocked the receiver on the other team like she was supposed to, but was obviously not sure what to do after that. The team played well and by the end they had won 36-0. Halle walked off the field with that huge smile again. This seemed to be working for her. I couldn't have felt more proud.

The next week was more practice. Layla was beyond tired of being a spectator. I couldn't blame her, I wasn't used to being the one watching either. I had rarely ever been a spectator in anything. I would always much rather be the one out in the arena or on the race track. But this was a little different since I was watching one of my own developing new skills and having the time of her life. It didn't bother her at all being the only girl and it helped that the coaches and team mates treated her like any other player on the field. I think it was refreshing for her to feel like anyone else, not a special case who needed to be handled with gentle care because of everything she had gone through. She wanted nothing more than to be just another kid playing football.

It wasn't long before our next game. The kids learned a lot from the previous game and the practices that followed. They all came out with more confidence than they had before. The team they were playing was from the city, comparable size but the mouths on these kids was new. They stood on the line calling our kids down, cussing them out and trying to get in their heads. I wanted to jump out on the field and teach some sportsmanship in a non-sportsmanship way. But I didn't have to, after a few plays I could see Halle getting irritated, clenching her fists and stomping around. She lined back up, waiting for the call.

"Hut, hut."

Halle lurched forward, grabbed her opponent by the face mask and drilled him into the ground, then bolted for the quarterback. He was quickly pounded down by another one of our players. I had a few family members and friends there with me watching and they all roared with laughter. I shook my head. She had always had her mother's soft hearted side, but now I could see she had Stacy's fighting side as well. The kid slowly got back up and walked over to the referee to plead his case of how he had been mishandled by the blonde girl wearing #11. The ref shrugged his shoulders and apologized for not seeing the illegal maneuver Halle had just done. Halle trotted off to get back into formation as if nothing had happened and continued to play. They had a tougher team to go against this time and they had to fight for it, but they still came out ahead, winning the game 26-14.

I met her at the corner of the field as she walked off, again with that huge smile. This had been a light bulb game for her. She hadn't stopped when she blocked the receiver this time. She pushed hard to tackle anyone with the ball. She was now understanding what she needed to do and with her speed, she was getting the job done.

"Dad, did you see me tackle?"

"Uh, yeah, you know that's not legal right? You guys could have lost some yards on that play if the ref would've seen it."

"Yeah, I know, but they were being very rude," she replied.

I laughed, I couldn't argue with her logic. I hugged her and held back a few proud tears, I hadn't seen her play any sports that she had thoroughly enjoyed as much as this. For as shocking as it was for her to come home and beg me to let her play. It was even more so to watch her come out and throw her shyness away when she stepped onto the field. She still never said a word, never got vocal about anything. But she didn't have to, her actions spoke volumes.

It wasn't much longer before Layla was finally able to put her cleats on and get out on the field to play soccer. Now I had soccer Mondays and Wednesdays, football practice Tuesdays and Thursdays and games on Fridays or Saturdays and sometimes both. I was now trying to work fulltime, make food, do laundry and try to keep the house in some sort of order on top of all the sports my girls were involved in. I was exhausted, but I wasn't about to miss a game or a practice. If they were enjoying it, I would stay there to support them. After a few soccer games Layla came off the field and told me she didn't really like the sport. I was confused, she had wanted to play so bad and now was not all that enthused about it.

"I don't get it, Layla, you wanted this and now you don't like it?"

"But, Dad, every time we play I feel like I should tackle someone!"

"Huh? But that's football, honey. You can't do that in soccer."

"I know, that's why I want to play football."

"What?"

"Yes, I want to play football like Sissy does so then I can tackle people."

Well, then, I wasn't sure what to say. I couldn't argue with her. I wasn't a fan of soccer at all but I wasn't going to push football onto either of them. I still held the same belief: if you start something, you have to finish it even if you don't enjoy it. Layla agreed to finish her soccer season, if she wanted to play football now, she was going to have to wait until next season.

Amid all the sports chaos, our racing club had asked if they could do the first race of the season as a memorial race in Stacy's name and I agreed. It was a nice idea, but I didn't really plan to be there. They had made a point to ask if I would at the very least bring the race truck there. It had been such a big part of who we were and they wanted us there with the truck, but I wouldn't have to race. That thought didn't last long. If the truck was there, I was damn sure gonna run it. I made a quick call to Ron, my engine guy, to pull my engine off the shelf, slam it back together and send it home. As if I didn't have enough to do, I just kept adding more in. I didn't have any other prep work to do to the race truck, it just needed a motor and it would be ready. As for myself, I was always ready to race; that's what I told myself anyway.

I was also ready to roll Stacy's F-100 out of the garage. The girls and I were pretty excited to get it out after all the work we had done to it. The final piece was a set of wheels Stacy had picked out. They were perfect, except they were a very deep offset wheel for the back, which meant having to cut and narrow the rear axle to make them fit inside the wheel wells. She never made anything easy, but she did have incredible taste. We finally rolled it out and headed for town. It was getting hot outside finally, so it was windows down.

Halle looked over at me and asked, "Dad, why doesn't this truck have AC?"

"It does, it's called 260 AC."

"Huh?"

"You roll two windows down and drive 60 miles per hour and the air conditions you." I smiled at her. My dad had said the same thing to me when I was young.

"That's the dumbest thing I've ever heard of," Halle replied, annoyed with my humour. I thought it was pretty damn funny.

We cruised around town for a bit, enjoying the warmth of the spring air and the feel of the old truck we had been putting a lot of time into. There was a sense of peace when we drove it. I had wanted so badly to get this truck done for Stacy, but I never got the opportunity to hand her the keys to the finished product. It still needed paint and we hadn't built the motor for it that she had wanted, but if she was still here she would be driving it herself. I missed her terribly.

More football games came and went, the team was doing really well and had not lost one game yet. Layla continued with her soccer games and, even though she wasn't really into it, she still tried hard when she was on the field.

My race engine was on its way home as well. I was going to have to find time to put it in right away so I could cross it off my list. This engine had always been a bit of a pain to deal with. It ran incredibly well, but was generally hard to start and brutal on parts. I had developed a reputation for showing up and blowing up over the last couple years. That thing would fight me every step of the way, from simply putting it in the truck to actually running it. But I just had to do this one last race for the memorial and then I wouldn't fight with it anymore.

A friend of mine had picked it up for me and drove all night to get it home. I got it from him in town and headed to the house. I sent a text to a couple friends who had helped me put this motor in several times before and would be the best ones to get this done. I pushed the race truck out of the garage. Matt backed into the driveway with his picker truck and got set to pluck the motor out of the back of the Dodge. We sat there assessing what the best plan of attack would be, but since we had done this so many times, we didn't think long. As Matt hoisted the motor from its perch, the motor became completely uneven.

"That ain't gonna work Matt. We're gonna have to reset it."

Matt looked at the motor hanging half sideways from the lifting cables.

"Well, let's just try it and see what happens."

I knew what was going to happen. It would fight us every step of the way, just like it always did.

"Alright, bring it in. Let's see what falls off."

Matt eased it closer while I watched for the dowel pins to match up to the transmission. It was actually fairly close on one side. Matt stopped, I gave the motor a little shove and it slipped right in on one side.

"Huh! Alright, well, that's sorta in the right place, but it's still pretty cock-eyed. Let it down some and I'll push on it," I instructed.

Matt eased down some more. Clunk! I stood back in disbelief, the motor just slipped into its home as if it was meant to be.

"Well, shit. I guess slack off and I'll unhook ya."

Jeff showed up moments later expecting to see the engine still in the box of the truck. None of us said much. We all knew where everything needed to be. We grabbed parts and tools and got busy putting things together. We were only at this for about two hours when Matt suggested I put fuel in it and fire it up.

"There's no way. We can't be ready yet. It hasn't fought us yet" I said.

Matt laughed. "Well, you haven't tried to start it yet so I wouldn't hold your breath."

Right, good point. I walked around and double checked each fuel line, electrical connection and bolt. I grabbed a fresh jug of alcohol and poured it into the tank.

"Fire in the hole!"

I pressed the start button, expecting it to crank for a long time and not actually fire up. But not this time. It barely spun the motor over and it was cackling away! I sat in the truck in disbelief. Two hours, no struggles and it fired up instantly. My eyes watered, but not from emotion. The alcohol fumes burned my eyes and made them water. I jumped out and searched all around for something to be wrong. It couldn't have been this easy; it was never this easy. I stood back and listened to that 1100 horse power monster's erratic choppy idle. I couldn't explain it, but it was ready to race. I shut the fuel valve and killed the ignition.

"Well, shit, fellas, I don't know what to say. I guess she wants to go racing," I said in disbelief.

We laughed. It had never been so easy to have the truck ready, but here we were. All I needed to do was load it up when the time came and head out. It needed nothing else but for me to get in and drive. But this time it would be without the support of my wife. My kids would be at the race without their mama to look after them while I ran the truck. My stomach turned a little, the truck was ready but I wasn't so sure I was.

Chapter 34

The craziness that had become my everyday life never seemed to slow up at all. Springtime was always busy for us but doing it on my own felt bizarre. I hated asking for help with anything, but luckily I had been blessed with some family and close friends who knew me well enough and would just step in when I was obviously struggling. I refused to miss any games. Layla was still not enthused with soccer but she kept on trying her best when she played. Halle was really getting a handle on what she needed to do on the football field.

Her next game was bright and early again and she wanted to take her mamas truck since we had it running now. It was also Layla's 8th birthday, so many places to be and only one of me. Sarah jumped in to take Layla for some sort of nail spa thing, something I knew nothing about. I helped Halle get geared up and she jogged out to the field to warm up with her team. We were in the first quarter when she hard-stopped a kid who was trying to gain some yards. It was a beauty of a tackle but she took a pretty good hit. She popped back up, though, and kept playing. In the third quarter she got in a spot to stop another player, but this kid was twice her height and likely three times the weight. Not much she could do but get in his way. The crushing sound of gear smashing together could be heard from across the field. She was sent flying, but had slowed the guy down enough to get stopped by a couple teammates. I was sure she wasn't going to get up this time, but she slowly got to her feet and kept on going.

With another win in the books for the team, she came off the field smiling again but walking a bit slower.

"Dad, my foot hurts."

"That's it? Just a foot? I was sure you were gonna be half busted after those few hits."

"I think I'm okay. It's just sore"

She stripped her gear off and got changed so we could get to Layla's birthday party on time. I had Sarah, my mom and Debbie there to help me wrangle the rowdy group of little girls. Again this was a foreign situation for me. Stacy was always in the middle of all this kind of racket while I stood out of the way and tried to be helpful. As far as all the firsts went, this one was not as bad as I had expected. The kids' energy and smiling faces made it a little easier for me to bear. Maybe it was the insane schedule of events we had going on and was still to come that kept my mind constantly pushing forward. I worried at times I was over doing things and would have a mental breakdown at some point, but for now I continued to push forward. Next morning I got up to make the kids breakfast. Halle came crawling up the stairs.

"Dad, I can't walk on my foot."

"Why? What's going on?"

Halle grimaced in pain. "I don't know, but it really hurts."

"Well, shit, I guess we better get it checked out."

After a few x-rays the doctor was still unsure if it was broken or if she had damaged some ligaments in her foot, but she was on crutches and had a boot on her foot. She was out for a few games for sure now and wasn't happy about it. She pouted and whined but there was nothing we could do about it but give it time to heal. Maybe she would get back before the end of the season.

A couple weeks passed and it was time for the memorial race. I had the old motorhome out and cleaned up somewhat. More things Stacy had usually looked after. I brought the race truck out that I still had not done any test runs with since the motor had been put in. I felt my stomach start to tighten up as I rolled into the grounds and pulled up to my usual pit area. It didn't feel right at all. Stacy would have been leaping out of the truck and running around greeting everyone with her beautiful smile and famous hugs that everyone looked forward to. But not today. Today it was just me.

I unloaded the truck and decided I should do a couple quick test runs in the field to confirm the tune I had in the motor. It had been ten months since the last time I drove the beast and I needed to feel that launch again to see if I could mentally do this. I rolled out to a secluded spot and turned it loose with my head pinned to the seat through all three gears as rooster tails of dirt flew behind the truck for a couple hundred feet. I killed the ignition and coasted to a stop, checked a few things and confirmed the tune was pretty close, close enough that a change wasn't necessary. Again, no drama. This was unusual. It should've been way off, or something should've been broken to cause me the normal hectic last minute scramble before the race. But nothing needed attention, except maybe my own emotions. I idled back to my pit and parked it. My head was spinning with so many thoughts. I needed to get out of there for a bit.

I pulled out and headed for the house to pick up the kids from school. I turned the stereo up to try and drown out the thoughts. But as I got to the highway, the same song she had played for me the night before she died came on. I lost it. I had been able to control myself for the last couple months, I could hold it back until I got to a better place to let go. But not this time. My eyes streamed as I sobbed the entire drive home. The feeling of going through this race without her here was unbearable. My heart was so empty and broken. That wound in my chest I had hoped had started to heal was torn open again and it hurt so bad to be without her.

I managed to get home and collect myself before the girls got home from school. They were very excited for the race just as they always were. They had grown up around these mud drag races and absolutely loved them. I didn't want to bring them down with my own emotions, so I did my best to be excited with them. We headed back out and got settled in our little camp filled with my mud family, lots of familiar faces, sounds of healthy motors and smells of race fuels and burning alcohol. It was a busy place. Word had gotten around that this race was for Stacy. The camp ground was full, the pit area was getting filled with a variety of race trucks and I was getting nervous. Every minute was another thought of what Stacy would've been doing or saying at this time. She would've been bugging me to change spark plugs, check my fuel, make sure my harness was set, make sure I ate something, chasing the girls around and visiting with everyone who stopped by to say hello. But not this time.

I stayed quiet. I didn't know what to say and not many people really knew what to say to me either. I got the kids to bed and tried to sleep. Once again sleep never came. I finally got up at about 4 a.m. and decided to check over things on the race truck. I knew it was ready, but what else was I going to do? Eventually the other drivers started getting up and moving their race trucks into place in the pits that were already stuffed full of trucks. I paced around mine, checking oil temps as the heater did its job, tire pressures, anything to keep my mind busy. It wasn't working.

Jamie stood up on the back of a four wheeler to do the drivers meeting. I knelt down by my truck with my head in my hands, trying to keep hold of myself. My tears kept rolling down my face as he spoke about the importance of this weekend and how the show was going to go. I was a mess. It was damn hot that day and I had put on my multi-layer fire suit already. I didn't want to forget anything and was trying to stay one step ahead of my thoughts. I rolled my truck up to my lane when the time was drawing near. My girls stood nearby as I paced back and forth. The trucks in my class all lined up and took their turns ripping through the two lanes of dark mud. As they finished the last couple trucks in my class all engines were shut off. My family was standing with me as the announcer drew the attention of thousands sitting in the stands to a sign that was covered.

The grounds we had been racing on had been dedicated to Stacy. They pulled the cover from a huge steel sign that had been built by a fellow racer. Stacy Krahn Memorial Motorsports Park was laser cut into the sign with birds cut into it and welded to the top to look as if they were flying away. I hadn't expected it but it was beautiful. A 20' big screen sitting across from the crowd brightened up with a picture of her that I had taken on our first vacation. One picture after another scrolled through as they played You Should Be Here by Cole Swindell. Every lyric so utterly profound in that moment, every word tearing at my heart.

I buried my face into my girl's hair as I bawled in front of thousands of people, family and friends, some of the toughest guys I knew. I couldn't stop it, my heart was so incredibly broken. She damn well should have been there. She should never have been taken from us. This just couldn't be real, there is no explaining it. It was never supposed to be like this, and yet here we were. My girls both hugged me, both a little shocked at my reaction to it all. They hadn't seen me break down in quite some time and now I was completely lost in tears. Thirty-three balloons were released as the tribute video ended, two of which became tangled together as they floated off. I smiled and shook my head. Of course, that had to happen. Why wouldn't it? Everything else had been so heart-breakingly perfect in this moment already. Why not have two balloons get tangled up and float away together just to finish it off?

I hugged my family and turned towards my truck. After all that, now I had to get in it and race. My good buddy, Mike, stood by my door, slapped me on the shoulder and said, "You got this, fella." He had been through this with me for so much of the way. If he had any doubt that I wasn't going to be able to handle this, he would've stopped me. I crawled in and strapped up, fired the motor up and looked over at him giving him a thumbs up. It was go time and suddenly I felt at peace. This was home for me. Being back behind the wheel was a good feeling and I was determined to get it done. I rolled up to the stage beams and pressed the trans brake button down, but the truck rolled right past the beams. *Well, fuck*, I thought to myself. *That's one thing I forgot to check.* I backed up. I would have to try and foot brake this run. *Oh. well*, I thought. *I wasn't here to break records.* I just needed a few clean passes and to not roll the truck. The lights started to drop. Just as the third yellow dimmed and the green light was about to light up, I slammed my right foot hard on the throttle and launched that bitch through the pit hitting third gear by half track. The truck leaped out the end and bounced hard as it landed. I coasted it out until I had it reined back in. I turned back and stayed on the crowd side as I returned to do my second pass.

I was on a mission now. One more pass and I was finished for the day. I revved the motor as I roared down the fence line against the crowd. I could hear the cheers over the racket of that 600 cubic inch motor. I had never heard them before, but I could hear them now. I spun around and lined up in the opposite lane. There seemed to be an issue with one of the sensors and the timing system was not working properly. Jamie opened my door and yelled into my ear what the situation was. I shrugged my shoulders and yelled back that I'd be out of fuel soon if we didn't hustle. He smiled back and said we would do it old school. He stepped up to the start beam and waved me in. I rolled up as he held his hat up in the air. He glanced back at me and dropped his hand. Throttle down hard again, I sailed through as I had just done. But this time, as I crossed the finish line, that feeling of

determination fled instantly and the tears flowed from my eyes again. I jerked the truck back around and raced up to where my girls were standing at the edge of the track. I killed the ignition and hopped out, throwing my helmet to the ground and wrapping my arms around them again as I wept. The roller coaster ride of emotions just kept on coming in waves and I had no control over it.

"I love you girls so much," I cried.

"I love you too, Daddy," Layla said as she wiped my face with a dirty hand.

Halle smiled at me as she knelt down to pick up a glob of mud, she smeared it under each eye like football war paint. "You did awesome, Dad! You were flying!"

I laughed at her as I wiped my face dry. "You girls wanna ride back with me in the race truck?"

They both ran to the door, crawled in and sat on the floor where the passenger seat used to be. They grinned ear to ear as I rolled back to the pits with them beside me. It had been an unbelievable chain of events in those few moments, but I felt like it had been necessary. Everything had happened for a reason--even the trans brake not working. I could feel Stacy elbowing me and saying, "I told you to check everything." I felt as if I had made it over a massive hurdle. I had been so wound up about that weekend and unsure how I would handle it. But the rest of the day would solidify my place here. So many faces I hadn't seen in many years were there, a few that I had never expected. Stacy's friend, Angie, came out of nowhere to come and say hi. I had not seen her in years. She had her three beautiful kids with her as well as her mom and dad. They all came and sat with us and told a few stories to my girls of how we knew each other. I told the girls how Angie had introduced me to their mama many years ago at an auction. It was an incredible feeling to catch up with so many old friends who were there when this all began.

I spent the evening sitting by the fire. I didn't eat much (which had been noticed by a few friends as they teased me about losing so much weight). But I couldn't handle much food after that much of an emotional dump. I headed to bed and tried to sleep, tomorrow was another race day.

The next day was much the same, but a fellow race partner had crawled under my truck and fixed the trans brake for me. Derrick had helped me a ton with my truck, many late nights were spent on my truck or his to get them race ready. He had my back when I needed it. We went through the same motions but this time I knew what was coming and was able to handle it much better. I crawled back in and rolled into the stage beams. This time with the trans brake locked in. The pits had become rutted and terribly rough but I wasn't going to let that stop me. The green light flickered and I let go of the button at

6000 rpm. The paddle tires shot chunks of dirt at everyone within range and I sailed through, getting kicked back and forth a few times before I exited the pit. Undeterred by the state of the pits, I turned back for my second pass, rolling into the beams just as I had done before. This lane had taken a ton of abuse and was looking pretty bad, but I was never one to feather the throttle for anything. It was on or off, there was no in between. I bounced through, fighting to stay in the direction of travel I wanted to go. As I neared the end, my rear tire contacted the edge of the pit kicking the truck sideways as I came out. *Oh, shit, here we go*, I thought. I cranked the wheel as quick as I could and stayed on the throttle, hoping to catch enough traction to not roll it. I braced for impact as I was sure I was in for a wreck, but just as I thought it would go over it suddenly straightened out again. No drama, or at least not as much as I thought was going to unfold. I slammed the throttle a few times and headed out. I was done. I had somehow gotten through this weekend without blowing anything up. I didn't know how it was possible but with the help of so many, we had made it.

I walked away with second place. Derrick had taken first and I couldn't have been happier about it. He had been busting his ass on his truck for a few years now and it had finally come together for him. If I had to lose to anyone, I was glad it was him. I packed up my stuff and started the process of getting everything home and cleaned up. It all seemed to take so much more time now without Stacy here to do more than her fair share.

The next day as I tried to get things back in order, my head was still reeling from the weekend's events. I decided to take her F-100 for a drive to clear my head. So many things had happened, so many emotions had come out that I hadn't been dealing

with. I needed to drive her truck. I rolled down a few of the quieter back roads with the stereo blasting just as she would have done, still wiping the odd tear from my eyes as I went. I was nearly back home after being out for a good while when I glanced up in the rear view mirror. I had put a memorial decal on the back window, but had never noticed before. Her name was in the center of my rear view. I stopped in the middle of the road and stared at it for a while. It never ceased to amaze me how every time something happened, or I was just having a terrible time getting through it all, there she was. Something would come up out of nowhere to tell me that she was still with me, forever watching over me. I rubbed my dirty plaid shirt over my face and headed for home. My heart still felt heavy, but there was just a little bit of light in there still. It had to be her.

Chapter 35

Halle's foot was healing slower than expected. The damage she had done was making it tough for her to get back in the game before the season was over. I had been taking her in for physiotherapy, which was helping, but she wasn't going to be able to play again before the final game. She was pretty disappointed. But when the final game day came, she threw on her game jersey and sat on the bench with her team to cheer them on. The team had been undefeated for the entire year, and by the end of the final game they were still on top. She had been a part of the team from the start, but I knew she felt a little left out when she couldn't get out on the field for the last one. Being there meant a lot to her. She still got to hold the championship trophy at the end and I was still proud of her. We handed in her gear and met up with her new coaches for next season. She wasn't giving up and wanted to sign up for bantam football in a month.

Layla was happy to be done soccer and ready to start her first football season, but she would have to wait until the following spring for her chance. School was nearly wrapped up and both kids were ready for it to be over. It had been a rough first year in the new school for them. Halle was starting to regret having a cell phone and many times would just leave it at home and ignore it while so many of the other kids were glued to them, learning all about Life from social media. They would come up with all sorts of weird ideas of what gender they were this week or how dumb everyone else was for having a difference of opinion. I hated to watch her struggle with it all. She'd ask me why people were like that and I'd answer her in my usual blunt fashion. I'd quit explaining things in a PG version and talked to her like an adult. It seemed to make more sense to her. I explained that we live in a world now where everything is tolerated - unless you disagree. Then, you were shunned and accused of being intolerant. Both my girls were starting to become happier being shunned instead of confused with who they were.

Aside from all the girl drama, I still had court dates looming around the corner. The man who killed my wife while intoxicated was due to appear in front of a judge to state his plea. I had found a lawyer to help me out and had the support of our police force through this terrible time. But it was just another thing to do, another step towards being done with all the negativity that had encroached upon my life.

I still had one major hurdle to get over and that day was coming very soon. I had Stacy's urn sitting on the nightstand in my room and it was time to set her free. I knew the day had been approaching, but with so much constant activity I had not really had a lot of time to think about it. I had made sure to explain everything to the girls to make sure they knew exactly what we were going to do and what it all meant. They seemed to understand all too well and had no questions to ask me. We spent a couple days preparing the spot, her favourite place, the place where we had been married. We cut the tall grass and built a new arch that we stood up in the same place one had stood for our wedding. I had decided I wanted to bury the urn in the exact spot we had stood when we said our vows. It was a sacred place for both of us and I knew this was the place she would have wanted to be laid to rest.

The night before we were planning to bring her to her final resting place the girls wrote letters to their mom. I never asked what they wrote and I will never prod them to tell me. It is something for them to know and only share if they really want to. I knew what I wanted to leave with her; I had known for a while now. I dug through the safe where I had left my wedding ring. I had put it in there months ago just for this purpose, but after emptying the box, it was not there. So many things had been shuffled around since the flood, I wasn't sure where it could have possibly gotten to. I opened up boxes that had been brought back home and started digging, doing my best not to panic. I set one box after another on the bed and emptied its contents, rummaging through every trinket and token that brought back so many memories. I came across a box filled with her old jewelry. I found the necklace I had given her for being my prom date and some expensive earrings I had bought for her for Christmas years ago. But it was not what I was looking for.

I opened up a faded old ring box and stopped. Inside was an old tarnished ring. It took me a moment before I realized what it was. This was the first ring I had ever bought for her. I had tied it in the hand of a cherub angel and given it to her when we had been dating for a year. I had looked for it after the accident but hadn't been able to find it and now here it was in my hands. I looked back down in the box and noticed a small blue ribbon. On it was a trinket ring, one that she had pulled out as a bridesmaid. The idea behind it was that whoever found the ribbon with a ring on it was to be the next one to get married. It had turned out to be true. I tied her ring to the ribbon and put it in my pocket. After searching for what seemed like forever, I had no idea what to do. My wedding ring seemed to have disappeared. I put the boxes back where they had been stacked in the closet while anxiety began to take hold of me. I hadn't felt it for a long time, but here it was again. I went back to my safe and removed everything again, I picked up a small zip up folder and opened it.

Clink.

My wedding ring hit the floor. I knelt down and picked it up, shaking my head as I held it in my hand. It had been in there the whole time, but I couldn't find it. I couldn't have found it until I found the first ring I had given her, the one she wore until I asked her to marry me. My mind rushed with thoughts and memories. I sat down on the floor and cried. I didn't want to do this, setting her ashes in place meant this was truly over. I knew she was never coming back, but I still didn't want it to be real. I pulled the ribbon from my pocket and tied my ring on with hers and set it on the urn. There was no way to avoid it. I had to set her free. I had to let her rest in her favourite place.

I slept very little that night, worrying about how this was going to effect the girls. They had done so much healing in the past few months and I wasn't sure if this would reopen all the wounds that had healed for them. I still felt as if the wound in my chest had not begun to heal, the pain was still there although not as constant. The girls woke up and began rushing around, packing things they would need for the day. They were falling in love with their mama's favourite place and loved spending time there. They grabbed the notes they had written for their mom along with some snacks for the road and headed to the truck. I carefully picked up the urn, it felt heavier than I had expected. I slid it inside of a royal blue velvet bag and brought it out to the truck, setting it on the center counsel. We started making our way out in silence. No music played and none of us spoke at all.

We slowly idled through one pasture trail after another, following the same route we had taken on our wedding day. The weather had been cold and rainy for the last couple days and grey clouds hung low in the sky, threatening more rain. We broke through the last stand of trees and were welcomed by that same gorgeous view overlooking the river. It had always been a place we would stop and stare, enjoying what this place had always meant for us. But today was going to be different. I had only wanted immediate family there for this, so it wasn't a huge crowd. I pulled up to the fire pit and shut the truck off. The girls bolted from the truck, excited to get out and run up the hills. I paced nervously, much the same way I had done before the wedding. My family was all waiting for me to be ready to do this and they gave me my space to think. I didn't know how to do it. I wasn't sure how this was supposed to be done. After a few moments I walked back to the truck, opened the door and reached in to pick up the urn. There was no easy way to do this, no instructions for me to follow. I just needed to nod my head and let events unfold as the chute gates of life cracked open.

I carried her urn slowly out to the sacred spot we had prepared, my girls by my side and my family following behind. I set the urn down and slid it out of the velvet bag, pausing before opening it. I took a deep breath and unlatched the box. My girls reached out and dropped their final letters inside the box and sat down on the ground. I reached into my pocket and pulled out the blue ribbon with the rings tied together. I told everyone how I had come across the first ring as I searched frantically for my wedding ring. I passed it around for them to have one last look at them. Once back in my hands I looked at them one more time before slowly setting them inside the box. I closed the lid and latched it shut. I gently picked up the box and placed it in the ground. Tears began to flow as I gently pushed dirt back in by hand. My girls moved closer to help me do what I had never wanted to do in my lifetime. They should have never had to do this at such a tender age.

I sat down beside her final resting place. There were no words I could speak right then. I held my girls tightly as I cried. My family came over to add a handful of sand. As they did, the clouds broke and the sun shone through on us, the warmth instantly apparent. We all sat in silence for quite some time. There really were no words that could have made this moment feel any better. As my family made their way back to the fire to let me have some time alone, I whispered, "I love you, I love you more, I love you most." and laid down beside her. The sun was warming me up. The calm breeze flowed around me as I lay there. Layla came to my side and laid her head down on my chest. It was only a few moments before she fell asleep. The beautiful silence of this place had an unmistakable peace about it. My heart, although still in pain, was feeling at peace.

Eventually Stacy's dog, Bella, found us enjoying the warmth of the sun and decided she needed to snuggle as well. Layla grumbled at the dog, but laughed as she had her face fully groomed by the fat-headed dog. We stood up and made our way back to the fire with everyone else. We spent the day just sitting and enjoying each other's company. It had been a long time since we had all just sat and visited. The kids all ran around the fields finding wild flowers and berries and catching grasshoppers. We stayed until late in the evening before heading home. We had one more day to get through before I could put a proverbial period at the end of this chapter.

I slept a couple hours, but not enough. I had been waiting for this day for a while now. Not that I was looking forward to it, but I knew it had to happen. We jumped in the truck and stopped for fuel. A group of trucks gathered and waited to follow me back out to the sacred spot. We traveled out and rolled into the field again, marveling at the view as the sun shone brightly, bringing the brilliance of Mother Nature into full view. My dad had his truck parked close to the center of the wooden arch. I guided Matt in with a picker truck and got things set to lift a stone memorial bench out of Dad's truck to set down exactly where we had stood when we said our vows. We gently placed the bench down, taking care to make sure it was as squared up as it could be. Once we were certain it was perfect, my girls came to my side and I slowly pulled the cover to unveil what I had written for the stone. Fifteen years ago today we had stood here hand in hand, looking into each other's eyes and saying our vows. Vows we had both taken to heart. Till death do us part had become all too real for me now, but it was the only way we would've ever become separated. The love we had for each other was so absolutely real and unapologetic, no one could ever deny what we had meant to each other. Now I stood in front of this stone bench expecting to feel the weight of emotion again, but it didn't come. Instead a sense of peace came over me, a feeling of accomplishment I couldn't explain. I knew what I had wanted to do to commemorate her life and the love she had given me. This stone would be here forever for people to come and visit in peace. I was surrounded by many who had known us from the start of our story. They all took a moment to read what I had written and understand

why I knew this was the place she needed to be. It was her favourite place, it was perfect.

I went back to the fire after spending some time to enjoy the place that had now become hers. I visited with old friends and family, some who hadn't been back here since the day we were married. The kids all ran and played and the dog did her best to keep up in the hot summer sun, but eventually retreated to the shade under my truck. I took a few moments alone sitting down to take in the view from her spot. It had become something I would cherish for the rest of my life. It was a place to feel grateful for having been a part of her life and fortunate to have had her as my wife. A person who had taught me to love so incredibly deeply, to love without boundaries or exceptions and to love as if there would be no tomorrow. I smiled as I ran my fingers over the bench one more time, I was sure she would have been happy with this.

I stood up and slowly walked back to the truck, the girls had been running all day and were getting tired. I was exhausted and ready to head out as well, so we jumped in the truck and turned towards the trail leading out. I paused one more time to look out over her place. It was perfect. We made our way back to the highway. As I drew near the intersection I stopped the truck. We had been through so much, life had become so incredibly busy and we had taken no time for ourselves. I looked back at the girls who looked back at me confused.

"Dad what are you doing?" Halle asked.

"Well, if we turn north we will be heading back home, but if we turn south...who knows what might come our way." I smiled.

They both were now completely confused. We still had so much more rough road to travel down in this life before we could ever get passed all the trauma we had been through. But looking back at all we had been able to accomplish together made me feel incredibly proud and fortunate to have these girls in my life. Without them I would have never made it this far. They were the driving force that kept pushing forward to keep living. I had to prove to them that although life will continually try to break you down, you can still remain focused and positive. You can still have an incredible life as long as you keep striving to live a happy life.

I knew we should go home, we had nothing with us. There were many things that needed to be done at home, but I also felt like we were starting fresh. Right now was the start of something new. I looked back at the girls who were still unsure of what was going through my head. I smiled back at them. It was time. We needed a new adventure together.

I turned south and slammed down on the throttle.

Epilogue

After the tragic loss of my wife I struggled, as most people who have lost the love of their life would. I searched for advice through friends, family and professional council on how to deal with the stress and extreme pain that had become of my life. So many people told me the pain would never go away, depression would become a way of life and I would just learn to deal with it. I appreciated all of their help but this wasn't helping me. I didn't want to just learn to deal with it! This pain would never go away? Depression? This wasn't who I was and I knew damn well that if I let myself slide down into that rut, I wasn't likely to get back out of it. I had a decision to make soon after Stacy died: I could slip into that hole and stay there (no one would have blamed me if I did), or I could choose to fight it. I could choose to live in a way that would honour Stacy. I could chose life.

It didn't come as an easy decision and I completely underestimated how hard of a fight it would be. But if I decided to play the victim and become a broken man for the rest of my life, it would've dragged my girls down as well. I was not about to do that. To stand up and fight this terrible life was to fight for my girls so they could have incredible lives of their own. They deserved to live lives that would be the envy of those around them and I would be damned if I wasn't going to make that happen.

The most depressing thing I was ever told after Stacy died was that the pain never goes away. I refuse to believe that. I do believe you never stop missing that person, but to tell someone that they will live the rest of their life in pain is a terrible thing to say. Yes it does hurt and I know it will for a long time yet, but I will not stop trying to become more positive and reduce that pain as I learn to live again. This will likely be the hardest battle for me to fight, but I know in my heart I will eventually overcome the pain and I will one day feel as if my heart has been healed. I will never stop missing Stacy, she was the biggest influence in my life, but I know she wouldn't want me to live the rest of my life with a constant feeling of having a gaping hole in my chest. There will be setbacks along the way, but I will not sit here and expect a hand out because of the situation I am in. I will become stronger every time I get back up and fight.

I honestly believe depression, anxiety and stress can be greatly reduced by simply standing up and making that conscious decision to fight it. Do something for yourself every day that will make you better than you were yesterday. Stand up and make a conscious effort to fight it, never let it beat you down. You are the only one that can make it happen. Drugs and alcohol won't make it go away, they will only put a bandage over the situation you are in. The power of a positive mind and a drive to never fail will carry you further than you could have ever imagined. It was about three months after my life got turned upside down that I looked back at how far I had come. I thought it would be a year before I reached the place I was at mentally. Of course I still had a long ways to go, and I still do. But I firmly believe that you never quit fighting. Even when you feel like you have arrived at the goal you may have set out for yourself to reach, take another step and push harder.

We all have setbacks. Every now and then you will get knocked back down. All you need to do is keep getting up. Don't sit there and say, "Why me?" That won't do anything for you. Stand up and scream, "TRY ME! YOU CANNOT BEAT ME!" Life will always try to beat you down. Don't ever think you are cursed or that there is nothing great in store for you. Great things will come to those who keep pushing forward. It will never just be handed out to you; there are no handouts in this life that you haven't earned.

Do not dwell on the *what-ifs* and the *it should have been me*. It will drive you crazy. It's not easy to do. I struggled with it myself for a while. When you stop and realize that you don't have control over outside events, but you do have control over how you react to those events, you will find the strength to keep pushing forward. Don't ask yourself who will help you. Help yourself by setting goals every day and fighting with everything you have to meet and then pass those goals. Keep striving to push past your limits every chance you get. Become a person so absolutely driven to succeed. Do it for someone you love. I push myself now more than ever before. Every day I wake up and ask myself, "What can I do today that would make Stacy proud?" Having that constantly on my mind has helped me get through my hardest moments.

If you have lost someone dear to you, you understand that lost, empty feeling and uncontrollable emotions that come with it. There are no words to describe it. If you know someone who has gone through an incredible loss, there isn't always something you can say to make them feel better. Just be there for them. It's the little things you do that mean the most. In my case it was the ones who stood by me when I was at my worst. Someone just being near me when I couldn't keep it together made a difference. They didn't always need to say something; sometimes a hand on my shoulder was enough to let me know that I wasn't alone.

Above all else, be a positive light for those who have lost someone. Get them up and outside. Go for a walk in a place that isn't crowded, get into a place that's peaceful and enjoy what God has created in this world. I know I will have some pretty serious questions for Him when I die, but until then I will enjoy what this world has to offer.

Stay positive. Never stop fighting those inner demons. Love others as if it was their last day on this earth. Do this and you will leave a legacy behind like that of my wife, Stacy Ann Krahn.

I love you, I love you more, I love you most.
I love you still.

ACKNOWLEDGMENTS

There are many people I need to thank for helping me create this book. Stacy is my inspiration through this journey, without her this book would not exist. She is the person who taught me how to live life everyday as if it were my last.
My daughters, Halle and Layla, who give me every reason to constantly push forward and keep fighting.
Ashley G. for giving me the nudge to start this process.
Nicky for the photography work.
Dawn and Toni for the hours of editing through my rough writing skills.
All of my family, by blood or by bond, who have stood by my side when I needed them the most. I cannot thank you all enough.

ABOUT THE AUTHOR

Myron was born and raised in Alberta, Canada. He resides there still with his two daughters. His life is filled with the daily grind like anyone else. Besides his work and raising his girls, he spends time racing, working in the garage and hunting. Keeping to himself most times, but the family goes out to enjoy what this world has to offer every chance they get. Their lives have been forever changed, but that doesn't stop them from constantly pushing for better things. They keep a positive outlook on life and never give up on each other. Tomorrow is never a guarantee, so they live for today.

Made in the USA
Middletown, DE
16 November 2018